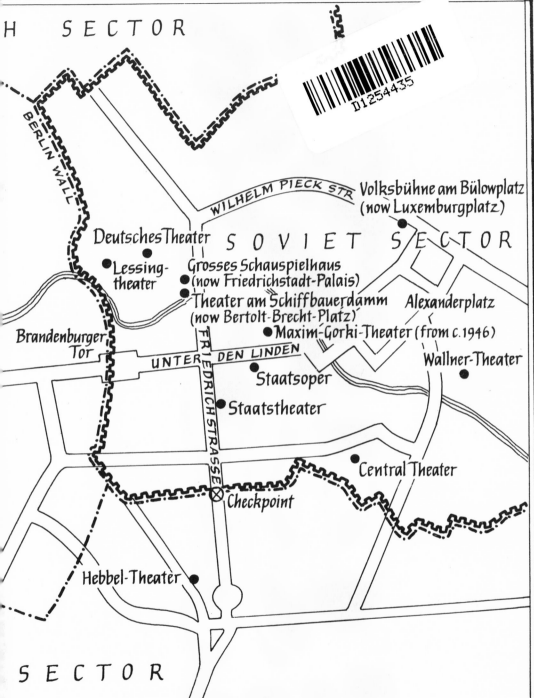

H SECTOR

BERLIN WALL

WILHELM PIECK STR.

Volksbühne am Bülowplatz
(now Luxemburgplatz)

SOVIET SECTOR

Deutsches Theater

Lessing-
theater

Grosses Schauspielhaus
(now Friedrichstadt-Palais)

Theater am Schiffbauerdamm
(now Bertolt-Brecht-Platz)

Alexanderplatz

Maxim-Gorki-Theater (from c.1946)

Brandenburger
Tor

UNTER DEN LINDEN

FRIEDRICHSTRASSE

Wallner-Theater

Staatsoper

Staatstheater

Central Theater

⊗ Checkpoint

Hebbel-Theater

SECTOR

Erwin Piscator is not only the most important theatre director since Stanislavsky and Reinhardt but a key figure in the history of the arts between 1916 and 1966. First in Weimar Germany, then as an exile in Russia, France and the U.S., and finally back in the Germany of Adenauer and Brandt, he engaged and often enlarged such talents as those of Gropius, Brecht, Grosz, Toller, Moholy-Nagy, Hochhuth, Peter Weiss, Tennessee Williams and the young Marlon Brando, linking them in a concept of theatre which aimed to reflect new technological advances and the social and political issues of its time. As a technical innovator in the 1920s he used film, sound reproduction, the animated cartoon, the treadmill stage and other devices in ways that remain influential even today. As a political commentator he had to come to terms with the great issues of Nazism, Stalinism and world war, and his success or failure in doing so needs to be pondered by all concerned with forms of political art.

This is the first book in English to cover Piscator's whole career. As one of the leading authorities on twentieth-century German theatre, John Willett is supremely well equipped to write it. Many rarely seen illustrations and documents accompany the text, almost half of which is devoted to the Weimar period. There follows chapters on his little-known activities in the USSR and France and a critical look at the more familiar story of his later career, before the whole problem of political theatre is discussed in a final chapter. There is also a bibliography and an illuminating chronology of events, productions and publications during these fifty historically crucial years.

The
Theatre of
Erwin Piscator

Half a Century of
Politics in the Theatre

The
Theatre of
Erwin Piscator

by

JOHN WILLETT

HOLMES & MEIER PUBLISHERS, INC.
New York

483-2089

First published in the United States of America 1979 by
HOLMES & MEIER PUBLISHERS, INC.
30 Irving Place, New York, N.Y. 10003
Copyright © 1979 John Willett

ISBN 0-8419-0501-0

PRINTED IN GREAT BRITAIN

Contents

List of illustrations

Sources of illustrations

from Libraries, Special Collections, etc.:
Deutsche Akademie der Künste, Berlin-East 37, 57, 73, 75, 76, 77, 78
Erwin-Piscator-Center, Akademie der Künste, Berlin-West 25, 54
Estate of George Grosz, Princeton, New Jersey 10
Fogg Art Museum, Harvard University, Cambridge, Mass. 35
Institut für Theaterwissenschaft, Universität Köln 4, 9, 22, 24, 27, 39, 40, 41, 44, 45, 52
Lee Strasberg Collection, New York 65
Lincoln Center Library of the Performing Arts, New York 67
Morris Library, Southern Illinois University at Carbondale 66, 68, 69, 70, 71, 72
Staatliches Filmarchiv der DDR, Berlin-East 58, 59
Theaterwissenschaftliches Institut, Freie Universität, Berlin-West 8, 12, 28, 29, 31, 32, 38, 43, 47, 49, 50, 51
Ullstein Bilderdienst, Berlin-West 1, 13, 14, 15, 16, 17, 18, 23, 42, 46

from Publications:
Walter Gropius, *Theaterbau* (IV Convegno 'Volta' – Tema: Il Teatro), Rome, Reale Accademia d'Italia, 1934 53, 55
Friedrich Kranich, *Bühnentechnik der Gegenwart*, Munich and Berlin, Verlag R. Oldenbourg, Vol. I 1929, Vol. II 1933 6, 20, 21, 48
Mishket Liebermann, *Aus dem Ghetto in die Welt*, Berlin, Verlag der Nation, 1977 61
New York Herald-Tribune, New York 64
Erwin Piscator, *Das politische Theater*, Berlin, Adalbert Schulz Verlag, 1929 2, 3, 5, 11, 33, 36, 56
Ernst Toller, *Hoppla, wir leben!*, Potsdam, Gustav Kiepenheuer Verlag, 1927 26
Leo Tolstoy, *War and Peace* adapted for the stage by Alfred Neumann, Erwin Piscator, Guntram Prüfer, English adaptation by Robert David Macdonald, London, Macgibbon & Kee, 1963 74
Theater im Exil 1933–1945, Berlin, Akademie der Künste, 1973 60, 62

Chronology

———◆———

Events, productions, publications (1893–1966)

The right-hand column lists theatre events and productions; the left-hand column gives historical and biographical information.

1893–1913

Erwin Friedrich Max Piscator was born on 17 December 1893 at village of Ulm near Wetzlar, to Carl Piscator, a merchant, and Antonia Laperose. The family moved to Marburg, where he attended the Volkshochschule till 1913. He then went to Munich University to study German, philosophy and art history, also attending classes of the theatre historians Arthur Kutscher and Max Herrmann.

1914–1918

Productions for army theatre units. Six anti-war poems published in *Die Aktion* (Berlin), 1915 and 1916.

2 Aug. 1914. Start of First World War.

1 Feb. 1915. Called up as private soldier in 32 Inf. Regt., and trains at Gera.

Spring 1915. Radio operator on Ypres front. Two years front-line service; wounded.

Summer 1917. Meets Wieland Herzfelde. Home leave.

1918. First visits Berlin on leave.

November 1918. Armistice and German Revolution. Piscator speaks at formation of Soldiers' Council, Hasselt (Belgium) before returning to Marburg.

Summer 1914. Piscator an unpaid extra at Munich Court Theatre.

2 Oct. 1914. Plays Astolf in Kleist's *Die Hermannsschlaht* there.

Summer 1917. Joins army theatre unit under Eduard Büsing.

End 1917. In charge of Deutsches Theater, Courtrai (Belgium).

18 Feb. 1918. First Dada evening at J. B. Neumann Gallery, Berlin

31 Dec. 1918. Joins newly-founded Communist Party (KPD) in Berlin with Grosz and the brothers Herzfelde.

1919

Helps organise one or more Dada meetings (with Grosz, the Herzfeldes, Walter Mehring, etc.) and goes to Königsberg (East Prussia) as an actor in the autumn.

5–15 Jan. Spartacist rising in Berlin. Murder of Liebknecht and Rosa Luxemburg by right-wing Freikorps.

19 Jan. Elections. 45% Socialist votes. KPD abstain.

February. Friedrich Ebert (SPD) elected president. National Assembly meets at Weimar.

21 Mar. Soviet government in Hungary under Béla Kun.

April–May. Bavarian Soviet Republic formed and bloodily suppressed. Imprisonment of playwrights Toller and Mühsam.

31 July. Republican constitution voted by Assembly at Weimar.

1 Aug. Fall of Hungarian Soviet, followed by White terror under Horthy.

October. Leopold Jessner, a Socialist, takes over the Prussian State (ex-Court) theatre in Berlin.

16 Feb. Piscator applies to the Volks-bühne for a job as 'young character actor' and assistant director.

Spring. League for Proletarian Culture formed in Berlin by Artur Holit-scher, Ludwig Rubiner and Alfons Goldschmidt.

March. First issue of irregular magazine *Die Pleite* edited by Herzfelde with Grosz illustrations.

1 Sept. Karlheinz Martin and Fritz Kortner found Die Tribüne as a political theatre in Berlin (with Hans Rodenberg, Rudolf Leonhard *et al.*).

30 Sept. Toller *Die Wandlung*, dir. Martin at Die Tribüne, with Kortner.

7 and 13 Dec. Piscator involved in Dada evenings at Tribüne.

14 Dec. Cranz: *Die Freiheit*, dir. Martin. First and only production of 'Proletarian Theatre' sponsored by League for Proletarian Culture.

1920

Productions: (1) Wedekind *Tod und Teufel* and H. Mann *Variété*, des. Otto Reigbert; (2) Wedekind *Schloss Wetterstein*, des. Piscator and F. Kaiser; (3) Georg Kaiser *Der Centaur*; (4) K. A. Wittfogel *Der Krüppel*, 'L. Sas' (Andor Gabor) *Vor dem Tore*, L. Barta *Russlands Tag*, des. Heartfield; (5) Gorky *Enemies*; (6) Upton Sinclair *Prinz Hagen*, des. Moholy-Nagy. Marriage to Hilde Jurezyss.

January. Suppression of *Die Pleite*, thereafter absorbed in monthly *Der Gegner*, of which Herzfelde becomes co-editor.

March. Suppression of right-wing Kapp Putsch. General strike, followed by left-wing rising in the Ruhr put down by the army.

10 Jan. Piscator plays Archenholz in Strindberg's *Ghost Sonata*, dir. Oskar Spaun for Spaun–Piscator theatre Das Tribunal, performing in Königsberg Town Hall.

20 Jan. (1) at Das Tribunal.

30 Jan. (2) ditto.

17 Feb. (3) ditto.

June. Majority Socialists (SPD) leave the government.

4 Aug. Police president Richter initially refuses application by Piscator and Hermann Schüller to found a new Proletarian Theatre in Berlin.

October. *Der Gegner*, vol. 2, nr 4, is a special Proletarian Theatre issue containing text of *Russlands Tag* and Piscator article 'Über Grundlagen und Aufgaben des proletarischen Theaters'.

5 June. First Berlin Dada exhibition at Burchard's gallery.

14 Oct. (4). Opening of Proletarian Theatre, which performs in various Berlin halls.

7 Nov. Verhaeren *Les Aubes*, dir. Meyerhold at RSFSR Theatre 1, Moscow.

10 Nov. (5) for Proletarian Theatre.

5 Dec. (6) ditto.

1921

Productions: (1) Franz Jung *Wie lange noch, du Hure Bürgerliche Gerechtigkeit?*; (2) Jung *Die Kanaker*.

8 Mar. Berlin police refuse to renew Proletarian Theatre's licence.

March–April. Communist rising at Mansfeld (central Germany) led by Max Hölz, fails.

August. Lenin initiates New Economic Policy, concluding the revolutionary phase in Russia.

12 Aug. International Workers' Aid (IAH) founded by Willi Muenzenberg at Lenin's request, with sponsors including Grosz and Paquet. First Berlin meeting held in December.

8 Jan. (1) for Proletarian Theatre.

April. (2) Last production of Proletarian Theatre, which closes on 21 April.

April. Grosz and Herzfelde prosecuted in Berlin for portfolio *Gott mit uns*.

1 Oct. Piscator secretary of newly-formed 'Artists' Aid for the Starving in Russia'.

1922

Productions: (1) Gorky *Der Kleinbürger*; (2) Romain Rolland *Le Temps viendra*, des. Otto Schmalhausen, with Paul Henckels.

April. Rapallo Treaty between Germany and the USSR.

June. Assassination of Walther Rathenau by nationalists.

Summer. Grosz to the USSR for five months under IAH auspices.

September. Meeting of Constructivists

25 April. Crommelynck *Le Cocu Magnifique*, dir. Meyerhold in Moscow, des. Popova.

12 June. Meyerhold in Moscow launches his theory of 'bio-mechanics' or gymnastic acting.

September. Last issue of *Der Gegner*.

and Dada at Weimar marks end of latter movement. Independent Socialist Party (USPD) fuses with the SPD.

November. Conservative government under Cuno.

29 Sept. (1), first production of Piscator's and Rehfisch's Central-Theater, Berlin, an attempt to form a 'proletarian Volksbühne'.

17 Nov. (2) at Central-Theater.

1923

Production: (1) Tolstoy *The Power of Darkness*.

January. French troops occupy the Ruhr.

April. Inflation becomes unmanageable.

July. At the first Bauhaus exhibition in Weimar Gropius proclaims slogan 'Art and technology – a new unity'.

August. Stresemann Government effects currency stabilisation.

21 Oct. Communist rising in Thuringia quickly put down. Ditto Hamburg two days later.

9 Nov. Beer-cellar putsch by Hitler and Ludendorff in Munich fails.

January. (1), Last production at Central-Theater, which is taken over by the Rotter brothers.

March–April. Ostrovsky/Tretiakoff *Enough Simplicity in Every Wise Man*, dir. Eisenstein at Proletkult Theatre, Moscow, with film interlude.

April. Guest season by Tairoff's Kamerny Theatre at Deutsches Theater.

Autumn. Fritz Holl becomes Intendant of the Volksbühne.

3 Nov. Georg Kaiser *Nebeneinander*, dir. Viertel, des. Grosz, with Viertel's 'Die Truppe', Berlin.

Also during 1923 the Blue Blouses are formed, the first Soviet Agitprop group. Tairoff stages Chesterton's *The Man Who was Thursday* in a constructivist set by Vesnin. Eisenstein's article 'Montage of Attractions' appears in *LEF*.

1924

Productions: (1) Alfons Paquet *Fahnen*, des. Edward Suhr, with Veit Harlan, Leonard Steckel, Gustave Fröhlich; (2) Piscator and Felix Gasbarra *Revue Roter Rummel*, music Edmund Meisel; (3) O'Neill *Moon of the Caribbees* and Alfred Brust *Südseespiel*, des. Paul Malik, music W. Zeller.

21 Jan. Death of Lenin.

16 Feb. Prosecution of Grosz and Herzfelde for *Ecce Homo*.

April. Ruth Fischer and Arkadi Maslow leaders of KPD, which gets 3.7 million votes in May elections (as against 6m. SPD).

16 July. Toller leaves gaol.

December. Bauhaus to leave Weimar, owing to rightward shift of provincial government.

19 Mar. Brecht directs his *Edward II* in Munich.

26 May. (1) at Volksbühne.

June. Piscator a member of 'Red Group' of Communist artists run by Grosz and Heartfield.

September. Brecht starts work in Berlin as dramaturg for Reinhardt.

22 Nov. (2) for KPD winter election campaign.

21 Dec. (3) at Volksbühne.

Also during 1924 Egon Erwin Kisch's book of reportage *Der rasende Reporter* is published. IAH takes over Russ film studio in Moscow to form Mezhrabpom-Russ.

1925

Productions: (1) Hans Rehfisch *Wer weint um Juckenack*, with Gerda Müller and Heinrich George; (2) Berta Lask *Die Befreiung* with workers' acting group; (3) Rudolf Leonhard *Segel am Horizont*, des. Traugott Müller, with G. Müller, Aribert Wäscher, Henckels, Gustav von Wangenheim, Albert Venohr; (4) Wilhelm Schmidtbonn *Hilfe! Ein Kind ist von Himmel gefallen*; (5) Piscator and Gasbarra *Trotz Alledem*, des. Heartfield, music Meisel; (6) Hanns Johst *Die fröhliche Stadt*.

29 Mar. Death of Ebert, followed by election of Hindenburg as president.

14 June–13 Sept. Neue Sachlichkeit exhibition at Mannheim.

July. First KPD party conference. Thälmann elected leader and accepts Moscow line.

October. Locarno treaties between Germany and the Western Powers.

14 Oct. Bauhaus reopens at Dessau.

1 Feb. (1) at Volksbühne.

8 Mar. (2) at Central-Theater.

14 Mar. (3) at Volksbühne.

28 April. Eisenstein's *Strike* first shown in Moscow.

2 May. (4) for Volksbühne at Central-Theater.

12 July. (5) at Grosses Schauspielhaus for KPD conference.

September (6) at Munich Kammerspiele.

20 Oct. Klabund *Der Kreidekreis*, dir. Reinhardt, with Elisabeth Bergner at Deutsches Theater.

22 Dec. Carl Zuckmayer *Der fröhliche Weinberg*, dir. Reinhard Bruck at Theater am Schiffbauerdamm.

Also during 1925 Grosz and Herzfelde publish their polemical book *Die Kunst in Gefahr*.

1926

Productions: (1) Ortner *Michael Hundertpfund*, des. Cesar Klein; (2) Alfons Paquet *Sturmflut*, des. Suhr, film I. A. Hübler-Kahla, with George, Venohr, Erwin Kalser, Alexander Granach; (3) Paul Zech *Das trunkene Schiff*, des. Suhr, projections Grosz, with Carl Ludwig Achaz, Leonard Steckel; (4) Strindberg *Fantasy*; (5) Schiller *Die Räuber*, des. Müller, music Meisel, with Carl Ebert, Erwin Faber, Paul Bildt; (6) Gorki *The Lower Depths*, des. Suhr, with George, Granach, Kalser, Maria Leiko, Agnes Straub.

January. IAH film distributors take Eisenstein's new film *Potemkin*. Meisel writes its incidental music, Piscator helps get it past censors.

17 Jan. (1) at Die Tribüne.

23 Jan. Sergei Tretiakoff: *Roar China*, dir. V. Fyodorov at Meyerhold's theatre, Moscow.

March–May. Toller tours the USSR.

5 Mar. IAH organises Intellectuals' Appeal for expropriation of German princes. Piscator signs.

29 May. At ninth congress of German Association of Workers' Theatres (DATB) a left opposition is formed on KPD initiative. Arthur Pieck chairman of Berlin section.

Summer. Piscator to Bandol (France) with Toller, Erich Engel, Wilhelm Herzog and Otto Katz.

Autumn. Tilla Durieux introduces Piscator to Ludwig Katzenellenbogen who offers to finance him.

20 Feb. (2) at Volksbühne.

4 Mar. Lunacharsky *Don Quixote*, dir. Holl at Volksbühne.

29 April. German première of *Potemkin*.

21 May. (3) at Volksbühne.

7 June. (4) at Munich Kammerspiele.

11 Sept. (5) at Staatstheater.

10 Nov. (6) at Volksbühne. Piscator meets Gorki.

Also during 1926 Grete Reiner's German translation of Hašek's *Schweik* is published. The Young Communists form an agit-prop group under Maxim Vallentin.

1927

Productions: (1) Heinrich Mann *Das Gastliche Haus*, des. Reigbert; (2) Gerhart Hauptmann *Die Weber*; (3) Ehm Welk *Gewitter über Gottland*, des. Müller, film Curt Oertel, with Granach, George, Kalser, Steckel, Venohr; (4) Toller *Hoppla, wir leben!* (see p. 84); (5) A. Tolstoy and P. Shchegolev *Rasputin* (see p. 87).

March. Gropius working on Total-Theater plans. Otto Katz administrator of Piscator's new company.

14 Mar. Meeting of young Volksbühne supporters demands a more political programme.

30 Mar. Herrenhaus meeting of Volksbühne members supporting Piscator, with Toller, Jessner, Martin, etc.

12 July. Formation of 'Sonderabteilungen' of Volksbühne membership to support new Piscatorbühne.

5 Oct. Soviet 'Blue Blouses' agit-prop group tours Germany till 18 Dec.

15–16 Nov. First conference of Revolutionary Writers in Moscow sets up international association (IVRS, later MORP).

21 Jan. (1) at Munich Kammerspiele.

15 Feb. (2) for unemployed stage workers, Berlin.

23 Mar. (3) at Volksbühne. Major controversy results from political interpolations by Piscator. He leaves the Volksbühne.

Spring–summer. Toller writes *Hoppla, wir leben!* Leo Lania writes first two acts of *Konjunktur*. Herzog sacked as Piscator's Chefdramaturg.

3 Sept. (4) at Theater am Nollendorfplatz. Runs till 7 Nov., then tours Frankfurt, Mannheim, Cologne.

16 Oct. Piscator Studio founded.

10 Nov. (5) at Theater am Nollendorfplatz. Runs till 20 Jan.

1928

Productions: (1) Hašek *Adventures of the Good Soldier Schweik*, dramatised by Max Brod and Hans Reimann (see p. 90); (2) Leo Lania *Konjunktur* (see p. 96).

January. Prosecution of Johannes R. Becher for his novel *Lewisite*.

February. Hannes Meyer succeeds Gropius as director of the Bauhaus.

March. Piscator rents Lessing-Theater as second theatre.

8–9 April. Communists gain control of DATB at tenth congress. Béla Bálazs, later Wangenheim, become artistic directors.

30 April–8 May. RAPP founded by first congress of Proletarian Writers, Moscow.

May. SPD win elections with 9m. votes, and lead new government with Stresemann foreign secretary.

7 July. Critical remarks by Meyerhold about Piscator reported in Paris *Monde*.

18 July. Release of Max Hölz.

19 Oct. Association of Proletarian-Revolutionary Writers (BPRS) set up as German section of IVRS. Piscator a member.

Autumn. Asja Lacis in charge of films at Soviet Trade Delegation, Berlin.

November. Piscator, Brecht and Fritz Sternberg discuss producing *Trommeln in der Nacht*.

December. Grosz and Herzfelde fined for *Hintergrund*, portfolio of Schweik drawings.

8 Jan. Jung *Heimweh*, dir. Steckel, des. Heartfield, music Hanns Eisler, as first Piscator Studio production.

23 Jan. (1) at Theater am Nollendorfplatz. Runs till 12 April.

1 Mar. Sinclair *Singing Jailbirds*, dir. Ernst Lönner at Lessing-Theater. Second Studio production.

10 April. (2) at Lessing-Theater. Runs till 3 May.

29 April. Mühsam *Judas*, dir. Leopold Lindtberg, as last Studio production.

14 April. J.-R. Bloch *Le dernier empereur*, dir. Martin, at Theater am Nollendorfplatz.

5 May. Marcel Achard *Marlbrough s'en va-t-en guerre*, dir. Kalser at Theater am Nollendorfplatz.

June. First Piscatorbühne bankrupted by suit for back entertainment tax. Piscator resigns licence to emergency committee of actors.

31 Aug. Brecht and Weill *Die Dreigroschenoper*, dir. Engel at Theater am Schiffbauerdamm.

16 Oct. Günther Weisenborn *U-Boot S 4* at Volksbühne, originally destined for Piscator's Studio.

23 Oct. Ferdinand Bruckner *Verbrecher* at Deutsches Theater.

Autumn. Berlin season of Moscow State Jewish Theatre under Granovsky.

2 Dec. P. M. Lampel *Revolte im Erziehungshaus*, dir. Hans Deppe at Thalia-Theater with Gruppe junger Schauspieler of ex-Piscator actors.

Also during 1928 the Sixth Comintern Congress in Moscow adopted 'left' policy of opposition to social-democracy. First year of the first Five-Year Plan. Trotsky banished from Moscow.

1929

Productions: (1) Maxwell Anderson and L. Stallings *What Price Glory?*, adapted Zuckmayer, des. Caspar Neher, music Walter Goehr, with Kortner, Hans Albers, Ernst Busch, Venohr, Kalser; (2) Walter Mehring *Der Kaufmann von Berlin* (see p. 98); (3) Schiller *Die Räuber*, des. Piscator; (4) Carl Credé § *218* (see p. 101). Writing and publication of *Das politische Theater*, Piscator's only book.

25 Mar. Piscator addresses Herrenhaus meeting of the Sonderabteilungen.

22 April. Discussion Piscator–Herbert Ihering broadcast by Berlin radio.

1 May. Berlin police fire on demonstrators.

1 Aug. First issue of *Die Linkskurve*, BPRS monthly review.

Late August. International Association of Workers' Theatres (later MORT) formed Moscow, with A. Pieck, Margarete Lode, Wangenheim and Bálazs as German representatives. Piscator to collaborate.

September. *Linkskurve* article on Piscatorbühne and non-revolutionary characters of its plays.

October. *Linkskurve* calls (2) 'a bad development'.

3 Oct. Death of Stresemann heralds end of moderate politics in Germany.

3 Oct. Ludwig Klopfer removes Piscator's name from Theater am Nollendorfplatz and bans him from the house, thus ending Second Piscatorbühne.

28 Oct. Wall Street crash initiates world economic crisis.

13 Feb. Mayakovsky *The Bed Bug*, dir. Meyerhold, des. Rodchenko, music Shostakovitch, in Moscow.

20 Mar. (1) at Theater in der Königgrätzer Strasse.

21 April. Mühsam *Sacco und Vanzetti*, dir. Lindtberg, with Busch, Friedrich Gnass and November-Studio group of ex-Piscator actors.

July. Performance of first two 'Lehrstücke' by Brecht at Baden-Baden.

Autumn. Martin takes over as Intendant of Volksbühne. Vallentin's agit-prop group, now called 'Das rote Sprachrohr', tours the USSR.

31 Aug. Brecht and Weill *Happy End* at Theater am Schiffbauerdamm.

6 Sept. (2) at Theater am Nollendorfplatz. Runs four weeks.

6 Sept. Friedrich Wolf *Cyankali*, dir. Hans Hinrich, des. Wolfgang Boettcher, with Gruppe junger Schauspieler at Lessing-Theater. Later tours the USSR.

Sept. (3) at Theater am Nollendorfplatz.

9 Nov. Tretiakoff *Roar China* at Frankfurt in translation by Lania.

23 Nov. (4) at Mannheim, first performance of West German tour by Piscator–Kollektiv.

Also during 1929 Ihering publishes his *Reinhardt, Jessner, Piscator, oder Klassikertod?* Hilde Piscator and Theodor Plivier dramatise the latter's *Des Kaisers Kulis*. In Moscow Lunacharsky ceases to be Commissar for Education.

1930

Productions: (1) Credé § *218* (as in 1929); (2) Plivier *Des Kaisers Kulis* (see p. 101). Piscator's wife Hilde leaves him.

January. Hostile review of *Das politische Theater* by Berta Lask in *Linkskurve*. Frick becomes Minister for Education in Thuringia, first Nazi to hold such a post.

March. SPD coalition breaks up. Brüning becomes chancellor, governing by emergency decrees.

11 April. Mayakovsky's suicide.

6 May. Sonderabteilungen renamed Junge Volksbühne after expulsion by the parent body.

End June. First MORT congress, Moscow. Piscator visits Moscow to sign film contract.

1 Aug. Hannes Meyer sacked from Bauhaus for IAH activities. Goes to a professorship in Moscow.

14 Sept. Elections: SPD 8½m. votes, KPD 4¼m., Nazis 6½m., giving them 107 deputies in lieu of 12.

6–15 Nov. Second international conference of Proletarian Writers (MORP) at Kharkov.

23 Nov. Piscator speaks at inaugural meeting of Junge Volksbühne, Wallner-Theater.

January. Jessner resigns from Staatstheater and is succeeded by Ernst Legal.

16 Mar. Mayakovsky *The Bath House* at Meyerhold Theatre, Moscow.

3 April. (1) at Wallner-Theater. Runs eight weeks.

4 April. Meyerhold Theatre starts guest season at Theater in der Stresemannstrasse. Piscator sees *Roar China!* there.

31 Aug. (2) at Lessing-Theater. Runs four weeks and later transfers to Wallner-Theater.

31 Aug. Toller *Feuer aus den Kesseln*, dir. Hinrich, des. Neher, at Theater am Schiffbauerdamm.

29 Oct. (1) revived at Wallner-Theater.

8 Nov. Friedrich Wolf *Die Matrosen von Cattaro* at the Volksbühne, with Busch.

19 Nov. Ernst Ottwalt *Jeden Tag vier*, dir. Friedrich Neubauer, with Venohr, Lotte Löbinger, Curt Trepte at Wallner-Theater.

28 Nov. Bill-Belotserkovski *Mond von Links*, dir. Martin Kerb, des. Böttcher, music Goehr, with Venohr, Trepte, at Wallner-Theater.

10 Dec. Brecht and Eisler *Die Massnahme*, with workers' choral society, Berlin.

1931

Productions: (1) Friedrich Wolf *Tai Yang erwacht* (see p. 104).

January. Piscator arrested for failure to pay entertainment tax since 1928. Tretiakoff visits Berlin on a German lecture tour.

15 Jan. (1) at Wallner-Theater. Subsequently goes on tour.

17 Feb. Anatol Glebov *Inka* (or *Frau in Front*), dir. anon. (in part Pisca-

February. Wolf arrested for breach of abortion laws.

March. Pudovkin in Hamburg making *Deserter* for Mezhrabpom-Film.

2 April. Berlin police told to ban agit-prop performances at political meetings.

Mid April. Piscator and Katz to Moscow. Latter to work in film section of IAH HQ.

May. Wolf to Moscow to write script for Mezhrabpom-Film. Ihering in Moscow for two months. Heart-field comes for show of his work and stays a year.

25 June–2 July. Presidium of MORT meets Moscow. Piscator paper 'on the International Workers' Theatre'.

24 Oct. Announced that Mezhrabpom-Film will employ Piscator, Hans Richter, Bálazs, etc.

28 Oct. Katzenellenbogen arrested in Berlin for falsifying accounts.

tor), des. Böttcher, with Löbinger, Kalser, Venohr.

5 Mar. Zuckmayer *Der Hauptmann von Köpenick*, dir. Heinz Hilpert at Deutsches Theater.

October. Meyerhold's theatre closes for renovation (for a year).

17 Nov. Berlin première of Pabst's film *Kameradschaft*, script by Ottwalt, Lampel and László Vajda, with Busch and Gnass.

9 Dec. Berlin première of Victor Trivas's film *Niemandsland*, music Eisler.

1932

No productions.

10 April. Hindenburg re-elected president.

23 April. Soviet Central Committee dissolves all artistic organisations.

Spring. Brecht visits Moscow. Grosz goes to teach in New York.

1 June. Von Papen becomes Chancellor and announces campaign against *Kulturbolschewismus*.

20 July. Dissolution of the Prussian government (SPD).

22 Aug. Dessau city council dissolves the Bauhaus.

31 July. Nazis get 14m. votes at elections, i.e. 235 seats against KPD's 89.

29 Oct.–3 Nov. Central organising

12 Jan. Brecht and Eisler *Die Mutter* at Wallner-Theater for Gruppe junger Schauspieler and Junge Volksbühne.

11 April. Berlin radio broadcasts Brecht's *St Joan of the Stockyards*, which no theatre will take.

30 May. Berlin première of Dudow's film *Kuhle Wampe*, script by Brecht and Ottwalt, music Eisler.

July. Lukács in *Die Linkskurve* attacks reportage, montage, the documentary approach and the work of Ernst Ottwalt.

August. Toller, Rehfisch, Wolf, Zuckmayer, Brecht, Credé, Lampel and Plivier on list of undesirable writers in Nazi *Völkischer Beobachter*.

committee of Soviet writers pro-
claims principle of Socialist Realism.
9–14 Nov. Second Plenum of MORT.
Piscator elected to Secretariat (with
A. Pieck) and Presidium (with
Wolf and Wangenheim).
November. Nazis, with 10m. votes,
lose 40 seats at elections.

23 Dec. Julius Hay *Gott, Kaiser und
Bauer* at Deutsches Theater, dir.
Martin, with Kortner, Kalser, Paul
Wegener.

1933

No productions.

30 Jan. Hitler becomes Chancellor.
27 Feb. Reichstag fire.
14 July. Suppression of all parties
except the Nazis.
August. Brecht settles in Denmark.
Piscator hopes to film *Schweik* in the
USSR.
14–16 Aug. Piscator addresses first
MORT congress, Moscow, 'Olympiad' of groups from nine countries,
including 'Kolonne Links' (German
agit-prop), who remain.

12 Jan. Grosz emigrates to the USA.
Spring. Volksbühne dissolved. Rainer
Schlösser appointed Reich Drama-
turg.

19 Sept. Première of Pudovkin's *The
Deserter* in Moscow.
24 Oct. Hans Otto, leader of Berlin
actors' union, murdered by Nazis.
30 Nov. Bruckner *Die Rassen* at
Zurich Schauspielhaus.

1934

Film *Revolt of the Fishermen* (Vostaniye Rybakov) for Mezhrabpom-Film, with
Alexei Diky, Vera Janukova. Piscator becomes president of MORT. *Das politische
Theater* appears in a Soviet edition.

January. Piscator a contributing editor
to *New Theatre*, New York (with
Alfred Kreymborg, Lee Strasberg,
etc.).
Summer. Piscator visits Prague (seeing
E. F. Burian) and Paris.
9–10 July. Mühsam murdered in
Oranienburg Concentration Camp.
August. First Soviet Writers' Congress, attended by Toller, Herzfelde, etc. Message from Piscator.
1 Dec. Murder of S. M. Kirov in
Leningrad, prelude to Soviet purges.

22 Jan. Shostakovitch *Lady Macbeth of
Mtsensk* at State Musical Theatre,
Moscow.
Spring. First showing of *Revolt of the
Fishermen*.

5 Oct. Première of *Revolt of the
Fishermen*.
8 Nov. Wolf *Professor Mamlock* at
Zurich Schauspielhaus.
10 Dec. Wolf *Sailors of Cattaro*, dir.
Irving Goldman for Theatre Union,
New York.

1935

No productions. First performance of Dreiser–Piscator *An American Tragedy*.

March–April. Wolf visits the USA and attends first congress of League of American writers (affiliated to MORP).

April–May. Piscator holds a theatre conference in Moscow. Brecht attends and meets Meyerhold, Tairoff, Eisenstein. Other visitors around this time include Harold Clurman, Gordon Craig, Granach, Teo Otto and Mei Lan-fang.

Summer. Piscator and Wolf discuss theatre plans with Volga Republic authorities.

21–25 June. First Writers' Congress in Defence of Culture, Paris.

14 July. Popular Front established in France.

November. Busch visits Moscow at invitation of MORT and Tretiakoff, and stays two years.

5 Jan. Clifford Odets *Waiting for Lefty*, League of Workers' Theatres, New York.

April. Dreiser–Piscator *An American Tragedy* at Hedgerow Theatre, Moylan, Pa.

May. German-language travelling theatre for the Ukraine established Dnepropetrovsk, with Maxim Vallentin, Curt Trepte and Kolonne Links members.

19 Nov. Brecht and Eisler *Mother* for Theatre Union, New York.

1936

No productions.

28 Jan. *Pravda* article attacking Shostakovitch initiates campaign against 'formalism'.

March. Hitler reoccupies the Rhineland.

Spring. Actors of the State Academic Theatre, Engels, brought to Moscow for training, while Vallentin, Trepte and Bernhard Reich work at Engels with local amateurs.

3 April. Mühsam's wife Zenzl arrested in Moscow.

May. Popular Front win French elections and form government.

January. Piscator and Julius Hay visit Volga Republic to plan film *Die Wahrheit* (unfinished).

13 Mar. Dreiser–Piscator *The Case of Clyde Griffiths* (new title), dir. Lee Strasberg with Morris Carnovsky, Luther Adler, Elia Kazan, John Garfield, and the Group Theatre, at Ethel Barrymore Theatre, New York.

End May. Eisenstein's new film *Bezhin Meadow* previewed by politicians and its destruction ordered.

Early Summer. Piscator, Plivier, and
Gustav Regler visit Volga Republic.

18 June. Death of Gorky.

8 June. Mezhrabpom-Film dissolved.

18 July. Nationalist insurrection in
Spain initiates Civil War.

Spring–summer. 'Living Newspaper'
programmes staged by Federal
Theatre in New York and other
US cities.

July–September. Piscator in Western
Europe on MORT business.

August. Trial of Zinoviev, Kamenev,
etc. in Moscow.

October. Wilhelm Pieck advises Piscator not to return to the USSR.
MORT dissolved.

4 Nov. Brecht *Die Rundköpfe und die
Spitzköpfe*, music Eisler, in Copenhagen.

Also during autumn 1936 Carola Neher, Granach, Maria Leiko and Ottwalt are
arrested in the USSR.

1937

No productions. Piscator marries Maria Ley.

January. Second major Moscow trial,
of Bukharin, Radek, etc.

January. Wolf *Das trojanische Pferd*, dir.
Reich at German State Theatre,
Engels. The company subsequently
dissolved and its German members
returned to Moscow.

February. Piscator and Max Jacobi
form company to film *Schweik*.
Lania, Brecht and Henri Jeanson
involved.

June. Jacobi withdraws from *Schweik*
scheme.

16 Mar. Brecht proposes a 'Diderot
Society' of theatre innovators, including Piscator. Not realised.

21 June. French Popular Front government falls.

27 Oct. Münzenberg expelled from
the KPD.

28 Sept. Brecht and Weill *The Threepenny Opera* at Théâtre de l'Etoile,
Paris.

19 Dec. *Pravda* article 'An Alien
Theatre' attacking Meyerhold.

During 1937 an Exposition Universelle is held in Paris. Arrests in the USSR
include Béla Kun (later executed), Tretiakoff (ditto), Reich and Asja Lacis (both
deported).

1938

No productions.

February–March. Together with Sam
Spiegel Piscator tries to organise a
German theatre tour of the US,
involving Steckel, Kalser, Granach,
etc.

8 Jan. Meyerhold Theatre liquidated
in Moscow.

June. Contract with Gilbert Miller for
adaptation of *War and Peace* by
Alfred Neumann and Piscator, to

11 Mar. Hitler occupies Austria.

7 Aug. Death of Stanislavsky.

1 Oct. Munich Agreement with Britain and France allows Hitler to occupy Czech frontier areas.

24 Dec. The Piscators sail to New York.

be directed by Piscator in New York and London.

November. Miller rejects Acts 4 and 5 of *War and Peace*. Brecht completes *Galileo*.

1939

No productions.

15 Mar. Hitler occupies all Czechoslovakia.

End March. Defeat of Spanish Republic.

22 May. Suicide of Toller in New York.

June. Meyerhold arrested in Moscow.

19 Aug. Nazi–Soviet pact.

1 Sept. German invasion of Poland starts the Second World War.

9 Mar. Second version of *War and Peace* completed.

26 May. Schiller *Wilhelm Tell*, dir. Jessner, with Granach and Ernst Deutsch at El Capitan Theatre, Los Angeles.

30 June. Federal Theatre Project terminated by Congress.

1940

Productions: (1) Shaw *Saint Joan*, des. H. A. Condell, music Felix Günther, with Luise Rainer and Washington Civic Theatre (amateurs); (2) Shakespeare *King Lear*, des. Antonin Heythum, music Henry Cowell and Harold Burris-Meyer, with Sam Jaffe, Herbert Berghof.

2 Feb. Meyerhold shot in a Moscow prison.

Spring. German armies overrun Denmark, Norway, Holland, Belgium and France. French intern Muenzenberg, Mehring, Busch, Wolf, etc. Busch handed over to Gestapo, Muenzenberg killed by unknowns, Wolf released to the USSR.

January. Dramatic Workshop opens at New School of Social Research, New York with Piscator as director.

23 Feb. Dorothy Thompson and Fritz Kortner *Another Sun*, dir. Kortner, with Kalser and Johanna Hofer, at National Theatre, New York.

4 Mar. (1) at Belasco Theatre, Washington.

September. Studio Theatre founded, using New School auditorium.

14 Dec. (2) at Studio Theatre.

1941

No productions.

13 May. Brecht leaves Finland to take up post at Dramatic Workshop.

24 Mar. Klabund *The Circle of Chalk*, dir. James Light at Studio Theatre.

19 April. Brecht *Mutter Courage*, dir. Lindtberg at Zürich Schauspielhaus.

22 June. Hitler invades the USSR.

21 July. Brecht arrives in Los Angeles via the USSR and settles in Santa Monica.

3 June. Philip Yordan *Any Day Now*, dir. Robert Klein at Studio Theatre.

Summer. Piscator discusses production of Brecht's *The Good Person of Szechwan* with the Theatre Guild. Also plans production of *Arturo Ui*.

November. Frank Gabrielson *Days of Our Youth*, dir. Light at Studio Theatre.

7 Dec. Pearl Harbor. The US enters the war.

20 Dec. Bruckner *Criminals*, dir. Sanford Meisner at Studio Theatre.

1942

Production: (1) Piscator and Neumann *War and Peace*, des. Condell, film Hans Richter, with Hugo and Dolly Haas.

March. Lessing *Nathan the Wise* adapted Bruckner, dir. Light, with Berghof, at Studio Theatre. Transfers to Belasco Theatre for 28 performances.

May. Tennessee Williams hopes Dramatic Workshop will stage his *Orpheus Descending*.

19 Nov. Start of Russian Stalingrad offensive leading to encirclement of German 6th Army.

May. (1) at Studio Theatre. Runs for four weeks.

28 Nov. Daniel Lewis James *Winter Soldiers* at Studio Theatre. Thereafter the theatre unions decide to treat the Studio Theatre as a normal professional theatre, leading Piscator to ask the New School for a $20,000 subsidy for it.

1943

Production: (1) O'Neill *Mourning becomes Electra* with students. Studio Theatre is discontinued.

February. Brecht arrives in New York and stays till May.

March–April. Piscator preparing production of Brecht's *Private Life of the Master Race*, which Equity will let Studio Theatre present on the old non-professional terms. It falls through.

Spring. Marlon Brando arrives in New York and enrols in Dramatic Workshop.

4 Feb. Brecht *The Good Person of Szechwan*, dir. Steckel at Zürich Schauspielhaus.

6 Mar. Brecht evening at Studio Theatre, with Herzfelde, Peter Lorre and Elisabeth Bergner.

July–August. Plan to produce *Schweik* for Theatre Guild leads to clash with Brecht and Alfred Kreymborg, whose rival plan is further advanced than Piscator's.

3 Sept. Allied invasion of Italy. Italian armistice.

October. Piscator abandons production of *The Innocent Voyage* (an adaptation of Richard Hughes's *A High Wind in Jamaica*) for the Theatre Guild.

June–July. Piscator Theatre Group performs at Sayville Playhouse (Long Island).

9 Sept. Brecht *Galileo*, dir. Steckel at Zürich Schauspielhaus.

15 Oct. (1) at Rooftop Theatre, New York.

15 Nov. Paul Osborn *The Innocent Voyage*, dir. Osborn, with Oskar Homolka, Berghof at Belasco Theatre.

1944

Productions: (1) Irving Kaye Davis *Last Stop*. New School board discuss closing the Dramatic Workshop but postpone their decision for another year.

March. Busch condemned in Berlin to four years' imprisonment for high treason.

6 June. Allied landings in Normandy.

25 Aug. Liberation of Paris.

21 Feb. *Nathan the Wise* revived for 22 performances at Studio Theatre, thanks to special concessions by theatre unions.

June–July. Piscator's group at Sayville includes Brando, whom he sacks.

5 Aug. (1) at Ethel Barrymore Theatre.

December. Brecht in Santa Monica begins work on *Galileo* adaptation with Charles Laughton.

Also during 1944 Fred Zinnemann's film of Anna Seghers' *The Seventh Cross* is released, with Spencer Tracy and cast including Granach and Felix Bressart.

1945

No productions.

January. Dramatic Workshop has 40–60 full-time and about 250 part-time students.

7 May. German capitulation follows Hitler's death and the fall of Berlin.

June. Piscator abandons direction of Brecht's *Private Life of the Master Race* for CIO-backed 'Theatre of All Nations'. Berthold Viertel takes over.

12 June. Brecht *Private Life of the Master Race*, dir. Viertel, des. Leo Kerz, music Eisler, at City College, New York.

15 Aug. Hebbel-Theater, Berlin, opens with Martin as intendant and a

6 Aug. Japanese surrender follows dropping of first atomic bomb on Hiroshima.

October. Dramatic Workshop moves to President Theatre, West 48th Street.

27 Dec. Bryn J. Hovde succeeds Alvin Johnson as president of the New School.

production of *Die Dreigroschenoper*.

7 Sept. Deutsches Theater re-opens with Von Wangenheim as intendant and a production of *Nathan der Weise* with Paul Wegener as Nathan.

November. Robert Ardrey *Thunder Rock*, dir. Martin, with Busch, at Hebbel-Theater.

1946

No productions.

4 June. Wolf, back in Berlin, invites Piscator to come and direct a film.

September. Wolfgang Langhoff succeeds Wangenheim at Deutsches Theater. Fritz Wisten becomes Intendant at Theater am Schiffbauerdamm. Gasbarra in Italy renews contact with Piscator.

1 Oct. Conclusion of the major Nuremberg War Crimes trial.

28 June. Gorki *The Lower Depths*, dir. Martin, with Busch, at Hebbel-Theater.

14 Dec. Zuckmayer *Des Teufels General*, dir. Hilpert, des. Neher, at Zürich Schauspielhaus.

Also in 1946 Otto Katz returns from Mexico to join the Czech Foreign Office press department.

1947

No productions.

6 Feb. Ruth Fischer denounces her brother Gerhart Eisler to Un-American Activities Committee as a GPU agent.

May. Hanns Eisler interrogated in California.

Spring. Wolf, involved in the revival of the Volksbühne in the Soviet zone of Germany, hopes to get Piscator to direct there.

24 Sept. Hanns Eisler before the Un-American Activities Committee.

31 Oct. Brecht, after testifying to the Committee, leaves the US for Zürich.

11 Feb. Wolf *Die Matrosen von Cattaro*, dir. Busch with himself and Gnass at Theater am Schiffbauerdamm.

17 April. Sartre *The Flies*, dir. Paul Ransom at President Theatre.

Spring. Dramatic Workshop takes over Rooftop Theatre as a 'People's Theatre,, initially with 1630 members.

31 July. Brecht *Galileo*, dir. Joseph Losey, music Eisler, with Laughton, at Coronet Theatre, Los Angeles.

3 Dec. Williams *A Streetcar named Desire*, dir. Kazan, with Brando at Ethel Barrymore Theatre.

Also in 1947 the Actors' Studio is opened in New York by former members of the Group Theatre. Joseph McCarthy is elected to the Senate.

1948

Production: (1) Robert Penn Warren *All the King's Men*, adapted by Warren and Piscator.

13 Jan. Death of Karl Heinz Martin.

1 Mar. New School decides to shed the Dramatic Workshop by end of 1948–49.

20 June. Currency reform in Western zones of Germany leads to Berlin blockade and final division of the country.

14 Jan. (1) at President Theatre.

22 Oct. Brecht returns to Berlin to prepare production of *Mutter Courage*.

1949

Production: (1) Wolfgang Borchert *Outside the Door*. Dramatic Workshop separates from the New School under its own trustees with Piscator as chairman.

February–March. Wolf, Brecht and Jhering unite in trying to get Piscator to direct at Volksbühne and Brecht's new Berliner Ensemble.

Autumn. Constitution of two separate German states, the Federal Republic (West) and the DDR or Democratic Republic (East), the latter with Wilhelm Pieck as president.

11 Jan. Brecht *Mutter Courage*, dir. Brecht and Engel, with Weigel, at Deutsches Theater.

1 Mar. (1) at President Theatre.

1 Sept. A separate West Berlin Volksbühne opens at the Theater am Kurfürstendamm.

Also during 1949 Brecht publishes his main theoretical work, the *Short Organum for the Theatre*.

1950

Production: (1) John F. Matthews *The Scapegoat* (after Kafka's *The Trial*), des. Condell.

March. The Rooftop Theatre has been given up.

Summer. Fritz Wisten becomes Intendant of the East Berlin Volksbühne.

19 April. (1) at President Theatre.

Also in 1950 Wolf becomes DDR ambassador to Poland. Eisler settles in East Berlin. Joseph McCarthy becomes chairman of Senate committee on Un-American Activities.

1951

Productions: (1) Shakespeare *Macbeth*, des. Zvi Geyra; (2) Fritz Hochwälder *Virginia*, des. H. G. Zircher. Piscator returns to Germany.

17 Mar. SED (or East German Communist party) passes resolution 'Against Formalism in Art and Literature'.

6 Oct. Piscator leaves the US for the German Federal Republic. Maria Piscator remains in charge of the Dramatic Workshop. He asks Neumann to revise *War and Peace* in view of interest shown by the Hamburg Schauspielhaus and the Schlosspark Theater in Berlin.

28 Feb. (1) in New York.

17 Mar. Brecht and Paul Dessau *Lucullus* at State Opera, East Berlin, to a closed audience.

4 Dec. (2) at Hamburg Schauspielhaus.

1952

Productions: (1) *Des Menschen Grundgesetz* (programme of one-acters); (2) Lessing *Nathan der Weise*; (3) Peter Ustinov *The Love of Four Colonels*, des. Ambrosius Humm; (4) Büchner *Leonce und Lena*; (5) Büchner *Dantons Tod*, des. Erhardt Klonk.

June. Sees Jean Vilar in Paris and tries to interest the TNP in *War and Peace*.

3 Oct. Death of Alfred Neumann in Lugano.

3 Dec. Otto Katz is hanged in Prague as a member of Rudolf Slansky's alleged conspiracy.

16 Mar. (1) at Hamburg Kammerspiele.

14 May. (2) at Marburg.

Summer. The Maxim-Gorky Theater, East Berlin, opens with Vallentin as Intendant.

11 Sept. (3) at Zürich Schauspielhaus.

27 Oct. (4) at Giessen.

2 Nov. (5) at Marburg.

1953

Productions: (1) Shaw *Androcles and the Lion*; (2) Hochwälder *Das heilige Experiment*; (3) Shakespeare *Macbeth*; (4) Sartre *Im Räderwerk* (adapted from *L'Engrenage* by Oskar Wälterlin) des. Hermann Soherr, music Aleida Montijn.

5 Mar. Death of Stalin.

20 May. Maria Piscator resigns from Dramatic Workshop.

June. Piscator visits Gasbarra in Italy.

17 July. Rioting in East Berlin.

5 Oct. Death of Wolf.

Winter. Piscator and Max Horkheimer discuss establishment of a theatre school in Frankfurt.

1 Jan. (1) at Komödie, The Hague.

14 Feb. (2) ditto.

May. Piscator works with Guntram Prüfer in Hamburg on revision of *War and Peace*.

Summer. Oskar Fritz Schuh becomes Intendant of the West Berlin Volksbühne for five years.

1 Sept. (3) at Oldenburg.

27 Sept. (4) at Frankfurt Städtische Bühnen Kleines Haus.

1954

Productions: (1) Shaw *Caesar and Cleopatra*; (2) Arthur Miller *The Crucible*, des. Paul Walter; (3) ditto, des. Walter Pietsch.

January. Hesse provincial government awards Piscator its Goethe Plaque.

12 April–14 May. J. Robert Oppenheimer examined by an Atomic Energy Commission Security Board in Washington.

23 July. Boleslaw Barlog, Intendant of Schlosspark and Schiller Theatres in West Berlin, invites Piscator to do a production.

Summer. East Berlin Volksbühne moves back to its old theatre on the Bülowplatz (renamed Luxemburgplatz).

2 Dec. US Senate condemns McCarthyism.

March. Berliner Ensemble takes over Theater am Schiffbauerdamm.

15 June. (1) at Komödie, The Hague.

July. Brecht *Mother Courage*, in the Berliner Ensemble production, at the Théâtre des Nations in Paris.

20 Sept. (2) at National-Theater, Mannheim, Kleines Haus.

October–November. (3) at Tübingen.

1955

Productions: (1) *The Crucible*; (2) Piscator, Neumann and Prüfer *War and Peace*, des. H. W. Lenneweit, music Boris Blacher, with Kalser; (3) *The Crucible*; (4) *Im Räderwerk*; (5) *War and Peace*; (6) William Faulkner *Requiem for a Nun*, des. Franz Mertz; (7) Paolo Levi *Der Fall Pinedus*, des. Walter.

17 Jan. Piscator's first return to Berlin.

12 Mar. Death of Plivier in Switzerland.

29 April. Piscator sees *The Caucasian Chalk Circle* in Frankfurt.

28 May. Addresses SPD Forum in West Berlin on 'Confessional Theatre'.

24–25 Oct. First return to East Berlin. Meets Jhering, Heartfield, Eisler, Wangenheim, Seghers, Langhoff, etc.

2 Nov. Sees *Mother Courage* at the Berliner Ensemble.

8 Feb. (1) at Volkstheater, Göteborg.

20 Mar. (2) at Schillertheater.

20 April. (3) at Marburg.

15 June. (4) at Tübingen.

19 Sept. (5) at Landestheater, Darmstadt.

4 Oct. Zuckmayer *Das kalte Licht*, dir. Barlog, at Schillertheater.

10 Nov. (6) at Schlossparktheater.

30 Dec. (7) at National-Theater, Mannheim, Kleines Haus.

1956

Productions: (1) *Requiem for a Nun*; (2) Büchner *Dantons Tod*, des. Neher; (3) *War and Peace*; (4) ditto.

February. Khrushchev makes secret speech to 20th party congress in Moscow.

Spring. English Stage Company under George Devine takes over Royal Court Theatre, London.

14 Aug. Death of Brecht in East Berlin.

October. Suez War: Britain, France, and Israel invade Egypt. Budapest rising suppressed by Red Army.

26 Oct. Piscator elected a corresponding member of the East German Academy of Arts.

16 Feb. (1) at Volkstheater, Göteborg.

4 May. (2) at Schillertheater.

Summer. Schillertheater production of *War and Peace* at the Théâtre des Nations, Paris.

24 June. (3) at Tübingen.

1 Oct. *The Diary of Anne Frank*, dir. Barlog, at Schlossparktheater.

21 Nov. (4) at Krefeld.

1957

Productions: (1) Schiller *Die Räuber*, des. Walter, music Montijn; (2) Pirandello *As You Desire Me*; (3) Tolstoy *The Root of All Evil*, Chekhov *The Bear* and *The Proposal*; (4) *War and Peace*; (5) Strindberg *The Dance of Death*, parts I and II, condensed by Franz Hoellering.

February. Piscator invited to direct *Richard III* with Busch at Deutsches Theater.

2 May. Schillertheater production of *Requiem for a Nun* given at Théâtre des Nations, Paris, against Piscator's advice.

1 Oct. Willi Brandt becomes mayor of West Berlin.

13 Jan. (1) at Mannheim National-Theater. Inauguration of new theatre and 175th anniversary of first performance.

16 May. (3) at Schlossparktheater.

25 Oct. (4) at Uppsala.

24 Nov. (5) at Thalia-Theater, Hamburg.

1958

Productions: (1) O'Neill *Mourning Becomes Electra*, des. Hans Aeberli; (2) Schiller *Wilhelm Tell*, des. Walter; (3) Georg Kaiser *Gas*, parts I and II; (4) Miller *The Crucible*, des. Piscator and Aeberli.

March. Vallentin wishes to stage *The Case of Clyde Griffiths* in East Berlin.

6–8 June. Congress of the Volksbühne movement at Mannheim. Lecture

Jan. (1) at Essen Municipal Theatre.

7 June. (2) at Mannheim National-Theater, Kleines Haus.

Summer. Steckel succeeds Schuh for

by Piscator on 'Author and Director'.

Summer. Piscator plan to set up a theatre section of Folkwangschule at Essen.

one year as Intendant of West Berlin Volksbühne.

28 Sept. (3) at Bochum Schauspielhaus.

23 Nov. (4) at Essen Municipal Theatre.

1959

Productions: (1) *Die Räuber*, des. Piscator and Aeberli, music Montijn; (2) Kaiser *Nebeneinander*; (3) Max Frisch *Biedermann und die Brandstifter*, des. Walter; (4) Schiller *Don Carlos*, des. Hannes Meyer, music Montijn; (5) *The Dance of Death* I and II.

24 Feb. (1) at Essen.

23 Mar. Brecht *Arturo Ui*, dir. Peter Palitzsch and Manfred Wekwerth, des. von Appen, at Berliner Ensemble.

May–June. Piscator at Dillenburg recording interviews with Gerd Semmer.

5–6 July. Grosz dies in West Berlin a few weeks after returning from the US.

16 Aug. Piscator speech to Deutsche Akademie der darstellenden Künste, Bayreuth.

4 May. (2) at Thalia-Theater, Hamburg.

22 May. (3) at Mannheim National-Theater, Kleines Haus.

Summer. Rudolf Nölte succeeds Steckel for one year at the West Berlin Volksbühne.

28 Sept. (4) at Munich Kammerspiele.

21 Nov. (5) at Essen.

1960

Productions: (1) Brecht *Mutter Courage*, des. Ekkehard Grübler, music Dessau; (2) Sartre *Huis-clos*, des. Aeberli; (3) Blacher *Rosamunde Floris* (text after Kaiser), des. Hans-Ulrich Schmückle; (4) Sternheim *1913*, des. Lenneweit; (5) *Huis-clos*.

20 Feb. (1) at Kassel.

2 May. (2) at Essen.

9 June. Death of Rehfisch in Switzerland.

Summer. Piscator negotiating to get the West Berlin Volksbühne but Günter Skopnik succeeds Nölte for two years.

21 Sept. (3) at Städtische Oper, West Berlin.

17 Nov. (4) at Munich Kammerspiele.

24 Nov. (5) at Marburg.

1961

Productions: (1) Jean Anouilh *Becket*, des. Aeberli, music Montijn; (2) *Huis-clos*; (3) Hans Henny Jahnn *Der staubige Regenbogen*, des. Mertz, music Montijn; (4) *1913*; (5) Miller *Death of a Salesman*, des. Mertz, with Steckel; (6) *1913*.

May–August. Mainly at Grado in NE Italy.

9 Nov. Death of Lania in Munich.

5 Jan. (1) at Essen.
9 Feb. (2) at Tübingen.
17 Mar. (3) at Frankfurt, Kleines Haus.
19 Sept. (4) at Frankfurt, Kleines Haus.
6 Oct. (5) at the Theater am Kurfürstendamm. Piscator's first production for the postwar Volksbühne.
29 Oct. (6) at Essen.

1962

Productions: (1) Brecht *Flüchtlingsgespräche* (adapted by Piscator); (2) *1913*; (3) Jean Genet *Le Balcon*, des. Johannes Waltz, music Montijn; (4) Gerhart Hauptmann *Atriden-Tetralogie* (adapted by Piscator), des. Mertz, music Montijn; (5) Anouilh *La Grotte*, des. Lenneweit.

February. Rolf Hochhuth first visits Piscator.

Spring. Piscator's appointment to be artistic director of the Volksbühne is announced.

6 Sept. Death of Hanns Eisler in East Berlin.

7 Oct.–30 Dec. Grosz exhibition at West Berlin Academy.

6 Feb. *War and Peace*, dir. Val May at Bristol Old Vic.
15 Feb. (1) at Munich Kammerspiele.
17 Feb. (2) at Tübingen.
31 Mar. (3) at Frankfurt Städtische Bühnen.
Summer. Wolfgang Heinz becomes Intendant of the East Berlin Volksbühne for one year.
7 Oct. (4) at Theater am Kurfürstendamm for Freie Volksbühne.
7 Oct. Brecht *Die Tage der Commune*, dir. Palitzsch and Wekwerth, des. Appen, at Berliner Ensemble.
16 Dec. (5) at Theater am Kurfürstendamm for Freie Volksbühne.

1963

Productions: (1) Rolf Hochhuth *Der Stellvertreter*, des. Kerz, music Montijn; (2) Romain Rolland *Robespierre* (adapted by Piscator and Gasbarra), des. Schmückle, music Blacher and Montijn; (3) Verdi *The Robbers*, des. Walter; (4) Shakespeare *The Merchant of Venice*, des. Schmückle, music Montijn.

26 Mar. *War and Peace* shown on Granada TV in England.
30 April. Opening of new Volksbühne

20 Feb. (1) at Theater am Kurfürstendamm.
10 April. *War and Peace*, dir. Wolf-

building in West Berlin. Speech by Piscator.

August. Republication of *Das politische Theater*, revised by Gasbarra.

October. Piscator addresses a conference of Dramaturgs in West Berlin.

20 Dec. Start of the 'Auschwitz Trial' of SS men at Frankfurt.

gang Heinz and Hannes Fischer at East Berlin Volksbühne.

1 May. (2) at Freie Volksbühne.

18 June. (3) at Teatro Comunale, Florence.

Autumn. Heinz takes over from Langhoff as Intendant of the Deutsches Theater.

21 Oct. (1) goes on tour.

1 Dec. (4) at Freie Volksbühne.

1964

Productions: (1) Sartre *Le Diable et le bon Dieu*, des. Lenneweit, music Montijn; (2) Richard Strauss *Salome*, des. Schmückle; (3) Herbert Asmodi *Mohrenwäsche* (with Willi Trenk-Trebitsch as co-director); (4) Heinar Kipphardt *In der Sache J. Robert Oppenheimer*, des. Schmückle, film Werner Krien; (5) Shaw *Androcles and the Lion*, des. Hein Heckroth, music Montijn.

21 May. (1) at Freie Volksbühne.

31 May. (2) at Teatro Comunale, Florence.

18 June. (3) at Freie Volksbühne.

11 Oct. (4) ditto.

16 Dec. (5) ditto.

1965

Productions: (1) *In der Sache J. Robert Oppenheimer*, des. Schmückle; (2) Hauptmann *Fuhrmann Henschel*, des. Roman Weyl; (3) Peter Weiss *Die Ermittlung*, des. Schmückle, music Luigi Nono.

14 May. Speaks at conference on theatre architecture in West Berlin Academy.

20 Aug. Conclusion of the 'Auschwitz Trial' at Frankfurt.

19 Jan. (1) at Théâtre Royal du Parc, Brussels.

1 April. (2) at Freie Volksbühne.

19 Oct. (3) at Freie Volksbühne.

22 Dec. *War and Peace* in Wolfgang Heinz's production revived at Deutsches Theater.

1966

Production: (1) Hans Hellmut Kirst and Piscator *Aufstand der Offiziere*, des. Schmückle, music Montijn.

March. Writes 'Postscript' for republication of the original *Das politische Theater* by the East German Academy.

15 Jan. Günter Grass *Die Plebeier proben den Aufstand*, dir. Hansjörg Utzerath, des. Lenneweit, at Schillertheater.

2 Mar. (1) at Freie Volksbühne.

20 Mar. Piscator dies in a nursing home at Starnberg, Bavaria.

*The
Theatre of
Erwin Piscator*

1. Setting the scene

Politics and the arts

As the First World War ground to its end, the centre of gravity of the modern movement in the arts was already shifting. Before 1914, when so many of its formal and technical discoveries were made, everything seemed to radiate outwards from Paris. After about 1917 a lot of the interesting ideas originated from central Europe and revolutionary Russia. France remained the home of the great individual innovators. But in the new stage of development – social, collective, technological and ultimately political – such figures had less to say.

For anybody who wants to follow the movement beyond this turning-point the achievements of the Weimar Republic are crucial. Here was a new, hopefully democratic Germany which sprang from the defeated Empire of Wilhelm II and lasted precariously throughout the 1920s before being overthrown by Hitler. The artists (in the broadest sense) who came to maturity there were generally well informed about the prewar French movements – much more so than their contemporaries in Britain and the United States – but because they had reason to be critical of the world about them they were not concerned so much to explore further as to relate the new formal conventions to pressing social and economic realities. Where in France there had been Apollinaire, Picasso, Matisse, the premiere of *Le Sacre du printemps* and the establishment of *vers libre*, in Weimar Germany there was Brecht, George Grosz, the Bauhaus, the tubular metal chair and the adoption of sanserif all-lower-case asymmetrical typography.

What was it gave the artists of the Weimar Republic their keen social concern, their collective drive and their cutting edge? In the first place it was their opposition to the war, which had been stronger and more widespread than in any other belligerent country except Russia. This feeling, courageously expressed throughout the war years in magazines such as Franz Pfemfert's Berlin weekly *Die Aktion*, led not only to their association with the revolutionary movement which overthrew the Empire in November 1918 but also to a lasting scepticism about the great Social-Democratic Party which at first supported the war. Many were attracted, like the young Ernst Toller, to the Independent Socialists or USPD who broke away to form their own parliamentary party; others were drawn to the small revolutionary Spartacus Union under Karl Liebknecht and Rosa Luxemburg, who held, with the Russian Bolsheviks, that the war would be ended by the working class seizing power. Few of those under thirty opted for orthodox socialism, let alone the conservative or nationalist parties.

The results of the German Revolution confirmed their scepticism, though without quite destroying their hopes. The main Socialist party or SPD opposed every left-wing attempt to seize power, and in order to do so was prepared to compromise not only with the traditional representatives of law and order but also with the Freikorps or right-wing private armies which later became a mainstay of the Nazi movement. So Liebknecht and Luxemburg were murdered by Freikorps members after the defeat of the Spartacist rising in Berlin, the eminent anarchist writer Gustav Landauer after that of the Munich Soviet in the spring of 1919, when the poets Toller and Erich Mühsam were gaoled. At the same time attempted right-wing coups were also defeated, notably Hitler's 'beer-cellar putsch' in Munich in 1923, and once the crazy currency inflation had been stabilised that year the country seemed to be settling down as a middle-of-the-road conservative democracy, with only the odd scandal or censorship controversy to suggest that its liberalism was skin-deep. Until 1925 it had a Socialist president, though after the stabilisation the SPD played little part in governing the country, and the economy remained almost wholly capitalist. But Prussia, the chief of its federated states, was under Socialist control, and so was its capital Berlin.

For the committed artist the chief source of tension in these years was the continuing struggle within the German Left, which became polarised into SPD and KPD (or Communists) following the break-up of the USPD in 1922. Often it seemed more important to be extreme than to be effective, so that a passion for sharp antagonisms developed which became fatal when the rise of Hitler's Nazis or National Socialists made a common front essential if they were not to capture power. The world economic crisis of 1929 gave the Nazis their chance and their mass backing, the uncompromising division of the Left allowed the democratic system to be suspended and Hitler to be handed the reins virtually unopposed. The artistic and intellectual climate, which thanks perhaps to the peculiar situation of Berlin had till then been astonishingly free and even revolutionary, changed as the Nazis progressed; signs of a cultural reaction could be seen as early as 1930. This was nothing to what happened once they took over the government in 1933. Their mixture of racialism, militarism, anti-intellectualism and extreme artistic conservatism drove practically every interesting artist into silence or (more often) exile.

One special aspect of artistic life in those fifteen years was the two-way traffic with the new Soviet Union. Beside obvious geographical factors there were other reasons why such links should be closer than for the rest of the capitalist world. Different as their effects were, the Russian and German Revolutions had set out from similar causes and seized power by similar methods; and there were some leaders like Luxemburg and Karl Radek who as it were straddled the frontiers. This ideological kinship, which led for a time to the maintenance of a Western Bureau of the Comintern in Berlin, was strengthened by the practical ties due to the Rapallo Treaty of 1922, the first attempt to normalise the USSR's relations with the outside world. As a result the immensely interesting development in Russia of the modern movement in the arts was more closely followed in Germany than anywhere else, exerting a direct influence through such visitors as Kandinsky and Lissitzky and through Ehrenburg's Berlin magazine *Veshch*. Communist artists came increasingly to take their cultural directives from Moscow, particularly once their opposition to the SPD became more aggressive; nowhere else was the militantly 'proletarian' phase of Soviet culture so strongly echoed. It became natural for German artists not merely to visit Russia but to take jobs there, notably in architecture and the cinema. And interwoven with this traffic was a unique organisation called International Workers' Aid or IAH, which had been set up on Lenin's instructions under Willi Muenzenberg in 1921 to organise famine relief for the new state and grew into a great complex for putting Germany in touch with Soviet ideas and needs.

The disillusionment, the unease and the special awareness of Russia were factors common to artists of every kind born in Germany between about 1890 and 1905. But where the theatre in particular was concerned there were special reasons why its artists could develop as they did. Unlike the practitioners of more individualistic arts, who were on the whole not technically impressive by comparison with the great Parisians, German theatre people had a marvellous instrument at their disposal. This was due in the first place to the country's origin in a great number of separate kingdoms or principalities, some of them very small, each with its court theatre which survived as an established cultural institution far above the provincial standards of centralised countries like England and France. No theatre in Europe could compare with the German in the resourcefulness of its technicians (who were the first to develop electric stage lighting, the revolving stage and other modern devices), in the security offered to its actors or in the opportunities open to its playwrights. It was quite simply more professional than any other.

In a sense also it was more popular, for nowhere had the late nineteenth-century movement for a People's Theatre been so effective as in Berlin, where the Freie Volksbühne organisation was set up in the summer of 1890 to recruit subscribers for performances which would bring 'Art to the People'. Almost from the outset this body was divided as to the political angle to be given to such Art, the one faction splitting off to form a Neue Freie Volksbühne which hoped that plays of real quality would enlarge the People's horizon, while the other still aimed to promote class-consciousness and the aims of the SPD. Even so the movement grew, till in 1914 the former alone had 70,000 members and could build its own theatre. In 1919 the two wings reunited but the less political policy prevailed and the membership became middle-class enough for the organisation to become in effect a huge cooperative ticket agency rather than a cultural–political force. For a time Max Reinhardt directed productions at the new theatre, then in 1918 he made way for Friedrich Kayssler, who was essentially a traditionalist. As a result, for the first few years of the Weimar Republic, the Volksbühne became a synonym for dullness. And this is the risk with the great non-commercial theatres for which Germany was and is famous: the guaranteed audience grows passive, the technical resources cost too much, the state- or municipally-employed actor starts to do a routine job and the theatre is no longer an adventure. But the strengths of the system are none the less there, and for the original artist responsive to his time they yielded spectacular results.

Piscator

When Erwin Piscator first came to Berlin on leave in 1918 he was twenty-four, a good-looking middle-class young man from Hesse-Nassau in the west centre of Germany, descendant of the protestant theologian Johannes Piscator whose translation of the Bible appeared in 1600. Strongly rooted in that area, which he always regarded as home, he had run away from a business career to study theatre history with Arthur Kutscher at Munich University in 1913, and been an unpaid small-part actor at the Bavarian Court Theatre. Kutscher was a friend of Wedekind, and his seminar was a famous one, attended by the poets Klabund and Mühsam and later by Brecht; while Ernst Possart, who for many years was *Intendant* (or director) of the court theatres, may have seemed the epitome of old-fashioned acting to the young, but had been admired by Stanislavsky; it was also under his regime that Karl Lautenschläger installed the world's first revolving stage there. Then came the war, and Piscator was called up into the army, where he served as a signaller in a front-line infantry unit from the spring of 1915. Previously something of a dandy, he found this a shattering experience – 'I date everything from August 4th, 1914' are the first words of his book *Das politische Theater* – and he reacted not only with a handful of bitter poems which appeared in *Die Aktion* in 1915 and 1916 but with a lifetime's hatred of militarism and war. Involved in the Ypres offensive of 1915, he was thereafter in and out of the Flanders trenches, with at least one spell in hospital, until seconded to an army theatre unit in the summer of 1917. By the end of that year, when the Bolsheviks had put a stop to the war in the East, he was in charge of the so-called German Theatre at Courtrai immediately behind the fighting, where his repertoire is supposed to have included *Charley's Aunt*. The armistice of November 1918 found him at Hasselt north of Liège, where he spoke at the inaugural meeting of a revolutionary Soldiers' Council (or soviet) before returning home.

Within a matter of weeks he was in Berlin again and was recruited to the Dada group centering on the graphic artists George Grosz and John Heartfield, whose publisher brother Wieland Herzfelde Piscator had met in Flanders. This was a younger and much more aggressive movement than the circle around *Die Aktion*, and it used the provocative, Happening-like techniques of the Zürich Dadaists not merely to attack all accepted bourgeois ideas but also to preach the practical political revolution which looked to be on the point of rolling over Europe. Piscator does not appear to have been especially active in the group, though he is said[1] to have directed one or two of the Dada meetings in Berlin halls and galleries over the next few months. Such contacts as he made however were to be fruitful ones: with Grosz and Heartfield, with Walter Mehring the poet and song-writer, and with the rather older writer-adventurer

1. *Piscator at thirty-three, near the height of his fame. A portrait taken in 1927 when he was setting up his own company.*

Franz Jung. On the last day of 1918, just before the unsuccessful Spartacus rising in Berlin, he went with Grosz and the two Herzfeldes[2] to join the Spartacus Union, then in the process of renaming itself KPD or German Communist Party.

The subject of this book is how Piscator came to be the great advocate of politics in the theatre, and what sort of theatre this led him to practise then and later. What happened once the Nazis took power? How far did the principles which he had evolved stand up during his years without a theatre, first in the USSR and then in France? Did they work in the very different climate of New York, where he ran his Dramatic Workshop from 1940 to 1951? Finally, what of his late achievements in West Germany (*not* the communist East where he never worked): did these represent an abandonment of his former approach, or its resurrection, or its further development in a new context? Piscator was one of the most remarkable artists of the second stage of the modern movement, whose work remains in many ways inspiring, yet at the same time brings under question the very notion of political art. The fact that not all our conclusions will support him should not be taken to mean that the notion is under all circumstances wrong, only that it is a lot less simple than at first appears. The value of his example depends on understanding its limitations.

2. Approaches to a political theatre (1919–1927)

First steps

During 1919 a number of events changed the face of the Berlin theatre. First Max Reinhardt, abandoning the Volksbühne's new theatre on the Bülowplatz, took over a former circus building which he turned into the Grosses Schauspielhaus, a 5000-seat theatre with an immense revolve and cyclorama, whose stalls could be cleared to make an arena. In the auditorium designed by Hans Poelzig the new mass public could see suitable older plays, from the *Oresteia* (the opening production) to Romain Rolland's *Danton*, together with a sprinkling of new works of which *Die Maschinenstürmer* by the gaoled Toller was the most important. Secondly, and rivalling Reinhardt, at least in the opinion of the time, Leopold Jessner was brought from the provinces to become Socialist Intendant of the former Imperial, now (Prussian) State Theatre, where he established his own style of direction a few weeks later by staging Schiller's *Wilhelm Tell* as a passionate and symbolic, yet austere declaration of republican feeling. Thirdly, there was a much smaller but even more deliberately committed theatre in the shape of the Tribüne under the brief directorship of Karlheinz Martin and the actor Fritz Kortner, who made their mark with Toller's first, highly expressionist anti-war play *Die Wandlung*.[3] The Tribüne was also among the sponsors of a League for Proletarian Culture set up that September under the writers Rudolf Leonhard, Arthur Holitscher and Ludwig Rubiner. This organised its own Proletarian Theatre, which staged a now forgotten work called *Die Freiheit* by Herbert Cranz and then packed up.

Up to this point Piscator, so far as we know, was not involved. In February he had applied unsuccessfully to Kayssler at the Volksbühne[4] for a job as actor and assistant director, but for the 1919–20 theatre season – German theatres perform roughly from September to the end of May – he had to go to the newly isolated province of East Prussia. Here at Königsberg (today's Kaliningrad) he began putting on his own productions in the town hall, plays by established modern authors which effectively antagonised the local audience, thanks in part to the austerity of the settings. ('When I go to the theatre', complained one citizen, 'I want to see boulders and my wife wants to see the dresses'.)[5] Two seasons later he tried to set up his own theatre in Berlin, this time in partnership with the writer Hans Rehfisch, who helped him to rent the otherwise undistinguished theatre in the Alte Jacobsstrasse where they presented a roughly comparable group of plays: Gorky, Rolland, Tolstoy. The interesting point this time was that the Central-Theater, as they called it, was to be a form of 'proletarian Volksbühne',[6] a rival foundation to the Volksbühne proper, based on supporters of Piscator's political productions in public halls together with a section of Volksbühne members who had paid to see operettas under the house's previous management. Though the critics indulged it as a worthy venture, with the withdrawal of the Volksbühne subscribers and the hectic inflation of spring 1923 it soon collapsed. The Berlin theatre world, reports one of his friends, remained indifferent. 'Erwin Piscator? Never heard of him. Must be some upstart . . .'[7]

Proletarian Theatre

Piscator's reputation in the early 1920s sprang much more from the uncompromisingly political productions which he organised outside the established theatre. Between his spell at Königsberg and the Central-Theater he joined with a Communist Youth leader called Hermann Schüller to start a new Proletarian Theatre which would perform in various halls outside the centre of Berlin. Though Schüller was an advocate of the Russian Proletkult, this theatre was independent of the previous League and supported rather by the former Dada group, now trying to put their nihilism to political use; 'Dada', wrote Piscator in an essay presenting the new theatre, 'admittedly saw where art without roots was leading, but it is not the answer'.[8] The committee included representatives of the USPD, the Communist splinter party called the KAPD, the International League of War Victims and a workers' rambling club called 'Friends of Nature'.[9] The KPD however only came in later, and Gertrud Alexander, critic of the party paper *Die Rote Fahne*, was not

Proletarisches Theater

Bühne der revolutionären Arbeiter Groß-Berlins

Geschäftsstelle. Halensee, Karlsruher Str 27.   Telefon: Pfalzburg 4515

Genossen und Genossinnen!

Die Seele der Revolution, die Seele der kommenden Gesellschaft der Klassenlosigkeit und der Kultur der Gemeinschaft ist unser revolutionäres Gefühl.

Das proletarische Theater will dieses Gefühl entzünden und wach halten helfen.

Die Erlebnisse, die sozialistische Kunst in uns hervorruft, stärken das Bewußtsein vom Ernst und von der Größe der geschichtlichen Sendung unserer Klasse.

I. Programm-Ausgabe.   20 Pfg.

2. The Proletarian Theatre presents itself. Drawing by George Grosz for the opening programme, 1920.

at all favourably disposed, finding the plays poor and the organisers bourgeois; art, she said, 'is too sacred to lend its name to cheap propaganda banalities'.[10] Though the KPD's subsequently rather less hostile attitude shows that they were none too clear about their position, they tended to adopt Lenin's criticisms of such 'proletarian' undertakings in Moscow, where the Proletkult conference was even then being brought under Bolshevik control. All the same the Proletarian Theatre collected

3. *The Proletarian Theatre performs. An episode from* Russlands Tag *by Lajos Barta, with scenery by John Heartfield, 1920.*

some 5000 group or individual subscribers, while Piscator himself was subsequently happier about it than about any other of his early ventures, writing in 1928 that 'It was as if the theatre were getting a completely new start'.[11]

Admittedly the main play of the opening programme, the one-act *Russlands Tag* by Lajos Barta, makes feeble reading today: thus its climax –

VOICE OF THE RUSSIAN PROLETARIAT: Proletarians, into the struggle.
WORLD CAPITALISM: Hell, devil, plague.
THE GERMAN WORKER: Struggle, struggle, struggle.
VOICES *from all directions:* Struggle, struggle, struggle.
WORLD CAPITALISM *going off right:* Down with Soviet Russia!
THE GERMAN WORKER: All for Russia. All for Russia. Long live Soviet Russia!

(After which the mob bursts on to the stage, tears down barriers, sings the Internationale and so forth till the audience join in.) Nor do the one or two surviving photographs convey anything but the most amateurish impression. But there was a prophetically documentary flavour to John Heartfield's use of a map for scenery, and the collective, anonymous adaptation of the original play (written by a refugee Hungarian communist) allowed Piscator to start formulating his ideas about the subordination of the author and his personality: 'he too will have to learn from the political leader' (the word being 'Führer', just as the word for 'Struggle', above, is 'Kampf'). Likewise the actors were anonymous, including Piscator himself, who took the main part in K. A. Wittfogel's *Der Krüppel* in the same programme (the third play was by Andor Gabor, another Hungarian). Some of them were working-class amateurs. The aim was to forget about 'Art' and build an ensemble on the basis of common revolutionary convictions.

In the spring of 1921 the (Socialist-appointed) police president of Berlin, who had raised objections from the start, refused to relicense the Proletarian Theatre, which accordingly had to close down. Economically it had made no kind of sense, since despite the actors' playing without salaries even full houses – and they were not uncommon – failed to cover expenses, thanks to the policy of letting the unemployed in free. But there were interesting plans for the future,[12] including plays by Iwan Goll and Paul Zech, Toller's *Masse-Mensch* (which the Volksbühne presented instead), three works by other Hungarian communists and a first play by Felix Gasbarra, later to become Piscator's principal *dramaturg*. And among the remaining works of the first season were a play by Upton Sinclair for which Moholy-Nagy designed the set[13] – it must have been one of his first jobs in Germany, within a few months of his arrival in Berlin – and two by the Communist (KAPD) official Franz Jung, which in Piscator's view 'were the most politically advanced, and also suggested new constructional possibilities'.[14] Everything was directed by Piscator himself.

Four seasons later, when he had begun to make his mark in the professional theatre, the KPD asked him to organise a political revue. If this shows that he had now become more acceptable to his own party, it was thanks perhaps to his association with Grosz in such enterprises as the IAH and the Red Group of artists, together with the evening entertainments which he had been directing on the IAH's behalf. The KPD now nominated Gasbarra to work with him, and the composer was Edmund Meisel, who likewise worked on several subsequent Piscator productions. This was the team that produced the *Revue Roter Rummel*, or first Red Revue, an important model for the agit-prop movement which grew up in the latter half of the 1920s. Once again the photographs suggest a fairly primitive charade, though with a new athleticism in the example reproduced here. The text has not survived, and may well have varied from performance to performance – fourteen in all, in different districts of Berlin. It seems to have consisted of about a dozen sketches, introduced by a pot-pourri of communist songs. Thus a tram-driver has an accident after working too long hours, a wife tries to stop her husband from attending a party meeting, there is a mock boxing match between politicians of the coalition parties, including the SPD, broken up by the militant communist Max Hölz (then in gaol, later mysteriously drowned in the USSR). Much of the second half was a scene of decadent Berlin night life, which the workers likewise break up, to culminate in a 'Victory of the Proletariat' scene. Thereupon (reported the *Rote Fahne*)

4. The Red Revue (RRR) *for the German Communist Party's election campaign of 1924. A pioneering piece of agit-prop.*

'enthusiasm became general and expressed itself in a resounding performance of the Internationale'.[15] Two things were significant here: first the framing of the scenes (at least of the first half) in a running argument between an Unemployed Man and a Master Butcher, who entered as members of the audience, and secondly the use of two projectors to illustrate some of the scenes with slides of police repression and portraits of political leaders, plus a selection of George Grosz drawings in the interval. Above all, Piscator had discovered the value of the revue form as a kind of elastic montage which embraced a wide range of theatrical devices and could continually be changed and brought up to date.

RRR was prepared for the election campaign of winter 1924/25, which

ended with the KPD losing about a million votes. That spring the same
team, of Piscator, Gasbarra and Meisel, began working on a vast open-air
political pageant for a workers' cultural organisation directed by Ernst
Niekisch, a friend of Toller's who, like him, had been imprisoned after

5. The historical pageant Trotz Alledem *for the Communist Party's Berlin conference, 1925. A photomontage from Piscator's book showing three shots from the
accompanying film with* (bottom) *the conductor Edmund Meisel and audience, all
against the background of the stalactitic interior of the Grosses Schauspielhaus,
dominated by a close-up of the head of Karl Liebknecht, murdered in 1919.*

the Munich Soviet. Before they had got very far however the KPD too
demanded a pageant for their first party conference; the scheme was
dropped and its material shortened to form *Trotz Alledem*! (after Liebknecht's famous article 'Despite All') which was staged for two performances in the Grosses Schauspielhaus in July 1925. This text has not

survived either, nor were the actors named on the programme, which describes the show as 'Historical Revue from the years 1914–1919 in 24 scenes with interspersed films'; its structure and its overwhelmingly documentary approach are however clear from the scene titles, virtually every character being historical (and in many cases still alive), aside from a few representative proletarians called Willy or Paul. Here are the titles, amplified in some cases by extracts from a police report:[16]

1. Berlin awaits the war / Potsdamer Platz.

A newspaper seller selling special editions containing 'Murder of the heir to the Austrian throne at Sarajevo'. The populace consists of social-democrats and right-wingers, who discuss the eventuality of war.

2. Session of the Social-Democratic group in the Reichstag on 25 July 1914.

. . . in which Liebknecht makes an emphatically anti-war speech.

3. In the Imperial Palace, Berlin 1 August 1914.

William II signs the declaration of war on Russia . . .

4. Session of the Social-Democratic group on 3 August 1914. Film: Mobilisation, moving off, the slaughter begins.

5. Reichstag session of 2 December 1914 (second vote on war credits).

6. In a Berlin munition factory.

Radical workers call for a strike. They fail because their employer threatens to have them de-reserved.

7. 1 May 1916 / Potsdamer Platz.

. . . Liebknecht speaks and is arrested by two policemen.

8. Landsberg proposes on 11 May 1916 that Liebknecht's parliamentary immunity be suspended.

9. Liebknecht before a court-martial on 23 August 1916. Film: The slaughter continues – authentic shots from World War battles.

10. In a shell-hole. Film: But the proletariat refuses to be abused further. Russia rises, Lenin speaks.

(Not performed, according to the police.)

11. The munitions workers' strike of 1918 / 30 January.

Ebert addresses the strikers, but the workers shout him down and boo him.

12. Berlin awaits the Revolution / Potsdamer Platz.

13. November 9th | In the Reich Chancellor's palace.

Ebert, Scheidemann, Bauer, Landsberg in discussion . . . Outside, a mob on the march, including sailors with rifles and red flags, with the newly released Liebknecht at their head . . .

14. Reich Chancellery | Landsberg's office | 5 December.

15. Chausseestrasse | 6 December.

The demonstration in the Chausseestrasse. There is a shot from the crowd, whereupon the troops fire on it.

16. Offices of Die Rote Fahne.

Liebknecht, Rosa Luxemburg and Radek discussing their course of action.

17. Reich Chancellery | Ebert's office | 9 January 1919.

Ebert, Scheidemann, Landsberg, etc. likewise are discussing what to do, since Noske has promised to send in the army.

18. On the Alexanderplatz.

Armed workers waiting to hear what their leaders have decided.

19. Session of the 'revolutionary committee' | 11 January.

20. The assault on Police Headquarters.

21. The final evening | 15 January.

Arrest of Karl Liebknecht and Rosa Luxemburg.

22. Foyer of the Eden Hotel | The same evening.

A lieutenant-commander tells Rifleman Runge what to do. The government think it important that Liebknecht and R. Luxemburg should die . . .

23. Tiergarten | By the Neuer See.

The car stops by the Neuer See. Liebknecht gets out, walks a pace or two and is shot.

Finale: Parade of the proletariat. Liebknecht lives!

Members of the Roter Frontkämpferbund [KPD paramilitary force] march on to the stage and form up about 50 strong with 8 flags.

The party paper's new critic had some bones to pick[17] with the performance, which took place on a plain construction of steps and platforms that Heartfield had built on the huge revolve: thus Rosa Luxemburg was too noisy, Liebknecht not dynamic enough, the SDP Minister of the Interior Noske too inoffensive. Above all, the approach was *too* documentary, with the workers not protesting nearly early enough and too many rousing patriotic songs being sung. 'That may be what's wrong, comrade director . . . Don't all stick so slavishly to "that's the way it happened".' But this was not the view of the *Berliner Tageblatt*,[18] which praised the account given as 'sober and factual', if seen through party eyes; while the impact of the authentic world-war films, provided by a friend in the state film archives, was generally agreed to be overwhelming. Both performances were so packed that Piscator wanted to prolong the run, and in this he was supported by the KPD Deputy Ernst Torgler who had initiated the whole idea. However, the party said no.

Politicising the People's Stage

These two political productions were undertaken at a time when Piscator was already establishing himself as one of the Volksbühne's principal directors. Looking back today it might seem that he was always in some

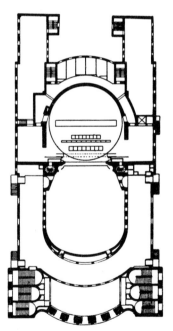

6. *The Volksbühne's theatre on the Bülowplatz, Berlin, built in 1914, where Piscator staged his first major productions between 1924 and 1927. The plan shows its large revolving stage and cyclorama; the slit-like rectangles are stage lifts.*

VOLKSBÜHNE E V

(VEREINIGTE FREIE UND NEUE FREIE VOLKSBÜHNE)

THEATER AM BÜLOWPLATZ

Dienstag, den 23. Februar 1926, abends 8 Uhr

STURMFLUT

Schauspiel in 10 Bildern von Alfons Paquet.
Regie: Erwin Piscator.

Prolog	. . . . ,	Adolf Manz
Granka Umnitsch	. . . .	Heinrich George
Rune Lewenclau	. . . .	Ellen Widmann
Ssawin	. . . .	Erwin Kalser
Gad	. . . .	Alexander Granach
Orvill	. . . .	Leo Reuß
Ostermann		Adolf Manz
Talbott .	Flüchtlinge, später Abgesandte . .	Ferdinand Asper
Sigogne .		Fritz Staudte
Zai . .		Peter Ihle
Bronkx	. . . .	Paul Kauffmann
Froljka .		Eugen Klimm
Narum .		Sigmund Nunberg
Pelagij .	Matrosen	Georg Kaufmann
Jewtichi .		Albert Venohr
Semtschuk		Karl Hannemann
Galon	. . . .	Armin Schweizer
Awdeja	. . . .	Marija Leijko
Marja	. . . .	Ilse Baerwald
Dotja	. . . .	Joh. Koch-Bauer

Petersburg und in den Wäldern zur Zeit der Revolution.

Bühnenarchitektur, Bilder und Kostüme: Eduard Suhr.
Filmische Leitung und Aufnahmen: J. A. Hübler-Kahla.
Technische Gesamteinrichtung: Hans Sachs.
Beleuchtung: Hugo Diesner.   Filmbeiträge: Filmhaus Mischke & Co.

Pause nach dem 6. Bild.

DIE KUNST DEM VOLKE

DER ZETTEL WIRD UNENTGELTLICH VERABFOLGT.
ZUSPÄTKOMMENDE DÜRFEN VON DEM SCHLIESSER
ERST NACH DEM ERSTEN AKT EINGELASSEN WERDEN.

7. *Programme for Alfons Paquet's play about the Russian Revolution, perhaps Piscator's most significant Volksbühne production. Note that organisation's motto 'Art to the People' printed white on black at the foot.*

way concerned with this great popular theatre organisation, even though critical opinion at that time found its productions dull by comparison with those of Jessner and the Reinhardt theatres, or of such individual directors as Engel, Fehling and Berthold Viertel, who had just begun to make their names. But in fact his first job as a guest director towards the end of the 1923–24 season seems to have been something of an accident. Under Kayssler the organisation had accepted a new play about Chicago anarchists in 1886–87 by Alfons Paquet, a Frankfurt journalist who had been with the German mission to Russia on the eve of the Revolution and was one of the first sponsors of the IAH; reputedly he was familiar with Meyerhold's theatre.[19] This had been awaiting production for a matter of years, neither Kayssler's successor nor his principal director being willing or able to stage it. Then, so one of the actors recalls,[20] 'along came this little man, looking like a gents' outfitter, a bit flat-footed', and found the way to pull it into shape. Perhaps it is unfair on the Volksbühne to suggest that this was entirely chance, for not only was Fritz Holl a more enterprising *Intendant* than Kayssler but there were members of the artistic board who wanted to see a more positive political commitment – the journalist Arthur Holitscher for one, who had helped found the original League for Proletarian Culture. When the wrath of the critics descended on the Volksbühne some three years later it was because they were at last beginning to respect it, and felt that they had to support its most remarkable director against the interventions of his governing committee.

However, Piscator was certainly lucky in his opening play. For Paquet described *Fahnen* as 'An epic drama', and it was the episodic succession of short scenes which this entailed that seems so to have baffled the other directors. Brecht, later to become the theorist of Epic Theatre, was not yet in Berlin, but his friend Alfred Döblin[21] while dismissing Paquet as a mediocre writer, called his work 'a half-way house between narrative and drama' claiming that this was a form always adopted 'wherever the coldness of the author's feelings stops him from associating himself intimately with the fate of his characters or the development of the plot'. Much the same was observed by other critics, for instance the *Berliner Morgenpost*, whose notice of the opening night[22] argued that although Paquet might lack Toller's passion or Gerhart Hauptmann's humanity 'he knows how to present the events tersely and accessibly to the senses, and if they often seem merely factual it should not be forgotten that even this demands a controlling hand'. Piscator made hardly any drama-turgical changes, and his solution to the problem depended on four main

devices, two of which came in due course to be specifically regarded as
'epic'. First of all the Volksbühne's designer Edward Suhr built him a
complicatedly divided permanent set on the revolve, with a street
running through it – no photographs seem to have been preserved, but
it reminded observers of Boccioni's Futurist painting *The Funeral of the
Anarchist Galli* – then he introduced a kind of huckster figure carrying a
pointer who spoke the prologue and commented on the characters. 'The
wall dividing stage from audience was swept away', said Piscator later.[23]
'The whole building a meeting hall. The audience drawn into the stage.'
Newer still, he projected portraits of the characters on the backcloth
during the prologue, and had further screens each side of the stage for
projections during and between the scenes, using these not only for
documentary illustration – posters, news cuttings and manifestos – but
also for cinema-like titles or captions. Thus when the anarchists came
up for trial the projector showed the anticipatory title 'Condemned to
death . . .'. Finally in the last scene a coffin bearing a Soviet star was
lifted up; a chorus of extras offstage swore allegiance to the hammer and
sickle; and red flags fluttered down from the flies.[24] To the journalist
Leo Lania, who reviewed the production for the Vienna Socialist daily
and later became a close collaborator, it was 'in a sense the first Marxist
drama',[25] the first production to expound the materialistic view of
history.

Much later Piscator revealed that the dress rehearsal was a disaster and
that he tried to resign, or at least to have the opening postponed, on
overhearing what Holl and other senior members of the theatre were
saying about it. Instead he managed to persuade his actors (and there were
fifty-six in the cast, not to mention the hard-pressed technicians), to
rehearse right through from 1 a.m. till after the curtain should have gone
up. The gamble paid off, they played with conviction, the audience was
enthusiastic. And in the following season, starting in the autumn of 1924,
Piscator was one of the Volksbühne's regular directors. Admittedly his
productions that year were not of such interest, even though two of the
plays were by authors sympathetic to him: to wit his former partner
Rehfisch, who had written a rather characterless conventional comedy,
and Rudolf Leonhard, one of the first Proletarian Theatre's sponsors,
author of a preposterous semi-expressionist drama about a Soviet woman
ship's captain. The new ideas tried out in *Fahnen* were developed rather
in the *Red Revue* and *Trotz Alledem*! However it was plainly of the greatest
importance to Piscator to be able to handle a well-equipped modern
theatre, built only ten years previously, as well as directing some of the

best actors in Berlin. 'The kind of cooperation demanded by my productions', he wrote in *Das politische Theater*, 'led them to develop a sense
of community on the human and artistic, and also to some extent the
political plane'. This was achieved, in his view, by such performers as
Erwin Kalser, Leonard Steckel, Fritz Genschow and Albert Venohr,
together with one major star in the massive shape of Heinrich George
(known to posterity in a particularly repellent portrait by Otto Dix).
Effectively, too, as he had worked with Suhr, he now met an even more
congenial designer in Traugott Müller, whose severely stylised set for
the Leonhard play was perhaps its most memorable feature. All these
people except George were to work with his companies later.

*8. Piscator's first season at the Volksbühne, 1924–25: the start of a collaboration.
Traugott Müller's set for* Segel am Horizont, *a play by Rudolf Leonhard.*

But in 1926 and 1927 his productions for the Volksbühne were among
the most exciting things he ever did. Right at the outset he was involved
in the manoeuvres to get a German distribution for a stunning new Soviet
film, Eisenstein's *Potemkin*, which was given a musical score by Meisel and
handled by a subsidiary of the IAH. This episode[26] was historically
important as introducing the great revolutionary masterpiece not only
to the outside world but indirectly to the Soviet public, which was
unenthusiastic until the film proved such a hit abroad. At the same time
it was significant for Piscator, since quite clearly it influenced his next
production, *Sturmflut*, Alfons Paquet's second revolutionary play. In itself
Sturmflut was a weaker work than *Fahnen*, as its documentary element (the

Bolshevik revolution) hung on an improbable story of a sailor (Heinrich George) selling the city of St Petersburg to a millionaire (Alexander Granach). But it had been written with the experience of Piscator's new methods in mind, and accordingly he felt justified this time in strengthening it to fit their possibilities and requirements. In less than four weeks of rehearsal the play was cut and reconstructed while the actors became a half-improvising ensemble and even the director himself was not clear what the final effect would be. This uncertainty resulted from the much

9. Sturmflut *at the Volksbühne, 1926. Use of film to provide the Russian re-volutionary background to Paquet's play. See ill. no. 7 for cast and details.*

greater role now given to projections, with a screen right across the back of the stage and six to ten film projectors – at least that was the number planned – providing a moving setting for a good part of the play. The set proper was a mere structure of steps and blocks behind which the screen showed floods, the sea, a naval battle and crowd scenes: 'a living wall', Piscator called it, 'the theatre's fourth dimension. In this way the photographic image conducts the story, becomes its motive force, a piece of living scenery'.[27] And it worked, combining (according to

Herbert Ihering's notice)[28] with 'exceptionally intensified ensemble scenes, to create an impact more intimate and profound than in the average chamber piece'.

10–11 Das Trunkene Schiff *at the Volksbühne, 1926. Use of George Grosz's drawings for Paul Zech's Rimbaud play. Above: original drawing. Below: its projection on a triple screen to provide a background to the prison scene. (The anti-clerical bird, far right, seems to have been suppressed.)*

Paul Zech's Rimbaud play, *Das trunkene Schiff*, which followed in the spring, was a 'scenic ballad' in eighteen scenes (or 'stations') by one of the most politically committed Expressionists, but it was no more a political play than Brecht's *Baal*, which it somewhat resembled in theme and language. Piscator's idea here originally had been to build a big rotating canvas prism on the stage, which would act as a multiple screen

for slide projections from three or more sides; the revolve would be used
to bring the characters on or off. When this proved technically impossible
a folding triple screen was substituted, on which George Grosz's water-
colour drawings for the play were projected as a kind of triptych. A
gauze was used for a film projection of waves in the fifteenth, shipboard
'station' (originally there was also to have been an introductory film
showing the historical background), while in the prison scene (or eighth
'station') the wings of the triptych were folded in and vertical bars put
across them to make an entirely enclosed cell, then unfolded so as to
show Grosz's pictures. Though this was one of Piscator's less controversial productions, there had apparently[29] been an awkward episode a
little earlier when Kayssler refused to appear under his direction in *The
Liberation of Don Quixote* by Anatol Lunacharsky, the Soviet Education
Commissar, who was not only a close associate of Lenin's but the man
responsible for the new theatre and cinema in that country. Instead the
production had to be taken over by Franz Holl.

In the autumn of 1926 Piscator first came into serious conflict with
conservative opinion when he staged Schiller's *Die Räuber*, a major
German classic, at the State Theatre under Jessner, who had borrowed
him for three productions. He now brought this highly unrealistic and
nobly tedious play up to date not by putting it into modern dress (which
would have been fashionable), nor by making its hero a revolutionary
leader (as Karlheinz Martin had done five years earlier), but by turning it
upside down and transforming the one interesting character, Schiller's
nastily subversive Spiegelberg, into a true revolutionary whose ideas and
followers are taken over by the hero for his own aristocratic, proprietorial
ends. This had a topical angle, as it followed a public campaign for the
expropriation of the German princes, which had been mounted by the
IAH and supported by Piscator. Accordingly he cut speeches and entire
characters, he rewrote, he telescoped the great rambling monologues by
playing two or even three such scenes simultaneously, the actors deliver-
ng their speeches like the singers in an operatic trio so that they were
more effective than intelligible.[30] The costumes were virtually timeless,
in the way common to Shakespeare productions in our own day; Traugott
Müller's set a massive castle for the hero's princely family, divided into
different areas and levels and defended by cruiser-like gun turrets, but
now and again cut off by trees for the bandits' forest scenes. Spiegelberg
was made up to look like Trotzky, the Internationale was heard when he
died, Meisel provided the rest of the revolutionary music, the whole
thing was over in two hours. 'A communist film drama', one hostile

headline called it, though in fact no use of film was involved; and again 'Schiller's *Räuber* as a Potemkinade'.[31]

Though Jessner himself was to follow this up with a *Hamlet* which likewise stressed basic political and class issues (the rottenness of the state of Denmark), *Die Räuber* had to be withdrawn after questions in the Prussian State Assembly – this was after all a state theatre and Schiller a national monument – and Piscator's other two productions never took place. Instead he staged *The Lower Depths* at the Volksbühne (a production chiefly remarkable for the fact that it brought him into personal contact with Gorky), did one or two minor jobs for other companies, then in the spring of 1927 worked on the production which brought his whole relationship with the Volksbühne to a head. This was of an otherwise obscure play by Ehm Welk called *Gewitter über Gottland*, which dealt with the struggle in the fourteenth century between the Hanseatic cities, pioneering capitalists, and a communistic league of 'Vitalians' led by a true revolutionary (played by Granach) and a mercenary adventurer (played by George) whose clash provided the main dramatic element. Its dialogue was rhetorical and old-fashioned, the performance about four hours long; the actors bawled; only Traugott Müller's fine sets redeemed things a little. As we shall see, Piscator knew that he could take risks this time, and he seized on the author's note 'The period of this play is not only *c.* 1400' as a pretext for loading it with political comment in the form of film; there were even projections in the auditorium. Thus the evening started with a long exposition of the mediaeval social and political background, then the characters were filmed walking towards the audience, their costumes imperceptibly becoming more and more modern till the identification of the Granach character with Lenin became complete. Shots of Moscow and Shanghai figured as part of the play's documentary background; finally a Soviet star loomed above the stage to the loud applause of enthusiasts in the audience, the non-enthusiasts having already left. About a quarter of this film material had been banned by the censors a few hours before the première (which Piscator anyway wanted to disown as insufficiently rehearsed); more was now removed by the Volksbühne management, who publicly accused him of an abuse of artistic freedom. 'This type of production', they said, 'is incompatible with the Volksbühne's principle of political neutrality'.[32]

The crunch had come, and it had two aspects, of which the less publicised was perhaps the more important. For throughout these three years Piscator had been preoccupied with the problem of finding plays which would live up to his demands. 'I have to ask for better texts from that poor creature, the author', he once noted. 'I have to be honest with the facts, truthful to the people who come to see these plays and who want to find an answer to their own problems'.[33] In his way he was, as Brecht was to recognise in *The Messingkauf Dialogues*, a highly original dramatist; but that way did not include the actual writing of plays. He had tried recommending scripts to the Volksbühne, sometimes success- fully as with Leonhard's play, sometimes not so as in the case of Lania's *Generalstreik*, which he wanted them to put on at the time of the British General Strike in May 1926. Then he had been drawn into the difficult negotiations with Ernst Toller, whose first play *Die Wandlung* they had

12. *Piscator's last Volksbühne production for thirty-four years: Ehm Welk's* Gewitter über Gottland, *March 1927. Set by Traugott Müller, then about to move with him to the new theatre.*

contracted to re-stage but now rejected as too radical for their governors. When Piscator proposed to Toller that they should substitute a new 'mass play', Toller at first refused. However that same summer the two men went off with Erich Engel, the writer Wilhelm Herzog (best known for the anti-war magazine *Das Forum* which he founded in Munich in 1914) and an advertising man called Otto Katz to plan the unfinished play *Blockade im Scheunenviertel* of which five scenes appeared in the Volks- bühne's magazine[34] just before the showdown. There had been the writers like Paquet, who understood Piscator's aims and technique and tried to write accordingly; there had been others, like Welk, who tolerated his imposing his new methods on what they had written. But neither had proved satisfactory, and by this time he felt the need for a more collective approach.

Ostensibly the battle that took place in March 1927 was for the future of the Volksbühne, and the issue a moral-political one. Toller had a lawsuit pending against that organisation for breach of contract, Piscator had been disowned and forced to resign. To many Berlin theatre people the situation seemed plain: here was the leading young director of the day – who had contributed so much to the move away from Expressionism, the renovation of the classics (about which Ihering was to publish a short book)[35] and the marrying of theatre and film – losing his post, and the Volksbühne would relapse into the old dull routine. A public declaration of support came from forty-two leading actors, critics, directors and authors,[36] including Feuchtwanger and Thomas Mann, and when a section of the Volksbühne membership called a meeting in the Herrenhaus on 30 March, with Holitscher presiding, it was addressed not only by Piscator and Toller, together with Kalser on behalf of the actors, but also by Jessner, Karlheinz Martin and Kurt Tucholsky, none of whom had any party-political axe to grind. Not that the disagreement as to the Volksbühne's basic function was a new one, for essentially it was the same old split between those who saw the organisation as a means of popularising great art and a minority who insisted that such art must be socially committed. However, since the KPD had now organised a left-wing opposition in the German Association of Workers' Theatres, with Wilhelm Pieck's son Arthur as its leader, the polarising of the Volksbühne conflict was clearly in line with its policy. The communists had little hope of capturing the whole organisation, which at that time had 140,000 members. But the 4000 who immediately supported Piscator, together with the 12,000 others who joined them by the start of the next season, must have seemed a nucleus worth gaining.

'The true People's Theatre', wrote Piscator in *Die Rote Fahne*, 'can only legitimately exist as a theatre of the people's most class-conscious section, the proletariat.'[37] This was the basis of the new 'political theatre', to quote the name which he first publicly used at the beginning of 1928. Uncompromising as the argument sounds, there was at the same time something a little stage-managed about the whole operation. For well before work started on the crucial *Gewitter über Gottland* production; even before Holitscher's *Weltbühne* article which set the ball rolling, Piscator knew that he was going to have a theatre of his own. Already Otto Katz was managing its affairs; plans for a new building were being drawn up; while the money had been secured the previous autumn, from the most capitalist of sources. Throughout the rest of his life Piscator never veered from what he saw as the Volksbühne's ideals. But he would have left it at this juncture in any case.

3. The Piscator companies (1927–1931)

———◆———

The first Piscatorbühne

In September 1926 the actress Tilla Durieux saw *Die Räuber* and wanted to meet its director. She was one of the grand ladies of the German stage, and as wife of the leading art dealer Paul Cassirer had lived for some years at the point where money and the arts meet; there is a portrait of her as a young woman by Renoir. She introduced Piscator to her friend Ludwig Katzenellenbogen, director-general of the Schultheiss and Patzenhofer breweries in Berlin, the Ostwerke and other enterprises. This newly rich tycoon gave him 400,000 marks (or 450,000; accounts differ) with which to start his own company. The one condition allegedly imposed was that its title should not include the adjective 'proletarian-revolutionary'.[38] Instead Piscator chose to use his own name, on the grounds (so he told an interviewer many years later) that 'the term "Piscator" stood for a whole political approach'.

His first idea was to build an entirely new theatre on a site near the Hallesches Tor, and on 22 March Otto Katz was able to tell Katzenellen-bogen[39] that an outline plan was being prepared for the building inspectorate, and that the architect estimated the cost at 1.8 million marks. This was the Total-Theater designed by Gropius, which would hold 2000 spectators and be built with practical help from the Bauhaus at Dessau. Piscator later emphasised[40] that its construction, even though it had to be postponed, was basic to his understanding with his backer, since the economics of the whole scheme would depend on accommodating a mass audience. Evidently Katzenellenbogen differed, but help came from another quarter when the Volksbühne agreed to offer tickets for the new Piscatorbühne to a proportion of its members. It was already that organisation's practice to make such arrangements with other theatres;

thus in the previous season it had offered seats for certain State Theatre performances, as well as for the opera and the Theater am Schiffbauer-damm. Now however it created 'special sections' of its membership, half of whose tickets would be for Piscator's productions. These 'Sonder-abteilungen', as they were called, were at first to be limited to 4000 members, then the figure was raised to 16,000. They had their own com-mittee and, while bringing in only 1.50 marks per head, became in-creasingly important to Piscator as time went on. Beside their practical

13. *Backers of the new Piscatorbühne, 1927: the actress Tilla Durieux and her subsequent husband the financier Ludwig Katzenellenbogen.*

value as a guaranteed audience they showed that the break with his former employers was not complete. He could thus still view the Volksbühne as 'the great gathering point for all proletarian forces relevant to the theatre'.[41]

The concept of the Total-Theater will be dealt with in more detail in chapter 5. It was never built, and the only work actually carried out by Gropius was the subsequent designing of Piscator's new flat, with its furniture by Marcel Breuer. Instead the company decided to make do with an existing Berlin theatre for its first season, and rented the Theater am Nollendorfplatz, close to the fashionable West End. This theatre had had an undistinguished history of late, but it was technically well-equipped (thanks in the first place to Otto Brahm), with a big revolve and much space backstage as well as a huge foyer, and it held 1100, which is a

14. Piscator's first wife Hilde photographed for a woman's magazine in the flat designed for them by Gropius and Marcel Breuer of the Bauhaus.

lot more than most London theatres. Of these seats the 'Sonderabteilungen' would take 200 to 300 a night, but even if they had filled the whole theatre it would only have meant some 1700 marks, which would have covered about half the estimated running costs. At that time a new production was reckoned to cost about 50–60,000 marks, and Piscator was offering tickets for seven such productions in his first season. A middle-grade actor would be paid about 500 marks a month, the average Berlin theatre rent was 200–300,000 marks a year. There was also entertainment tax, though the city authorities were prepared to

15–17 Three of the best-known Berlin actors of the 1920s engaged by the new company. Max Pallenberg (strolling) who played Schweyk; Paul Graetz (driving a car) and Alexander Granach (driving a well teed-up golf ball) who both played in Hoppla, wir leben! *For photos of these performances see ills. 29 and 33.*

remit this in some cases, including apparently that of the Reinhardt theatres. But whatever Piscator's luck with the tax people (and it is fairly clear that he trusted it) he would have to sell plenty of expensive seats in order to meet his budget. The mass audience could not come yet.

Independently of the Piscator company there was to be a Studio, training actors in collaboration with writers, musicians and technical staff. This was a plan which Piscator had already wanted to put into effect at the Volksbühne: each group there would choose its own play and director and decide the casting, then work on it as long as necessary before offering it to the public. Lectures and classes would be arranged around the particular play. Furthermore, rather than appoint a dramaturg (or two) as was the practice in German theatres, the company was to have a 'dramaturgical collective', in other words a whole team of writers to supervise the literary programme and go over the texts of the plays. Originally the head of this was to have been Herzog, but he apparently[42] proved himself so incompetent over the preparation of the first programme magazine (the *Blätter der Piscatorbühne*, as they became called), that he was sacked before the season began. Instead the collective was run by Felix Gasbarra, the German-Italian communist who had collaborated on Piscator's political productions, together with Lania as his chief aide. Walter Mehring, Brecht, Mühsam, Jung and Alfred Wolfenstein were among its other nominal members, while Döblin, Tucholsky, Johannes R. Becher and the film critic Béla Balázs (Herbert Bauer) were at one time or another drawn into its consultations. A villa on the Wannsee was rented so that planning sessions could be combined with the

18. *The short-lived composer and conductor Edmund Meisel* (standing centre right) *and the Piscatorbühne's band.*

healthy outdoor life while the problem of finding suitable plays was at last systematically tackled.

The first idea was to open the season with a specially written political revue by Herzog, to be called *Rings um den Staatsanwalt*. In July this was rejected as hopelessly undramatic: 2000 marks down the drain. Lania by then had finished two acts of his new play about the oil companies, *Konjunktur*, but though this had been accepted for the programme it would not do to start, since rehearsals were to begin on 1 August. The rights had also been acquired to stage the first performance of Hašek's *Adventures of the Good Soldier Schweik* (or *Svejk*), adapted from the novel whose German translation had made a great impact the previous year;

in Prague however the adaptors were still at work.[43] But meanwhile Toller had come along with a new idea for a play based very much on his own disenchantment with German socialism on emerging from prison; in June he gave a reading of the first draft; after which Piscator and Gasbarra went off with him to get it into final shape. This was *Hoppla, wir leben!*, with which they finally decided to open. In addition to the other plays included in the first season – Jean-Richard Bloch's *Le dernier empereur* and Alexei Tolstoy and Shcheglov's *Rasputin* – together with the studio productions of Upton Sinclair's *Singing Jailbirds* and Jung's *Heimweh*, the company's prospectus[44] listed a play by Wolfenstein (*Henkersdienst*); Büchner's *Woyzeck*; *Troilus and Cressida* and the unfinished *Weizen* (or *Joe P. Fleischhacker aus Chicago*) by Brecht, none of which were ever performed. We know too of negotiations with further writers: thus Günther Weisenborn's *U-Boot S 4*, a documentary work about an accident to an American submarine, was accepted for a studio production,[45] while P. M. Lampel's *Putsch* would (by its author's account)[46] have been similarly accepted if he had been willing to join the KPD.

Traugott Müller, Grosz and Heartfield were to be the designers, Meisel and Franz Osborn the composers, Kurt Oertel (who had worked on *Gewitter*) in charge of film. Besides the actors who actually played with the company, of whom Sybille Binder, Tilla Durieux, Ernst Deutsch, Graetz, Granach, Max Pallenberg and Hans Heinrich von Twardowski were the best known, the prospectus also named Helene Weigel and Fritz Kortner who did not (and omitted Paul Wegener who did). Scarcely any of them had been in Piscator's previous productions, anyhow not in those where the actors were named. No director was listed except Piscator, whose name, understandably enough, was several sizes larger and bolder than anything else on the prospectus. As for the company's manifesto, which introduced the first issue of the programme magazine, it began with the somewhat startling pronouncement that 'This theatre has been founded not in order to make politics but in order to free art from politics'.[47] This ingenious phrase, which puzzled some of Piscator's political allies at the time but was to come in useful later, was intended to convey that only the political situation was to blame for the introduction of politics into the theatre; the overthrow of the social order would clear the way for art to return to a state of freedom, for 'Pure art is impossible under present-day conditions'. It appears that Gasbarra was its author, and some selected passages from Trotsky's *Literature and Revolution* followed, arguing the importance of traditional culture and the pointlessness of talk about proletarian art.

19. Programme of the opening production, with manifesto (right) *and accompanying ad.*

From the first Piscatorbühne to the second

The first company opened its doors on 3 September 1927. By the following June it was bankrupt. The four major productions which it presented between those two dates are landmarks in theatrical history, and they will be dealt with separately as such in the next chapter, together with the most interesting productions of the succeeding Piscator companies. What we are concerned with at the moment, however, is the much less exemplary history of these enterprises as a practical undertaking. Admittedly the first three productions in many respects went well. *Hoppla, wir leben!* ran for two months, then set out on a rather ill-planned tour of the Rhineland, where dates were few and far between. *Rasputin* played from mid-November to mid-January, gaining much publicity when the exiled Wilhelm II successfully sued to prohibit his continued representation in the play (rumour had it that Piscator was offering him a contract to appear in person). *Schweik*, which followed with Max Pallenberg in the name part, was the biggest draw of all, taking between 7–9000 marks a day so long as Pallenberg was available. All three of these plays involved immense casts – thirty-nine, forty and forty-two characters respectively – and elaborate stage apparatus, whose removal for the next day's rehearsals called for much extra work by the stagehands. Despite the costs which this entailed, once *Schweik* was in its second month Katz and Piscator felt that the season was going to be a financial success, and accordingly put up a deposit to rent the theatre for another four years.

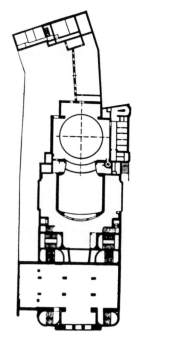 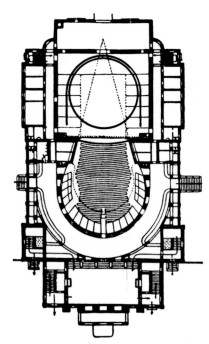

20–21. Plans of the two Berlin theatres used by the first Piscatorbühne, 1927–28. Left, the Theater am Nollendorfplatz; right, the Lessing-Theater. Both had revolving stages.

But they still had to offer their subscribers four more plays that season to fulfil the terms of their prospectus. Being loth to stop the run of *Schweik*, they rented a second theatre for Lania's *Konjunktur* – unnecessarily as it turned out, since by the time this play was ready Pallenberg had to go to another job. In the interim they filled it with the studio production of *Singing Jailbirds*, then brought back *Hoppla!* once more. Both operations lost money, and Piscator found it a rude shock during the *Konjunktur* rehearsals when he was suddenly told that he must find the actors' wages out of his own pocket. From that moment everything went downhill. *Konjunktur* opened at the second (Lessing) theatre and did badly; it was a less lavish production than the others and so, he felt, disappointed the fashionable public; it was also in some ways a pretty foolish play. Back at the Theater am Nollendorfplatz *Schweik* almost simultaneously came off, to be replaced by Karlheinz Martin's production of *Le dernier empereur*, a royalist-Ruritanian-revolutionary farrago whose acceptance by the dramaturgs is impossible to understand; this was extravagant enough, in terms both of technique and of star actors, but flopped all the same. At this desperate moment the local authority decided to sue the company for back entertainment tax, a matter of some 16,000 marks which proved impossible to find. First the Lessing-Theater, then the Theater am Nollendorfplatz had to be sublet to another management; Piscator abdicated his authority to an emergency committee of the actors, and the First Piscatorbühne went into liquidation.

Its debts were reported at the time[48] to amount to 950,000 marks, of which 450,000 were owed to Katzenellenbogen and 53,000 for unpaid taxes; its assets covered less than a quarter of the whole. Otto Katz, the 'nymphomaniac playboy'[49] whom Piscator largely blamed for the fatal decision to rent a second theatre, resigned and was given a job by Muenzenberg running an IAH book club at Piscator's request. No new backers could be found in time for the next season, nor is it at all clear what Piscator did for the rest of 1928 aside from making plans. Among these can be included his discussions with Brecht and the sociologist Fritz Sternberg about possible adaptations of *Julius Caesar*[50] and Brecht's own *Trommeln in der Nacht*,[51] the latter with a complex permanent set divided into different rooms and symbolising all Berlin. Later a list was published[52] claiming that he had forty plays under consideration, including Brecht's *Mahagonny* and the unfinished *Fatzer* (one of the most impressive of Brecht's abandoned works), a second instalment of *Schweik*, Friedrich Wolf's *Cyankali* and *Die Matrosen von Cattaro*, Ivanov's *Armoured Train*, Karl Kraus's *Die letzten Tage der Menschheit* and a dramatisation of Dreiser's *An American Tragedy*. By the spring of 1929 he had begun to come out of his shell again; thus he staged Maxwell Anderson's *What Price Glory?* successfully for another management that March and contracted to write his book, with Gasbarra and Lania helping. He appealed to an audience of his 'Sonderabteilung' subscribers to understand the reasons for his crash and support him in the 1929–30 season. He recognised that the sensation created by the first company's productions had been too dearly purchased, and promised 'a calmer and more systematic continuation of our work'.[53] But he could only succeed in his aim of helping the proletariat create a new social order if the workers themselves decided that the Piscator-bühne, 'and in a sense the Volksbühne along with it' were worth fighting for.

The possibility of more modest but no less political productions had already been implicit in the work of his Studio, under such younger directors as Leopold Lindtberg, and this had begun to bear fruit. *Singing Jailbirds* was not a success, partly because it had unexpectedly been used to plug a breach in the main company's programme, partly because there was union trouble over the original plan to use an amateur chorus, and as a result seventy extras had to be paid. Rombach's *Der heilige Krieg*, put on by a second group, was a failure. But Jung's *Heimweh*, which set out to give an almost plotless exposition of the theme of homesickness, using a mixture of different languages and musical turns, an English soap-box orator and a military band,[54] was a piece of quite original 'theatrical theatre' even though Piscator and his aides walked into one of the last rehearsals and cut its eccentricities so that Jung walked out. And Mühsam's *Judas*, which the emergency committee had staged for the author's fiftieth birthday after the crash, led Ihering to write that the energy and sense of common purpose put into this slightly old-fashioned revolutionary piece could well be taken up and developed by the main Piscatorbühne. Something of the sort indeed happened when the Studio actors themselves at the end of 1928 formed the Gruppe Junger Schau-spieler or 'Group of Young Actors', which thenceforward sponsored some of the most interesting Berlin political productions, including Wolf's *Cyankali* (1929) and Brecht's *Die Mutter* (1932). Their first play was Lampel's *Revolte im Erziehungshaus*, which had been written for them when they wanted to take up the old Piscator plan to do the same writer's *Putsch*. Lindtberg with a similarly formed 'Novemberstudio' staged Mühsam's Sacco and Vanzetti play which had been on Piscator's list of forty. Weisenborn's submarine play too was taken over by the Volksbühne, now visibly shifting leftwards, after presenting the Berlin première of Brecht's *Mann ist Mann* at the beginning of the year; in 1929 Martin became its new Intendant. Thus, despite Piscator's misfortunes 1928–29 was an active season for the political theatre, and it was also when Brecht had his great success with *Die Dreigroschenoper*, Wolf joined the KPD, and an Association of Proletarian-Revolutionary Writers was founded in Berlin (in line with the Soviet RAPP). Piscator meantime made his first trip to the USSR, and when the International Association of

Workers' Theatres (IATB) was set up in Moscow in August 1929, with
Arthur Pieck as chief German representative, it was announced that he
would be working with it.

Despite these developments the short-lived second Piscatorbühne of
1929 proved to be no more than a continuation of the first. The money
this time was raised largely from another businessman, Felix Weil, who

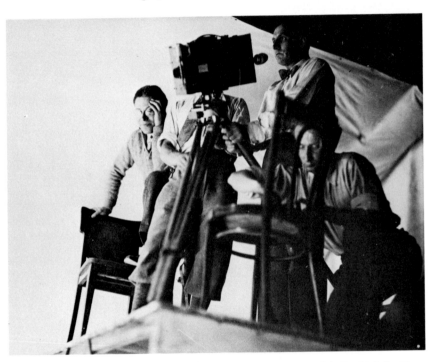

22. *Climax of Piscator's technological revolution, 1929. László Moholy-Nagy*
(left) *with camera operators during rehearsals for Mehring's* Der Kaufmann von
Berlin *with the second Piscatorbühne after the bankruptcy of the first.*

was one of Grosz's principal patrons and had financed Herzfelde's publishing firm; but in order to prevent everything from being drained off by
the first company's creditors the licence for the theatre was made over
to one of Weil's friends, a cinema owner called Ludwig Klopfer. The
stage machinery for the opening production on 6 September[55] was more
complicated than ever, while the play selected had about twice as many
characters as *Hoppla!* This was *Der Kaufmann von Berlin*, subtitled 'a
historic play of the German inflation' and written by Piscator's old Dada
friend Mehring, author of the theme song for Toller's play. Not only

were its characters and situations unconvincingly schematic; it was also not very happily conceived. Inspired, it seems,[56] by the visit to Berlin of the Moscow State Jewish Theatre under Alexander Granowsky, the leading part was conceived for Michoels, their great star and an actor whom Piscator always admired. The theme was the unexpected rise to power and riches of a poor immigrant Jew in Berlin during the inflation of 1923; but there could hardly have been a trickier subject in a country whose racialists blamed virtually all Germany's mishaps in the 1920s on Jews from Eastern Europe. Moreover if (as seems possible) the story was partly suggested by the meteoric career of Katzenellenbogen, the joke was turned retrospectively sour by his extermination in the Second World War. On top of this there was a controversial episode at the end of the play, where three street-sweepers are seen to clear away first a pile of paper money, then a steel helmet, then finally the dead body of its wearer, to three verses of a song to Hanns Eisler's music whose refrain goes 'Dreck! Weg damit!' ('Muck! Chuck it out!'). At the dress rehearsal, according to Albert Venohr, Piscator decided that the dead body should be dispensed with as too provocative; however on the night the actors not only forgot this but gave the corpse's head an extra clout for good measure, thus infuriating nationalist opinion without much pleasing their supporters. Klopfer as licensee reacted by banning use of the red flag in the production, then had the name Piscatorbühne taken off the theatre and finally barred access to Piscator. With that the second company too was finished.

The collective and the third company

Historically this occurred at a turning-point. For on 3 October 1929, Stresemann died, marking the end of six years of moderate politics in Germany; then on 28 October Wall Street crashed, initiating the world economic crisis and the spiralling German unemployment that brought Hitler to power. Meanwhile the USSR too was moving into a new phase with the adoption of the first Five-Year Plan and the exiling of Trotsky. In many ways the basis of the Berlin theatre was altering; already Piscator had complained that a theatre must be three-quarters full to cover its costs, instead of only one-third as before. The 'Sonderabteilungen' too had been cut from 16,000 to 9000 for the whole 1929–30 season, which meant that Piscator was forced to set his sights much lower and follow very much the line initiated by his own young actors. Led by Kalser and

Venohr, those who remained formed themselves into a so-called Piscator Collective, with Piscator virtually as their employee, and in November went off on a well-organised tour of thirty West German towns, playing another work on their list, Carl Credé's play § *218* (so called after the section of the criminal code dealing with abortion, at that time a particularly controversial subject). On their return they rented the Wallner-Theater near the Alexanderplatz, where the Nazis had tried to organise a Volksbühne of their own, and ran the play there successfully for two months before deciding to take that house over as a third Piscator company, and one no longer responsible for the debts of the first two.

23. *The third (collective) company at the Wallner-Theater, 1930–32. Piscator (left) with his author, actor and rival Theodor Plivier, dressed for* Des Kaisers Kulis, *a play about the High Seas Fleet.*

The Wallner-Theater was a moth-eaten old Berlin theatre with poor equipment, dating from the 1860s, and a rent of only 50,000 marks a year. 'All I can remember clearly', wrote Gasbarra,

> is the fusty smell everywhere and the faded photographs in the foyer, one of them showing my mother as a young actress. Otherwise there were endless discussions, as is usual with collectives, and dreadful coffee in the theatre restaurant.[57]

Jung, who now became another of the company's dramaturgs, claimed[58] that he had to meet bills for cleaning and repairing the audience's clothes because of the state of the seats. But the collective installed new lighting and other apparatus, and in July 1930 the new company was announced. According to reports in *Die Rote Fahne* all Piscator's administrative actions were in future to be subject to the agreement of the collective; the bourgeois audience was in principle to be dispensed with; while the party suggested forming a supervisory committee from the IAH and other communist cultural organisations 'to exercise practical influence on the line and repertoire . . . and prevent ideological lapses'.[59] The actors of the collective shared the takings; others were paid at union rates; there were no longer to be any star salaries. Under these conditions the com-

24. *The political theatre at its most 'political'. Audience for Friedrich Wolf's China play* Tai Yang erwacht *at the Wallner-Theater, 1931, showing Communist slogans.*

pany presented Plivier's *Des Kaisers Kulis* – which had to be performed in another theatre, as the Wallner could not show film – is an adaptation by its author, who also played the main part and was privately in the process of going off with Piscator's wife Hilde.[60] In January 1931 Wolf's *Tai Yang erwacht* followed, another notable Piscator production to be discussed in the next chapter. Piscator himself, according to Jung, 'kept surprisingly much in the background',[61] taking no interest in any plays for which other directors were responsible. His next production apparently should have been the adaptation of *An American Tragedy* on which Gasbarra was already working. Other plays performed included *Jeden Tag vier* by Ernst Ottwalt, a young communist writer who later worked with Brecht, and (at last) two genuine Soviet plays: Bill-Belotserkovski's *Mond von Links* and Anatol Glebov's *Inga*, the latter in an anonymous production for which Piscator was partly responsible. With it the Piscatorbühne came to an unexpected end.

He was clearly not happy in this period, which he later termed his 'lowest ebb'.[62] Nor can he have been earning much; thus the records of the collective[63] show his share of the initial four months tour as only

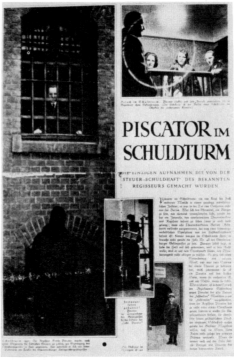

25. *Effects of financial imprudence and official vindictiveness: Piscator gaoled in 1931 for failure to pay municipal taxes.*

246 marks. During the summer of 1930 however he went back to Moscow to arrange to film either *Des Kaisers Kulis* or *An American Tragedy* there. This was just when the first German left-wing films were being made: for instance Pabst's *Threepenny Opera* and *Kameradschaft* (with the Piscator actors Granach, Gnass and Busch), and Trivas's *Niemandsland* (with Eisler's music), all three of them released in 1931. Sound film had now come in, and, given his growing experience of the film medium, it was logical that Piscator too should take part. At the same time he must

already have recognised the political writing on the wall, since not only had the Nazi representation in the Reichstag shot up from 12 seats to 107 in the September 1930 elections (while the KPD's increased from 54 to 77) but the first symptoms of a cultural reaction were manifesting themselves, starting with Jessner's resignation from the State Theatre at the beginning of that year. That November the Volksbühne expelled Piscator's supporters the 'Sonderabteilungen', who now formed a new organisation under the name Junge Volksbühne which later presented its own shows, with Hans Rodenberg as one of its leaders. No doubt as part of the same climate, the tax authorities thereupon came back to the Piscatorbühne, first making Otto Katz responsible for the whole sum due, then causing Piscator himself to be briefly imprisoned in the Charlottenburg gaol only a few days after the *Tai Yang* première. To rescue Katz, Muenzenberg sent him off to Moscow as a director of the IAH film studio there, and by April Piscator had followed. This meant abandoning his collective in the middle of their preparations for *An American Tragedy*, leaving the Gruppe Junger Schauspieler, the Junge Volksbühne, von Wangenheim's Truppe 31 and ultimately the Volksbühne itself to carry on the struggle for the political theatre as best they could.

4. The eight productions

Hoppla, wir leben!

With the first of his productions at the Theater am Nollendorfplatz Piscator was dealing, for once, with a major contemporary playwright, and despite all criticisms the result was a surprisingly effective fusion of Toller's approach with his own. Exactly how this took place would be difficult to reconstruct, since no manuscript seems to have survived and the text published in 1927, which is dedicated to Piscator and Walter Mehring, already reflects many of their suggestions. But the use of film for prologue and interludes is outlined there (indeed one of the most interesting sequences, showing the taking over of men's jobs by women, was cut in the production), as is the simultaneous stage. 'All the play's scenes can be performed' (says a prefatory note) 'on a scaffolding of several storeys which can be used unchanged'. Another marked difference from Toller's earlier work is the recognition that revolutionary prospects were no longer what they were at the time of the Bavarian Soviet; hope is still alight, says the heroine, but 'it glows differently. Less emotionally'.[64] None the less we know that Piscator and his advisers remained dissatisfied with Toller's poetic language and his still typically expressionist ego-hero. First his original ending was scrapped, then the published ending was cut and amended, finally Piscator struck at the root of the matter by making Granach play the hero as a solid, walrus-moustached proletarian, not at all the 'little son of a bourgeois' specified in the prologue.

What impressed critics and audiences alike was not so much the acting (aside perhaps from Graetz as a fussy provincial lobbyist) as the use of film, set and sound effects. One room after another in Traugott Müller's four-tiered structure would be individually lit for the many short scenes in the various ministerial offices or the hotel rooms of the third act, ending with the social-democratic minister's assassination. Larger episodes like the polling station scene which takes up most of Act 2 and leads to the election of a War Minister as President – the allusion was to Hindenburg in 1925 – were played across the whole stage, with the film interludes or illustrations projected on the tall screen in the middle. For this a whole film had been made, on a script written by the dramaturgs using newsreel material and specially shot scenes with the actors. Though it was still being cut when the curtain went up, Brecht thought the film the best aspect of the performance. Before the prologue, with the hero and the minister as political prisoners together, there was a mixture of First World War shots, leading up to the stripping of a bemedalled tunic. Act 1 was introduced by a documentary (over-long, said Ihering), showing world history during the hero's eight years in prisons and mental hospitals: Lenin (applause), Mussolini, Sacco and Vanzetti, Hindenburg and so on. Then came the scene of his release, followed by another sequence showing the social problems to which he returned. The polling station scene seems to have been accompanied by visual comments, fluttering ballot papers and crowd faces leading to the moment illustrated on p. 87, then on to the lowering of another screen for a film on the new president's past career.

The second half of the play was introduced by Mehring's specially written theme song,[65] which Käte Kühl sang to Meisel's setting (accompanied apparently by a piano and a quarter-tone harmonium); and it included two of the most interesting technical effects. The first was when the hero, now working as a hotel waiter, goes up to the radio station on the roof and listens to the heartbeats of a sick passenger on a transatlantic aeroplane (i.e., nearly twenty years in the future) being transmitted for diagnosis by specialists; apparently he also saw a television demonstration. The second came right at the end, where the hero and his fellow-prisoners tap messages on their cell walls till he no longer answers, having hanged himself; here the laconic text of the messages could be seen projected between the cells: 'flickering words from one person to another',[66] as a critic put it. Such devices, which Piscator clearly handled with artistry, made an overwhelming impression even though they dragged out the play to a greater length than an English or American audience would stand: four hours, said one report. How far they helped the script is not so easy to judge; Toller himself preferred other productions, but this may have been in part due to resentment at the criticism of him in Piscator's book. Certainly the author got little

(i) **Hoppla, wir Leben!**, *THEATER AM NOLLENDORFPLATZ, 1927*
*Toller's text (1927 edition, dedicated to Piscator and Mehring) specifies that all
the scenes should be 'playable on a scaffolding of different storeys without change
of set'.*

					Grand Hotel							
					Radiostation							
87	88	89	W/C	90	91	92	93	94	95	96 offen	97	98
26	27	28	29	30	31	32	33	34	W/C	35	36	37
Separé					Vestibül				Klubraum			
Dienstboten- zimmer und Office									Schreib- zimmer			

26. *This is his diagram for the Grand Hotel in Act 3. ('Séparé' means private
room; 'Dienstbotenzimmer und Office', servants' quarters and pantry; 'Schreib-
zimmer', writing-room.)*

27. *Traugott Müller's design for Act 2, the Polling Station, showing use of the
central area for a projection of the successful presidential candidate in uniform.*

28. *Act 2, scene 2, the polling station as realised. Kilman, the Socialist candidate, is defeated by the bemedalled Minister for War whose tunic is seen projected in the central area.*

29. *A scene in the lower right subdivision. Paul Graetz (left) as a provincial politician and Granach (right) as the disillusioned hero, waiting in Kilman's outer office.*

credit for his contribution, though the text still stands up well enough for this to be patently unjust. Perhaps Toller was simply no longer enough of a novelty. The new thing, in Ihering's words, was that 'An amazing technical imagination has worked miracles'.[67]

Rasputin

For *Rasputin, the Romanoffs, the War and the People that rose against them*, to give it its full title, Piscator harnessed his new 'dramaturgical collective', calling the result 'Adapted by the Piscatorbühne'. The original play by Alexei Tolstoy and the historian Pavel Shchegolev was generally recognised to be a trivial piece of work, but the dramaturgs – including certainly Gasbarra, Lania and Brecht – were determined so far as possible to turn it into a political documentary. Piscator's book lists the sources they claimed to have used, some thirty-odd works ranging from Churchill's *The World Crisis* to Stalin's *The October Revolution*; he also reproduces part of the elaborate month-by-month 'synchronic table' which they drew up to guide them. Accounts differ as to exactly how much they altered, but it looks as though at least half the scenes were written by Gasbarra and Lania, and at least half the characters added, including such major historical figures as Lenin, Trotsky and the German and Austrian emperors. Rasputin himself was played by Paul Wegener, one of the great names of the period, now best remembered for the silent *Golem* film and

(ii) **Rasputin**, *THEATER AM NOLLENDORFPLATZ, 1927*

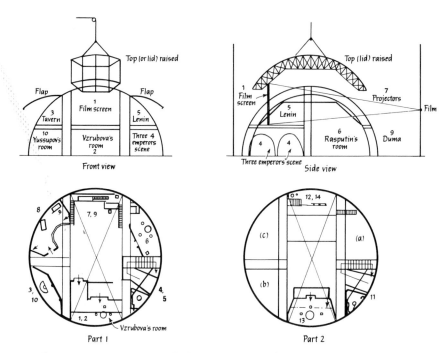

30. Diagrammatic sections and plans to show use of the hemispherical stage.

   Scenes and direction of stage rotation. 1. Lower part closed; film projected on screen suspended from removable top. 2. Vzrubova's room – then rotates anti-clockwise. 3. Tavern (upper level) – then clockwise. 4. The three emperors (lower level, with two small flaps opened). 5. Lenin (upper level) – then clockwise. 6. Rasputin's room – then clockwise. 7. Projections on closed upper part – then clockwise. 8. The Tsar's HQ – then rotates clockwise while the flaps of 8 are closed, and back anti-clockwise allowing projections to be thrown on the closed surface. 9. The Duma – then clockwise with more projections on the closed surface. 10. Yussupov's room (lower level). During the interval which follows, numbers 2, 4 and 9 are struck, and 13, 11 ond 12 set up in their places, the rest of the hemisphere being closed to form projection surfaces. The second part, then, begins with the stage rotating to bring on the first scene: 11. The Villa Rode – then clockwise as text is projected on closed surface (a). 12. The Yussupov palace – then clockwise, through 180°. 13. The Tsarina's room (lower level, with film projected on suspended screen above). 12 meanwhile is struck and 14 set in its place. Anti-clockwise rotation as film and text are projected on surfaces (b) and (c). 14. The Smolny Institute, with film and projections above.

31. Rasputin's room (6), with Wegener as Rasputin barely visible by the gramo-
phone, far left.

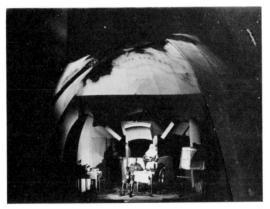

32. The Tsar's HQ (8), with a map being projected on the closed part of the
hemisphere.

the drawings of him by Emil Nolde; the Tsarina was Tilla Durieux. From
photographs and criticisms it seems as if both these performances were
distinguished but old-fashioned; Erwin Kalser as the Tsar and Anton
Edthofer as Prince Yussupoff made more impression. But once again it
was not the playing so much as the combination of film with an interesting
set that made theatrical news.

Traugott Müller this time had devised a great hemisphere, symbolising
the world and painted silver, which turned on the revolve, with thick
flap-like doors opening at different points to reveal various scenes and
rooms. On it, surprisingly effective considering its balloon-like surface,

the accompanying film was projected, or sometimes on a screen above its top. Much of the film material was drawn from Soviet sources, the German archives this time being less helpful; and Lunacharsky himself saw a rehearsal of the production, which was timed to coincide with the USSR's tenth anniversary celebrations. The curtain went up, the globe started to revolve, it seemed to catch fire and glow red. The film prologue began, showing four centuries' worth of Tsars, and leaving Nicholas II standing on top of the world with Rasputin's shadow looming above. Then came shots of Tsarist oppression, ending with an infantry attack on the Eastern front. From that point the film seems to have been used primarily as illustration or comment within the scenes, accompanied this time by projected texts on a separate screen to the side of the stage. Thus where one of the ministers assured the Tsarina that all would be well once the war had been won the side screen showed a long list of lost battles (see fig. 49), while above her head ran film shots of the shooting of the imperial family at Tsarskoye Selo. The true, vulgar news value of the production lay in the scene with the three emperors which Lania had written into the early part of the play, since this led ex-Kaiser Wilhelm (via a Colonel von Kleist in Berlin) to sue for defamation. Just a fortnight after the première Piscator was forced to take the imperial figure out of the play, and thenceforward substituted for his lines a reading of the court's order. Similarly Dimitri Rubinstein, one of the Tsar's former financial advisers, had to be deleted as the result of another suit. Such incidents were of all the more value to Piscator because they showed that his work was scoring political hits.

The Adventures of the Good Soldier Schweik

Both these productions were really a continuation of the work already done at the Volksbühne, but executed with a freer hand and before a different kind of audience. *Schweik* by contrast was something new. What Piscator had to deal with here was a great episodic comic novel, which its author had not lived to finish, and whose licensed adaptors, Max Brod and Hans Reimann, had dramatised it along conventional lines. Somehow he persuaded them to allow the dramaturgical collective to start again on different principles, throwing away the imposed plot and adapting the scenes to the rambling, step-by-step structure of the original: a pure montage from the novel, Brecht later called it.[68] Reimann seems to have washed his hands of the whole undertaking, being content simply to have his and Brod's names left on the programme and to collect the agreed royalties. The actual script was written anonymously by Gasbarra and Brecht, together with Piscator himself, and consists (so far as its structure can be clearly established)[69] of twenty-five scenes. Only one character moves consistently through them, Schweik, whose performance by the great Viennese actor Max Pallenberg dominated the show: the first time any of Piscator's actors had been able to do that. To help him in his progress, past a wide variety of scenes and figures, Piscator at an early stage conceived using two treadmills, or endless belts, which would roll Schweik on or off and allow him to march blandly into the bloody war without moving from the spot. The scenes in turn could pass across the stage as cut-out objects and people, or be seen moving past on the projection screen; there was no set in the usual sense. Instead Piscator called in George Grosz and made him draw whatever was needed in his characteristically spiteful, yet light, comic, economic style: cut-out marionettes, projected backgrounds, sequences of cartoon film. Though some real film shots were worked in – of the streets of Prague, for instance – the general effect was of a highly mobile show being illustrated in passing by one of Europe's most brilliant draughtsmen. Meisel was responsible for the music, which was entirely recorded. The element of top-heaviness in both previous productions had gone.

It opened with a cartoon-film prologue: Grosz's wriggling line tracing a German and an Austrian general, a death's-head judge and a priest juggling with a crucifix, symbolising the forces with which Schweik has to contend. The short first scene in Schweik's lodgings began as in the novel, followed by the episode at The Chalice (or The Flagon) with Brettschneider the police spy. As he and Schweik talked, a cartoon sequence started playing satirically with the § or paragraph sign familiar to all who have dealings with the German law. 'First', said Grosz's instructions,[70]

> a stupid-looking head is drawn with quick lines; the top springs open and paragraph signs swarm out, moving off to the left. The accompanying lines are to suggest hissing and steam.

Continuing till the screen was covered with squirming signs, this ran on into the next scene, where Schweik in his lodgings decides to volunteer; a tree becomes a structure of §'s, with hanged men dangling. The fourth scene shows Schweik waving a crutch (for he is rheumatic) being pushed off in a wheelchair by his landlady to the recruiting office; they move against the treadmill, while the great cut-out figures slide past them,

(iii) **Schweyk**, *THEATER AM NOLLENDORFPLATZ, 1928*

33. Four scenes from Piscator's book. Clockwise from top left: *Pallenberg as Schweyk before Dr Grunstein (scene 6); Schweyk under military arrest (scene 8); Barrack square, with the colonel, Lt. Lukasch and Schweyk (scene 14); Schweyk (invisible) in a rural latrine, under guard (from the Anabasis in part II). Showing animated and still projections by Grosz. The latrine is on one of the treadmills, as is Schweyk himself in scene 14.*

34. Strip with frames from Grosz's animated film (now unfortunately lost).

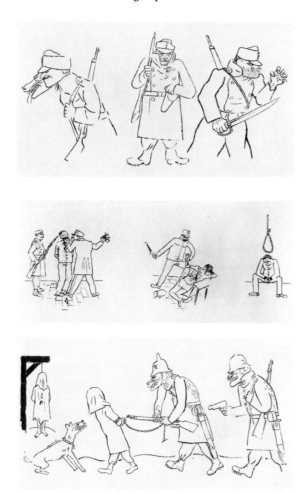

35. *Drawings by Grosz for the film. These relate to part II, probably to Schweyk's Anabasis through the rear areas of the Austrian army.*

36. *Parade of war victims before God: from the discarded closing scene.*

each reading the news of the declaration of war. Then come the medical examination and the military hospital, first with the huge snarling face of the doctor, animated on the screen above and simultaneously played on the stage below by the Austrian actor Joseph Danegger, then with a cartoon of the decrepit recruits which shows their ravaged internal organs and their treatment by sadistic orderlies. Back through the Prague streets into prison (for malingering), with Schweik swept in on the treadmill before an ironically welcoming banner held up by peace doves. Prison walls appear and fade into a sequence showing brutalisation by the warders. The drunken prison chaplain preaches his sermon to a congregation of debased cut-outs, scratching, fidgeting, passing notes, playing cards. When this reduces Schweik to spurious tears, he becomes the chaplain's batman.

For the rest of the first part of the play, which shows Schweik being won off the chaplain at cards by Lieutenant Lukasch, elegantly played by Edthofer (another Austrian), then stealing a dog for him, all photos, notes and drawings seem to have disappeared – apart from Grosz's collage for the lieutenant's bedroom wall, with its crossed sabres and postcards of period nudes. For the second part too the surviving script is slightly confused. This is where Schweik starts his so-called Anabasis towards the Galician front, along country roads where the screen fills with pursuing policemen as milestones, privies and other isolated objects sweep past on the treadmill; for much of it there was little dialogue, so that the march seemed unending. A horrifying cartoon sequence by Grosz (which may possibly have come later) showed soldiers arresting spies or hostages, their faces changing into those of snarling dogs; their prisoners are hanged and a dapper officer gets out his box camera to photograph the result. Schweik finds his unit and goes on by train with his friend the gluttonous Baloun and other notabilities from the book. Again a filmed landscape rolls by on the screen, then for the scene where Schweik and Baloun are made to do physical jerks beside the tracks a careful full-scale mock-up of a waggon comes in on the treadmill, with cut-out figures representing the 48 Men (or 6 Horses) it might contain. At this point Pallenberg tells the story of the waggon he has sent astray: a virtuoso monologue, delivered with all Schweik's obstinately subversive gentleness. Then as they get nearer the front Grosz's images become grimmer and less caricatured: a bombed village is carried past, a Red Cross waggon with wounded soldiers changes on the screen into a coffin, a solitary sentry stands in the snow-covered landscape as the moon goes down; after which come almost Goya-like cut-outs of fighting, a skeleton releasing poison gas, with on the screen a pit full of bones and skulls, and one last paragraph sign dwindling into a question mark.

The problem was, how should the play end? In the script there is simply the battlefield scene with Schweik and Volunteer Officer Marek (the character who largely represented Hašek himself) lost in the muddle.

SCHWEIK: I think we've gone the wrong way. The battle's next door.
MAREK: It'll take me weeks to forget this war.

Schweik finds a Russian uniform, puts it on, is arrested as a spy by a Hungarian unit, but a shell bursts and he is killed. Lania wanted a scene in Prague after the war, with Schweik being arrested by Brettschneider exactly as in 1914; the social order has not changed. Then it was decided rather to have a scene with Schweik in heaven, based on the incident in the book where Cadet Biegler dreams he is marched by militarised angels before an Austro-Hungarian imperial God, to be divinely court-martialled for his sins. Max Brod was asked to write this, and produced a satisfactory answer: some twenty mutilated war victims (apparently including real cripples as well as actors) march past God on the treadmill to the tune of the Radetzky March; meanwhile God, a poor old gentleman drawn by Grosz with epaulettes and a gouty foot, shrivels to nothing on the screen in face of Schweik's remarks. This scene was played once, at a private preview for the 'Sonderabteilungen', but it proved too long and insufficiently rehearsed, and it seems that for the première the version subsequently published by Brod was used. This has Schweik and Marek arriving at the gates of Heaven, where the angelic sentries turn them back. However, they sneak in behind a general's car; whereupon God as Commander-in-Chief cross-examines Schweik as to why he is wearing a Russian uniform. Marek strikes God as an honest atheist, so he is allowed to stay, but Schweik 'would mess up any outfit', and therefore has to be sent back to earth, where he arrives just in time to meet Vodička 'at six o'clock after the war' for the promised drink. It is typical of Piscator that half an hour before the curtain went up he had a further idea: he would show a slide of mangled corpses with a moving procession of crosses projected on top of it. The projectionist forgot to take the cover off the lens, so the corpses alone were seen. What happened at later performances is not recorded.

Konjunktur

Lania's 'comedy of economics', as he termed it, was originally to be a
light play about a Chinese general and an English businessman's attempt
to make use of him. At the planning stage of the Piscatorbühne it had
been decided to turn this into a vehicle for Tilla Durieux, whose aid in
setting the company up had earned her the right to a big part; she would
be a Soviet economic representative dealing not with a Chinese general
but with an Albanian dictator. The production at first was to follow
Hoppla! However, when Lania's colleagues came to look at it more
closely they judged that the story's new setting, the international oil
industry, was much too superficially dealt with; expert advisers like
Alfons Goldschmidt were drawn in, and the first act was rewritten to
Piscator's satisfaction. The rest was more difficult, as the star part could
not very well be abandoned; moreover the surviving photographs suggest
that even the revised script involved too many stereotyped comic situations. On top of this the new plan involved a piece of remarkable
political ineptitude in that it showed the imperialism of Soviet economic
interests and, by making the heroine at the same time a representative
of the Comintern, it emphasised the way in which the Communist parties
were used to further them. Only a day before the dress rehearsal Piscator
invited a select political audience to see the result – representatives of the
Soviet embassy and trade delegation and of the KPD and its paper *Die
Rote Fahne* – with only too predictable effects. The play must be changed.
According to *Das politische Theater* the one person to enjoy himself in this
situation was Brecht, who immediately came up with the preposterous
solution. The heroine had only been passing herself off as a Soviet agent
and right at the end, after speaking the lines unchanged up to that point,
could be unmasked as a secret representative of the South Americans.
What this piece of manipulative surgery did to Tilla Durieux's interpretation of the part can only be guessed. But it postponed the première
by another forty-eight hours and made the play even less credible than it
had been before.

Once again Müller's set played an important role. Starting with an
almost bare stage, symbolising unexploited land, structures multiplied:
huts, machinery, and a growing forest of drilling towers, all made of
authentic materials like corrugated iron and creosoted wood. So it
helped to develop the theme. Real motor-cars confronted a real donkey.
The use of projections too was different, since this time they appear

(iv) **Konjunktur**, *LESSING THEATER, 1928*

37. An Albanian rural pub, with transport facilities.

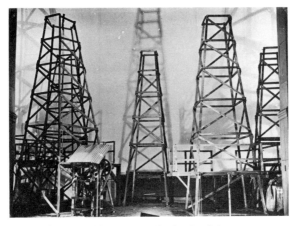

38. An oil rig somewhere in Albania. At the back of the stage is a vast projection screen.

to have consisted entirely of real or feigned newspaper cuttings thrown on to a screen the size of the entire stage opening and divided into columns. These, said Piscator, were to come up or fade into the background, so as to show the next incident on the stage exactly at the point where the relevant column had finished: something that was presumably less practicable once the drilling towers began to go up. Gasbarra too wrote a song in honour of Shell[71] ('I shell, you shell, he shell!') which Kurt Weill set to music; and both Ihering and Piscator felt that the whole production was more unified than its precursors. The audiences were less impressed, and it played for four weeks to dwindling houses.

Der Kaufmann von Berlin

Unlike the first, the second play by one of the dramaturgical collective was written very much with the possibilities and requirements of the Piscatorbühne in view. The basic drawbacks of Mehring's inflation saga have already been mentioned, but undoubtedly it gives a panoramic view of Berlin at that time even though the published text (which is meant to be read as a book)[72] is far too long for performance. From Piscator's point of view its weaknesses were first that it failed to explore the causes and effects of the inflation at all thoroughly, secondly that it criticised capitalism and militarist reaction without ever showing the working class. Accordingly he brought in such advisers as Alfons Goldschmidt, Sternberg and Richard Lewinsohn, who seem to have found the documentary material for some of the projections, while fresh songs by Mehring were added, partly to give a more proletarian emphasis, to those already in the text (the music being by Hanns Eisler). In the fourth and last part the scenes following Kaftan's arrest were cut; the final 'Oratorio of War and Inflation' being switched to form a prologue sung by a male choir. Even so the play ran more than four hours. Moreover although Kaftan had been conceived as a role for a great actor he was a far less richly rounded wanderer than Schweik, so that once again the acting fell into the background. The part was played with considerable subtlety by Paul Baratoff of the New York Yiddish Theatre, but necessarily spoken (as written) in a dialect which not all the audience could understand. Reinhold Schünzel too gave an effective but hardly unexpected performance as the right-wing lawyer who pulls Kaftan's strings, first making then breaking him as a financial tycoon. Otherwise the important actors were the members of the crowds: the porters, whores, dealers,

(v) **Der Kaufmann von Berlin**, *THEATER AM NOLLENDORF-PLATZ, 1929*

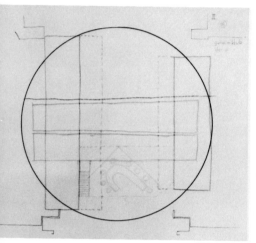

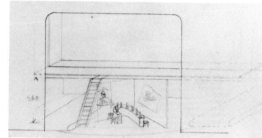

39–41. Act II, scene 16, 'The Secret Club of Eight', *a right-wing conspiratorial group meeting in a subterranean bar.* Above, Moholy-Nagy's plan *showing the revolving stage with, horizontally, the two stage lifts or bridges, and, vertically, the two treadmills (not used in this scene).* Above right, *an isometric projection of this. The bridges are raised half-way up the proscenium opening, with a stairway leading down to the bar. Dotted lines on the right show one tread-mill offstage, the other being visible behind the stairs.* Right, *the scene as realised. The projection screen can be seen at the back, both above and below the bridges.*

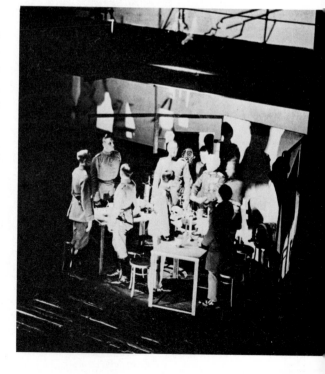

newspaper readers, Jews, black-marketeers, officers, bystanders and so on who were collectively listed in the programme and functioned almost as part of the Berlin setting.

This setting was the thing. To devise it Piscator went back to Moholy-Nagy,[73] who had left the Bauhaus just over a year before and was again working in Berlin. The combination of physical movement and social mobility led to a threefold solution of a brilliantly kinetic kind: first, the revolve was used; then on it were carried two treadmills, which could also be independently shifted; finally there were platform-like bridges or lifts stretching right across the stage and able to be used as acting areas at any level. At the same time the height of the stage opening could be adjusted to cut off whatever was not needed. A great number of different arrangements and movements was thus made possible: twenty in the first half alone. The lighting was selective, so as to pick out the area of the action; no fewer than four projection screens[74] could be brought into use, as well as a gauze. Moholy-Nagy this time directed the film, which was not so much used for comment as knitted ingeniously into the stage action by projecting it on the gauze, then lighting up the stage behind as the gauze was raised, thus smoothly transferring the action to the stage. Another feature in which Moholy's hand can surely be seen is the use of signs and symbols of various kinds: advertisements, shop signs, the illuminated entrance to an underground station, Hebrew letters, the board marking up the stock exchange prices: all the unconscious literary paraphernalia of the big city. Finally there were the sound effects. 'What an apparatus! . . .' exclaimed the critic Bernhard Diebold.

> Traffic intersection on the stage. Reality of the instant. The elevated railway crosses the bridge to the Alexanderplatz station. The underground's U sign lights up. Trams sound their bells. Cars hoot.[75]

Mehring, it now appears, would really have preferred a simpler, revue-like production on a mainly bare stage. But what stuck in the mind was not the flimsy story but the director's use of space, the life of the streets, the whole 'social panorama of the inflation'. To Diebold the beginning with Kaftan's wanderings through the East End of Berlin, first on the screen, then on the stage, was unforgettable. To Piscator himself there was a particular symbolic significance in the use of the bridges, particularly at the end of the play, to raise and lower the social classes.

§ 218

Carl Credé was a doctor from Celle near Hanover, who had been gaoled for offences against § 218, the abortion paragraph of the criminal code. His play was naturalistic and somewhat sentimental. Rehearsing it in a mere ten days with the remaining loyal actors after his second company had crashed, Piscator set it in a didactic, argumentative framework which turned it into a new form of discussion with the audience. This was done by seating actors in the auditorium to get up and speak from the standpoints of a lawyer, a magistrate, a panel doctor, a clergyman and so on. A new prologue and interlude were added, in which the house lights were turned up while these actors exchanged comments, which could in some measure be improvised. Otherwise the play was presented as written apart from the odd audience interjection.[76] There was a simple set by Müller's assistant Wolfgang Roth which represented two rooms divided by a wall; there was also some use of projections, for instance a letter from a working-class mother which was screened during the interlude between Acts 1 and 2. The ending however was new, involving a fight between some of the characters as the auditorium actors began to come up on stage arguing. 'The audience must decide', says the magistrate, after which the actors withdraw shouting slogans, the house lights again go up and a general debate follows. Where possible the performance included a speech by a real-life local figure such as a doctor about the play and the social problem with which it dealt; then at the end genuine members of the audience were encouraged to join in, with a vote on the abolition of the paragraph being taken by a show of hands: it was the first time, wrote Kurt Pinthus in a review of the Berlin production, that 'the ending of a play corresponded to a public meeting'.[77] The success of this approach was considerable, there being some three hundred performances – more than for any other Piscator production. This included the provincial tour and the two runs at the Wallner-Theater in Berlin.

Des Kaisers Kulis

Even before Theodor Plivier's successful novel about the German Navy had appeared he and Piscator were at work on its dramatisation. Though he seldom went to the theatre except to work as an extra, he had seen *Der Kaufmann von Berlin* and been fired by it to write his own play; mean-

(vi) § 218, *1929–30*

42. A scene from this more economically produced play, as performed in various provincial cities and the Wallner-Theater, Berlin. Set by Wolfgang Roth.

(vii) **Des Kaisers Kulis**, *LESSING- AND WALLNER-THEATER, 1930*

43. Photomontage design by Traugott Müller, showing cross-section of a First World War battle-cruiser.

time Piscator, who had been lent a copy of the book by one of his students who was a friend of Plivier's, read it at a sitting, asked if the author was a party member and arranged to meet him.[78] The contract seems to have been signed even before the second company collapsed. Thereafter the work went slowly, with Plivier writing the first draft and Piscator then going over it; and clearly the book, which is a sweeping yet condensed lower-deck's-eye view of the First World War, as fought at Jutland, in harbour, on lonely raids and in the glasshouse, would have been difficult to stage even with Piscator's full resources. Their answer was to make three separate acts of it. The first shows a crew coaling ship when the battlecruiser *Seydlitz* arrives back from the Dogger Bank battle with her two after turrets burnt out with the crews inside them; the dock workers bring out the calcined bodies, which disintegrate when touched. A booze-up on shore leads into the second, showing the battle of Jutland as experienced in various areas of the battleship *Lützow*, from boiler-room to bridge, down to the torpedo room in which forty men are trapped and drowned. The third shows the growing discontent and eventual mutinies of the fleet subsequently tied down at Kiel, together with the trial and execution of the two sailors, Alwin Köbis and Max Reichpietsch, to whom Plivier dedicated his book. Though the novel ends with the November Revolution the play apparently[79] went on to sketch what followed: the disillusionment of the returned sailors as they saw what had become of it, right up to the unemployment of 1930.

A cartoon film was made to show the manoeuvrings of the fleets at Jutland, simultaneously expounded by a lecturer on stage. This was amplified by newsreel material and some specially filmed sequences. The music was by Meisel (who died the same year in his mid-thirties), the set once more by Traugott Müller. At the première in the Lessing-Theater (which took place the same day as that of Toller's naval play *Feuer aus den Kesseln*; it was a great year for stage battleships) the last act was largely unrehearsed, the final scene actually being written in the interval, while Piscator had previously made Plivier rewrite the trial scene without ensuring that all the actors knew about the changes. The distractions of the two men's personal relationship doubtless contributed, but clearly the production was not carefully enough prepared, and this was hardly helped by the decision to cast Plivier himself as Köbis, since for all his first-hand naval experience he was a poor actor. However, this was another of those productions where the acting was not meant to be the main attraction. What stuck in Ihering's mind, for instance, was the docking of the *Seydlitz*, the petty officer's horrified exit through the audience after seeing the contents of her turrets, the exposition of the tactics at Jutland and the use of choruses. This was at least the fourth Piscator production to end with the singing of the 'Internationale', this time by an agit-prop group stationed as a claque in the balcony. Though it ran for only four weeks at the Lessing-Theater, the play was later revived in the Wallner-Theater, presumably with still further reduced means. Ihering, who thought that it would have been less ambiguously staged there in the first place, called for a further simplification of Piscator's whole approach.

Tai Yang erwacht

In the last of these productions Piscator dispensed with stage machinery and elaborate sets and made little use of film. The play this time was announced as a 'Lehrstück',[80] a form of cantata-like didactic exercise whose chief exponent was Brecht. Friedrich Wolf, its author, though a new recruit to the KPD, had established himself as the other leading communist playwright with *Cyankali* (on the same theme as § 218) and *Die Matrosen von Cattaro* (third of the 1930 crop of revolutionary naval plays – even the fourth if you count Meyerhold's visit to Berlin with *Roar China*), and ever since seeing *Gewitter über Gottland* he had been fascinated by Piscator's work. Though his two previous plays had been on Piscator's list in 1929, they had been produced instead by the Gruppe junger Schauspieler and the Volksbühne respectively. During 1930 however he had written a new work on the theme of Chinese labour conditions and the failed revolution of 1927, conceiving it as a 'counter-play' to Klabund's over-sweet *Der Kreidekreis*, and even calling his heroine at first by the same name, Hai-tang. Based on a Shanghai textile worker described in the *Süddeutsche Arbeiterzeitung* in mid-June 1930, this girl 'wakes up' to the intolerable conditions in the spinning mill where she works, and uses her position as the director's mistress to help the revolutionaries organise her fellow-workers to strike. The part was written for Constanze Menz, the Frankfurt actress who had distinguished herself there in *Cyankali* and in Lania's translation of *Roar China*, and she now came to play it in Berlin.

It was a much shorter play than usual with Piscator, having eight scenes and a mere nineteen characters all told. And the excellent photographs suggest a much lighter style of presentation. Thus John Heartfield's set consisted almost entirely of fluttering banners, which bore political (or

(viii) **Tai Yang Erwacht**, *WALLNER-THEATER*, 1931

44–45. Two photographs taken during a performance, showing the reversible banners which formed the basis of John Heartfield's design. The scenes are difficult to identify, since the author's stage directions are ignored and the banners were not specified in his text.

statistical) inscriptions on one side and nothing on the other, so that they could be turned round and used for projections; the music was by Eisler. There was no curtain; by continuing the inscriptions round the auditorium the production aimed to create a new relationship with the spectators. The play opened with the actors coming in from the street, chatting about the political situation and the play itself, then sitting down on stage to dress and make themselves up. As each became ready he took one of the banners, placed it in position for the first scene (Tai Yang's family shack) and slid into the dialogue. Much was expository, and to that extent akin to the 'Lehrstücke'; thus there was a short lecture by Alfons Goldschmidt during the play, while at the end the actor Ernst Ginsberg, dressed in his ordinary clothes, came out of his role and stepped forward to draw parallels with Germany's problems in 1931. The movements appear[81] to have been to some extent choreographed, under the direction of the communist dancer, Jean Weidt; film was used at a call from the auditorium suggesting that the abuses referred to might not be authentic – the players thereupon held their banners to act as a screen. For Ihering, who considered this to be 'Piscator's simplest and shortest performance',[82] its weakness lay in the incidents of the plot, particularly Tai's scenes with her boss and her young sister. The actors, he found, were stronger as soon as they became didactic. For Alfred Kerr, the doyen of the critics, who was not meaning to be complimentary, 'What moved one last night was neither the play nor the performance, but the state of the world'.[83]

5. The political theatre

Writing the epic play

On addressing the 'Sonderabteilungen' before setting up the second company Piscator had thus summed up the changes which he had effected in the existing theatre:

> In lieu of private themes we had generalisation, in lieu of what was special the typical, in lieu of accident causality. Decorativeness gave way to constructiveness, Reason was put on a par with Emotion, while sensuality was replaced by didacticism and fantasy by documentary reality.[84]

Looking back, however, at all that he had been able to do before he left Germany in 1931, we can see (as he could not) that such changes would go no further. For it was to be over thirty years before he was again master of a theatre with comparable resources, and in the meantime his view of many of his methods and objectives had altered. What he achieved later, as a man around seventy, will be dealt with in due course, but this is now the obvious break – in Piscator's own career, in German history and in the story of the modern movement. It is the moment to take stock of his innovations and the approach to art and politics which they represented.

From his first production for the Volksbühne he had become associated with the concept of epic theatre, an old term newly refurbished for our century. Whatever this may owe to the 'accident' of his working with Paquet on *Fahnen*, it was Piscator who more than anyone was subsequently responsible for linking epic dramaturgy to the new areas of subject matter with which he wished the theatre to deal. Despite his addiction to the Internationale, direct communication of revolutionary feeling did

not interest him for very long; instead he became more and more concerned with the social and political background and the economic basis
on which it rests. The history of the German Revolution and its aftermath, the conflicts of the oil companies, the inflation, the abortion law,
the tactics which slaughter men at sea, the wages of Chinese textile
workers: these were the kind of new subjects which for him 'burst the
form of the stage and the form of the drama too'.[85] The problem then
was how to find the new forms which would still contain this material
within the theatre. Unfortunately, if understandably, there seemed to
him as yet to be no playwright capable of doing that. 'The lack of any
great imaginative writing', he told readers of *Die Rote Fahne* in 1928,

> which would express the present day with all its forces and problems
> is no accident but results from the complexity, dividedness and in-
> completeness of our age.[86]

This did not mean that the aim must be abandoned. But if the right forms
were not to be found by the writer then they must be arrived at by
director and writer together, possibly (as in *Sturmflut*) with all the
resources of the stage being used for trial and error. The epic play, in
other words could only be created by adaptation, and ultimately by the
practical efforts of an entire team, using a form of montage (montage
being ultimately a Dada technique). Because they rambled more and were
less likely to be burdened with an artificial, conventionalised plot, novels
such as *Schweik* and *Des Kaisers Kulis* were likelier to respond to this
process than most existing plays.

This got him the reputation of being brutal to authors. Of course he
denied it, saying that the need to portray socio-political material in
depth meant that bourgeois dramaturgy had to be smashed; but his
'dramaturgical collective' was certainly not always as tactful as it might
have been in its interventions. Moreover his feeling that authors had to
accept a certain amount of discipline dates from well before his concern
with this kind of material, since already his essay on the Proletarian
Theatre argued that the playwright must 'subordinate his own ideas, his
own originality', so as to 'learn from the politicians'.[87] The effect of
such discipline on his writers varied. Paquet, so Piscator said, accepted it,
though it is noticeable that after *Sturmflut* the two men did not work
together again. Welk argued; but in a very decent statement[88] at the
time of the Volksbühne controversy said that he shared Piscator's
aims and accepted his changes, despite feeling that the actors had mangled
the words and that the whole evening added up to 'an immense produc-

tion versus a play'. Toller seems to have gone along with Piscator and Gasbarra on the formal side, but fought for his words, whose frequently poetic flavour they positively resented (deriding them in *Das politische Theater*,[89] in return for which Toller, in his book of reportage *Quer Durch*,[90] ridiculed the flatness of their proposed alternatives). He too stopped collaborating with Piscator after that; a loss perhaps for both men. Of the *Schweik* adaptors, Reimann shrugged the whole business off as ridiculous; Brod on the other hand remained friendly. The only playwright, apart from those involved in the collective, to remain an ally (for life) was Friedrich Wolf, who was by disposition an optimist,

46. *Adaptors adapted. Piscator with Hans Reimann* (left) *and Max Brod* (right), *the authorised adaptors of Hašek's Schweyk novel, whose stage version was trans-mogrified by the first Piscatorbühne's 'dramaturgical collective' in 1927/28.*

accepted party discipline, and had stood up well to the multiple re-writings of *Tai Yang erwacht*.

The puzzle of course is why did Piscator stage nothing by Brecht, who shared many of his convictions and actually believed in the individual's subordination to the collective. What Brecht got from his experience with Piscator in those years is fairly plain, and he acknowledged it. The emphasis on Reason and didacticism, the sense that the new subject matter demanded a new dramatic form, the use of songs to interrupt and comment: all these are found in his notes and essays of the 1920s, and he bolstered them by citing such Piscatorial examples as the step-by-step narrative technique of *Schweik* and the oil interests handled in *Konjunktur* ('Petroleum resists the five-act form').⁹¹ Who actually wrote the *Schweik* adaptation is not clear; Brecht later said that he did, Piscator claimed it as his own, the surviving script bears the names 'Brecht, Gasbarra, Piscator, G. Grosz', but pencilled in Brecht's hand. This at any rate was Brecht's most important job with the collective, though he contributed to *Rasputin* and, as we have seen, *Konjunktur*; he should have translated a song in *Singing Jailbirds*, but found he could not.⁹² If *Schweik* led to Brecht's own Schweik play fifteen years later *Konjunktur* developed more immediately into a joint scheme with Lania for a new version to be called *Das Ölfeld*, of which an incomplete script survives, with a fine last chorus. *Tai Yang erwacht* too has a certain bearing on *Der gute Mensch von Setzuan*. But of all the tentative plans to do a Brecht play at the Piscatorbühne not one came to anything, nor did his wife Helene Weigel ever act there. It is true that he was then having difficulty in finishing the large-scale epic works which he was writing at this time – *Fleischhacker, Fatzer, Der Brotladen* – while neither the smaller didactic Lehrstücke nor the satirical operas with Weill were best suited to Piscator's approach. At the same time even Brecht wished in certain respects to be his own master, for although he could collaborate with Lania (who helped on the *Drei-groschenoper* film) his relations with Gasbarra were not good. 'I am not prepared to work under Gasbarra's direction where literary questions are concerned', says an undated note from him to Piscator, 'only political.'⁹³

Brecht apart, it was not so much the epic structure which influenced contemporary theatres and writers as the subject matter itself. After the Piscatorbühne's first season, 'the times' suddenly became a fashionable theme, driving out 'Man' and 'I', those two favourite poles of the Expressionist drama, and quite overshadowing the reinterpretation of the classics which Jessner, Engel and Piscator had made briefly contro-versial. Weisenborn's submarine play, Ferdinand Bruckner's *Verbrecher* with its simultaneous stage a la *Hoppla!*, Feuchtwanger's *Die Petroleuminseln* with its Brechtian songs and thematic resemblance to the slightly later *Konjunktur*, Lampel's play about a reformatory and his subsequent *Giftgas über Berlin* (banned after one performance by the Gruppe junger Schau-spieler) were all staged in the year following the collapse of the first Piscator company, and with them the term 'Zeittheater' and 'Zeitstück', or 'theatre of the times' and 'play of the times', passed into the Weimar vocabulary. The 'Zeitoper' followed with operas like Hindemith's *News of the Day* and Max Brand's *Maschinist Hopkins*, both produced at the end of that season; that same year Eisler wrote his cantata *Tempo der Zeit* or *Pace of the Times*.

Piscator himself, then sitting on the sidelines, was not happy, and complained that radical democrats had taken over his themes making the *Zeitstück* 'modish, commercially attractive, in short stageable'.[94] This was not entirely fair to the groups putting such plays on, who included stranded actors from his own ventures and were quite as responsible as the third Piscator company for the steady politicising of the repertoire in the republic's last years. What remained special to his productions however was their dramaturgical handling of a whole succession of scenes using a variety of theatrical techniques in such a way as to suggest (for instance to Bernhard Reich when he saw *Der Kaufmann von Berlin*) that the subject matter was not just being put on show but examined by a Marxist. It was the difference between presenting 'the times' and trying to get under their skin.

Technology in the theatre

If Reich, when he got to know Piscator better in the USSR, decided that he was at bottom a playwright, he was one who used non-verbal and to a great extent elaborately mechanical means. Hitherto such means had been devised and used primarily for simplifying changes of scene, many having been in fact first used in opera houses, e.g. to meet the extravagant scenic demands of Wagner. With Piscator on the contrary the function of the set was not illusionistic but dramaturgical, and the whole elaborate German backstage apparatus was called in to help. 'For years', wrote Traugott Müller in his brief statement for the *Hoppla!* programme, 'I have been working to get rid of scenery.'[95] Beginning with the use of the revolve in *Segel am Horizont* to show the progress of the ship against projected clouds scudding the other way, he and Piscator became increasingly daring. The simultaneous *Hoppla!* set was not in itself a new idea, since a nine-room set had been seen in an American farce, while in Metz in the fifteenth century there had been a stage showing nine storeys.[96] Its immediate inspiration could well have been Vesnin's somewhat similar design for *The Man who was Thursday*, which Tairoff staged with the Moscow Kamerny Theatre in August 1923; though originally Müller's tall scaffolding was to have been covered with white screens which would be drawn back on runners to show the relevant acting area as it were popping out of the film; it was only when the screens kept

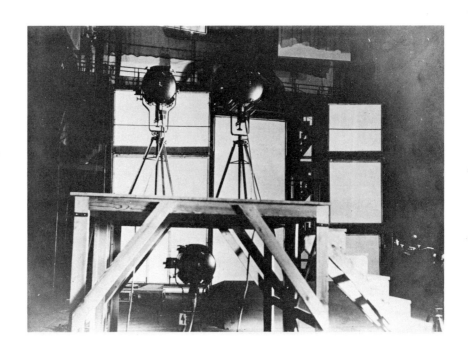

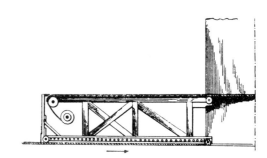

47–48. *Theatre technology 1927/28.*
Above, *projectors behind the* Hoppla,
wir leben! *set (see ills. 27–28),*
showing screens for projection at the
back of its various subdivisions. Right,
diagrams *of the treadmill stage, as*
provided for Schweyk by the firm of
Cl. Werrn, Dortmund.

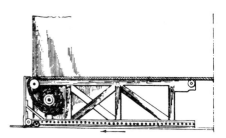

sticking that the skeleton was stripped and left as a bare structure of gas piping. In *Rasputin* the novelty of the design was not so much drama-turgical as symbolic; startling as it was, it can hardly be said to have followed from the narrative demands of the play. The use of the treadmill in *Schweik* however was logical and original, even if the device itself was not new. It had already been used in one or two opera houses, notably for a gala performance of *Orpheus* in Berlin in 1906 on the occasion of the Kaiser's silver wedding.[97] Piscator now turned it into a dramaturgical principle, the key to a picaresque adaptation which without it could only have been conventional, like Brod's and Reimann's, or indeed like the much more static *Schweik im zweiten Weltkrieg* which Brecht was to write in 1943.

Everything was grist to his mill. 'I know of no means', he wrote at the time of *Sturmflut*, 'that can be termed inartistic so long as it communicates a spirit of movement, tension, expression – in other words, of life.'[98] If the Volksbühne had been equipped for film at the time of *Fahnen*, he would have used it then; since the way had been paved by Berthold Viertel's production of Georg Kaiser's *Nebeneinander* (3 November 1923), which began with the title and cast being projected on a white screen, using an artificially induced flicker to give the effect of the movies (costumes and sets were by Grosz). Well before the First World War film had been used in opera houses for illusionistic purposes, while a Hamburg revue of 1911 called *Rund um den Alster* had shown a film of Neptune arriving in a submarine and touring the Hamburg streets till the screen showed the two leading actors entering the theatre door, only to appear in flesh, blood and three dimensions on the actual stage.[99] But no other director used film so extensively or thought about it so sys-tematically as Piscator, who came to employ front projection, back projection, and simultaneous or overlapping projection from more than one source. In his view slide projections were 'the literary element' (compare Brecht's views on 'the literarising of the theatre' by projected titles in the *Dreigroschenoper* notes) while film could be of three kinds: instructional, dramatic or commentary-cum-chorus. Instructional film was documentary, historical; it 'extends the subject matter in terms of time and space'. Dramatic film furthered the story and saved dialogue; commentary film pointed things out to the audience and emphasised the moral.[100]

For all his protestations that such techniques were dramaturgically necessary, Piscator undoubtedly enjoyed handling them, and was easily tempted into excess. Not only did his productions become extremely

49. *'Literarisation of the theatre.'* Rasputin, *1927: scene in the Tsarina's bed-room, accompanied by projected text on side screen, right.*

long, but he would also use gadgets which did not yet function smoothly; thus the lifts in *Der Kaufmann von Berlin* were a threat to life and limb, and the *Schweik* treadmills far too noisy:

> We had the impression of a steam mill working flat out. The bands clattered, rattled and puffed till the whole building shook. However hard you shouted you could scarcely make yourself heard. Dialogue on these whizzing monsters was out of the question. So far as I remember we sank into the stalls laughing desperately. That was twelve days before the première.[101]

The best the technicians could do, by reinforcing the stage, inserting strips of felt and using great quantities of grease, was to reduce the noise so that very loud words could get through. But there was the problem of expense; for these devices were costly even given the lavish scale on which German theatres were used to working. Piscator's technical director Julius Richter described what was involved in striking the sets each night for the next morning's rehearsal.[102] The *Hoppla* scaffolding

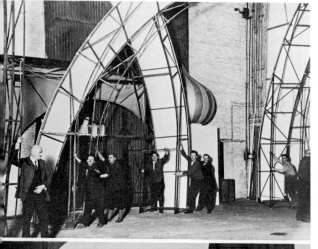

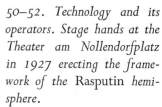

50–52. *Technology and its operators. Stage hands at the Theater am Nollendorfplatz in 1927 erecting the framework of the* Rasputin *hemisphere.*

The finished hemisphere, taken evidently at a dress rehearsal, with its top raised (see diagrams Fig. 30).

Piscator (with raised leg) showing Ernst Busch (left of him, with hands in pockets) and others the Kaufmann von Berlin *set at the same theatre in 1929. They appear to be gazing up at the bridges, with the two treadmills behind them.*

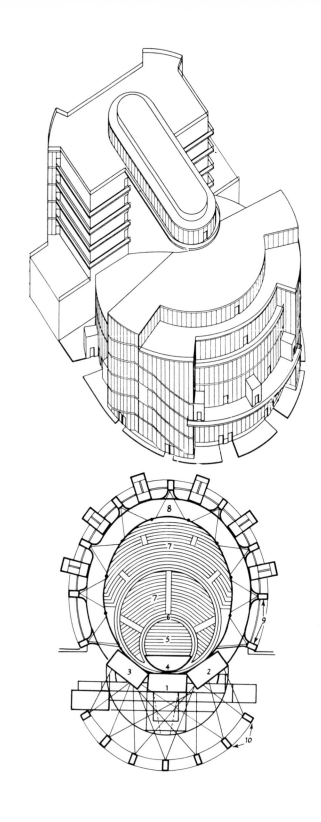

was 26 feet high and weighed four tons; each half of the *Rasputin* hemi-sphere some 50 feet wide and about a ton; so replacing the one set by the other took roughly 100 man-hours. Similarly with the *Schweik* rehearsals, where each treadmill was 55 feet long and weighed five tons. The cost of these operations alone was over 10,000 marks. It took something like the bravado of Mr Toad therefore to follow the first company's bankruptcy with a production on the scale of *Der Kaufmann von Berlin*, which used treadmills, lifts and the revolve as well as film and sound effects and a live dance band. In fact it was suicidal.

Piscator tended to blame his financial and his technical problems alike on the limitations of what was even by German standards a pretty well-equipped theatre. For he still wanted the Total-Theater which Gropius had designed. Ante-dating Barkhin and Sergei Vakhtangov's plans for the Meyerhold theatre in Moscow, which share some features with it, this treated both the audience and the stage in a new way. First of all it rejected the idea of class differentiation by tiers, as in the old court theatres, in favour of a single vast bank of 2000 seats, none at a sharper lateral angle than about 45° to the centre of a proscenium stage. Then the stage itself could be arranged in any one of three ways. There could be a proscenium stage for traditional plays (or a triple proscenium stage as in Van de Velde's exhibition theatre at Cologne in 1912), or a circular arena stage which itself could revolve; or by revolving the whole half of the theatre containing this, seats and all, the circular stage could be brought round in front of the proscenium stage, to be used as a thrust stage or else covered in whole or in part with seats. Behind the vast cyclorama were to be seven projection rooms; round the auditorium a further nine, so that the audience could be entirely surrounded by back-projected still or moving images – while yet another projection turret could be lowered from the auditorium roof. The aim (which had surely been discussed with Moholy too) was that of

> building in mechanical and light-generated fields of force which can be shifted in all three spatial dimensions and by their components and

53–54. Gropius's 'Total-Theater', designed for the Piscatorbühne when it was first set up. Axonometric projection and plan. 1, 2 and 3 are stages, 4 a forestage on an inner turntable which can be rotated to act as a small arena stage. Alternatively the surrounding seating, 7, can be rotated, thereby carrying this inner turntable to the centre of the auditorium so as to act as a full arena. 6 is an inner aisle. Round the broad outer aisle, 8, are placed projection boxes, 9, and staircases. There are further boxes, 10, for back projection.

their cubes of light permit the director to conjure up the dreamspaces of his imagination with infinite variability within the invisible network of coordinates imposed by the neutral blacked-out auditorium.[103]

Though these plans were exhibited at the congress of German workers' theatres in April 1928, already Piscator must have been clear that they would not be realised. There is also a plan of that year[104] for a smaller and simpler theatre which Traugott Müller drew up under their influence and with Gropius's evident approval. Though its relevance to Piscator's schemes is uncertain, this ingeniously put all the offices beneath the audience in order to gain space for scene changes backstage. The roof was to be a single shell from behind the stage to the far side of the auditorium: one vast cyclorama covering the whole theatre.

Actors with a cause

Piscator however did not like being thought of primarily as a theatre technologist, any more than he cared for his role as father of the 'Zeit-theater' and the 'Zeitstück'. Nor was he pleased to be told that this meant neglecting the actor. All the same there is something in what Brecht said about the transition from *Der Kaufmann von Berlin* to the bare simplicity of Credé's § *218*:

> It was a huge success, but he himself didn't like it at all. As its producer he was like a bacteriologist whose microscope has been taken away from him.[105]

Certainly Piscator was from the first insistent that the actor, as well as the author, must be part of a team, 'a kind of collective human being', he wrote in 1927,

> one who draws his whole strength from his involvement in the common cause. In course of time this attitude will produce a new form of acting . . .[106]

Two years later he told Ihering that building an ensemble was 'one of the most important objectives for my theatre, if not the primary one'. But then, as Albert Venohr says, Berlin in those days was one big ensemble, and there was a wealth of skilled acting talent – subsequently scattered to Zürich, London, New York and Hollywood – on which any theatre operating at Piscator's level of expenditure could draw. Within this rich pool, with its Granachs and Georges, its Pallenbergs and Wegeners, there was a sizeable circle of actors of more or less left-wing convictions, and it was from these that the various political groups and productions of 1930–32 were assembled. Kalser, Busch, Venohr, Gnass, Genschow, Trepte, Steckel, Bienert, Loebinger, Weigel, Widmann, Erpenbeck – there is a whole string of such names: all names that recur in the subsequent history of this kind of theatre, right down to the present. Piscator

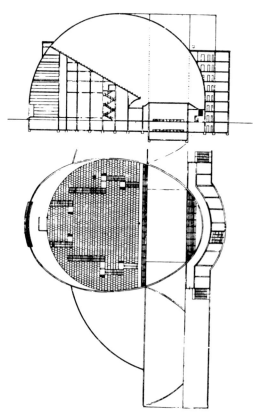

55. *A more economical version. Traugott Müller's theatre project of 1928. Section (above) and plan.*

felt that his style was cramped by the star system, for which he blamed Max Reinhardt, and by the lure of film work; at the same time, according to Venohr, he tended to underpay his supporting actors and on that account had trouble with the actors' union. As a director of actors both Trepte and Venohr admired him, while the critics praised his work with the established stars in *What Price Glory?* But he never worked out a new approach to acting to match his new approach to dramaturgy and stage technology, so that Meyerhold was surely right when he complained in 1928 that Piscator 'has built a new theatre but makes old actors perform in it'.[107] The concept of epic, 'gestic' acting was independently elaborated by Brecht.

Fritz Sternberg the sociologist once described Piscator complaining how hard it was to set up a company in view of the high fees demanded by star actors. Brecht thereupon is supposed to have said 'they would act for me if I promised to give them extra rehearsals', taken the telephone and got a number of the leading Berlin actors promptly to agree to perform in a hypothetical production for less than they were asking Piscator.[108] If this is true, it shows which of the two men was expected to be the more stimulating to work with. None the less Piscator did wish to train actors

56. *Mens sana in corpore sano. Piscator's Studio in 1927–28, with Fritz Sommer in charge of PT.*

in his own way, and the Studio which he set up for the purpose not only became important for his own later teaching but also turned out a number of notable talents, such as Leonard Steckel, Günther Haenel (of the Vienna Volkstheater after 1945, and Leopold Lindtberg, director of the Second World War film *The Last Chance* and later at the Burgtheater. 'I've long been known as a Piscator pupil', wrote Lindtberg in 1953,

> and if I don't use the techniques you taught me in my own work there is something more valuable which I got from your school, have treasured and tried to pass on: namely the principle that one should always work outwards from a moral and spiritual core, should put the cause first and one's own self second, and should aim not for what is effective but for what is right.[109]

This Studio was divided from the first into three groups, of which Haenel and Lindtberg were in the second; it was they who wished to do Lampel's *Putsch*. The first group, directed by Ernst Lönner, meanwhile prepared *Singing Jailbirds*, while the third, 'a teaching studio concentrating entirely on the training of young actors',[110] organised a matinée in honour of the gaoled revolutionary Max Hölz in November 1927. By 1 December Tilla Durieux and Granach, who had undertaken to teach there, had not turned up, while Erwin Kalser had only appeared twice. Though they were supposed to organise the daily PT classes for all the actors, according to Jung the established professionals abstained.[111] What the young actors got, he said, was mainly courses by KPD officials; 'one's party card became a certificate of competence'.

Politics of a political theatre

> 'Never was it more essential than now to take sides: the side of the proletariat. More than ever the theatre must nail its flag fanatically to the mast of politics: the politics of the proletariat. More and more insistent grows the demand: theatre is action, the action of the proletariat. The stage and the masses, a creative unity, not in the "Zeittheater" but in the militant theatre of the proletariat.
>
> Erwin Piscator'

So proclaimed the opening programme at the Wallner-Theater in April 1930.[112] It is the extreme statement of a case which originated in the need to learn the political and economic lessons of the First World War, modified by a sense (shared with ex-Dadaists like Grosz) that 'art for art's sake' and 'Art with a capital A' were in effect devices for stopping one from doing so. An 'unpolitical theatre' accordingly, such as the Volks-bühne was aiming to be when Piscator went there, was playing a highly political role, only to be countered by the conscious proclamation of a 'political theatre'. A first article under this title was published in a magazine a few months before the Piscatorbühne was set up,[113] and from then on the term became a kind of slogan. 'Politics', it said, 'represents the creative centre of our work', such politics being defined as 'social-isation of the means of production and the creation of the classless society'. So far this still implied that the theatre would do its own political thinking. So indeed it wished to, but the case of *Konjunktur*, besides showing that it did not always think very clearly, proved that in case of disagreement it would hand over the responsibility to the politicians. 'I had made up my mind', said Piscator of his decision to wrench that play into a new context, 'to close the theatre sooner than allow a production that would cast the slightest doubt on the company's political attitude'.[114] Five years later he told Soviet readers of his book that his theatre 'was always political, that is to say political in the sense approved by the Communist Party'.[115] The first two companies he saw as 'revolutionary theatre . . . deepening the class-consciousness of our own party comrades'. The third, at the Wallner-Theater, was 'proletarian-communist'.

What made some people, including some communists, query the sincerity of such statements was the fact that the political theatre was so largely directed to a bourgeois public. Even as the first article appeared, with its ringing conclusion –

> The masses have realised the importance of our theatre . . . Those who still see us merely as 'the latest thing' will soon realise their mistake.[116]

– Piscator was arranging to base his theatre in Berlin's West End and to operate on a scale which made the support of capitalist backers and a smart novelty-seeking audience essential. Certainly he reproached the workers more than once with their failure to support him better, but the conclusion he draws in *Das politische Theater*, that 'the proletariat, for whatever reason, is not strong enough to maintain its own theatre',[117] was already the initial assumption of his planning. He was in fact trying to have things both ways – never a very good position for somebody who insists that the theatre must take sides – wryly recognising 'that one has to accept as the precondition of one's work the very business one wants to do away with'. Not surprisingly the picture which reached Reich in Moscow at this time was hardly favourable; the glossy magazine *Die Dame* had published photographs of his 'princely' new flat by Gropius, while 'in communist circles people were asking . . . Is he a militant comrade or a parlour communist?'.[118] Similarly, though Brecht always denied that the satirical poem 'Der Theaterkommunist' which he wrote in his first year or so in Berlin[119] was directed against Piscator, it is not easy to think of any alternative candidate, and Piscator himself evidently thought that it was. Even his old editor Franz Pfemfert, in *Die Aktion*, disowned him because of the nature of his supporters.

Around 1929, wrote Reich again, 'neither the RAPP in the Soviet Union nor certain German representatives of the Association of Proletarian-Revolutionary Writers had much use for Piscator'.[120] At first the Association's organ *Die Linkskurve* was critical of his big productions and also of his book; 'I have often enough been attacked in these pages' says the only article which he wrote for it, which appeared at the end of 1930,[121] and indeed he had been taken to task at least three times.[122] By then a modus vivendi seems to have been reached; the Association (which included such writers as Becher, Anna Seghers and Ludwig Renn) would collaborate with the third Piscator company, in a spirit of 'frank comradely criticism', meantime certifying, on the strength of the production of *Des Kaisers Kulis* and Ottwalt's play (he being a member of the Association), that this was 'the theatre of the Berlin workers'.[123] With the workers' theatre movement proper relations seem to have been better. This was in part due to Piscator's KPD productions of 1924–25, which had influenced the whole flourishing agit-prop movement: i.e. the militant groups with names like 'Red Megaphone' and 'Column Left', which thereafter sprang up on the model of the Soviet 'Blue Blouses' and performed songs and agitational sketches from political platforms or the backs of lorries. Though Gustav von Wangenheim, who became one of this movement's artistic directors after its capture by the communists at the congress of 1928, was never close to Piscator (either then or later), Arthur Pieck and his wife Margarete Lode appreciated his value and accepted him as an ally when the corresponding international organisation was set up in Moscow the following year. However, the principal party offshoot with which Piscator was associated was the IAH, whose position in the Comintern's scheme of things was an odd one, since Muenzenberg's authority came direct from Moscow, by-passing the KPD; it was thus what Lenin had deliberately stopped the Proletkult from becoming – a form of cultural private army not all that strictly supervised by the party. At what point Stalin and his colleagues began looking askance at this is not clear, but during the 1930s its position became increasingly equivocal, with Katz as its most equivocal figure; it may be remembered that it was the IAH for whom Christopher Isherwood's Mr Norris made his speech on behalf of the Chinese communists. According to Franz Jung (that other very strange character) even Goebbels once submitted a play called *Der Wanderer* to Piscator,[124] who recalled knowing him well.[125] There was actually a plan for a radio discussion which he and Goebbels intended to broadcast around 1930, their ghost writers being Jung himself and Brecht's nationalist friend Arnolt Bronnen. Though it is not known why this oddity was never delivered its very possibility shows how the blurred lines could then be.

In the end however what mattered to the party was the relationship of the political theatre to the Soviet Union. This again is not as simple a question as it now seems, since even on the artistic level every Soviet influence or connection had its political implication according to the standing of that influence judged by the canons of the Soviet Communist Party. Plainly Piscator's record as a supporter of the October Revolution and the Soviet regime was a good one; from the days of the Proletarian Theatre onwards he had been caught up in the wave of pro-Soviet feeling of which the IAH was one manifestation. That was the main thing. But the only Russian play staged by the first two Piscator companies was by a fellow-traveller and had been elaborately overhauled by the (German) dramaturgs, while Lunacharsky, whose smiling face was photographed alongside Piscator's at that time,[126] was never appreciated by Stalin and lost his job in 1929.

Reich, who saw *Der Kaufmann von Berlin* and considered it 'formalist' by RAPP standards, found him at that time largely ignorant of the new Soviet theatre. He therefore recommended him the same two plays by Glebov and Bill-Belotserkovski which his own wife Asja Lacis showed to the Association of Proletarian-Revolutionary Writers and which were then accepted by the Third Piscatorbühne for production by other directors. In the summer of 1930 Piscator was able to see the first of these, *Inga*, at the Revolutionary Theatre in Moscow, as well as Vishnevsky's *The First Cavalry Army* (at the same theatre), Olyesha's *The Three Fat Men* (at the Art Theatre) and Romashov's *The Fiery Bridge* (at the Maly). But he seems not to have been in touch with Russian theatre people previous to that visit, and for a long time he was anxious to stress that his techniques owed nothing to the work of Meyerhold or any other avant-garde Soviet director.

Whether he can have been quite as ignorant of their ideas as he claimed seems doubtful, for it was hardly necessary to see actual productions in order to get some notion of their use of projection screens and constructivist sets. Paquet, for one, had been in Russia, as had such other Piscator associates as Jung and Grosz, while Alexander Tairoff had visited Berlin with the Kamerny Theatre in 1923, when a German edition of his book came out. Nor of course could Piscator speak for his designers, whose kinship with the constructivists has already been mentioned. All the same, where he did come to see what the Russians had been doing he often took exception to it. Thus his *Rote Fahne* article argued that while Eisenstein's use of montage possibly derived from that of Heartfield and Grosz his aim of electrifying the mass audience could equally well be achieved by filming a boxing match instead of the Odessa steps; instead of confining himself to what happened on the Potemkin he should have shown the historical background of 1905. Again, when Meyerhold first brought his company to Berlin in 1930, Piscator criticised their handling of the Chinese scenes in Tretiakoff's *Roar China* as, providing 'detail, not elucidation':[127] the point to him was not that Chinese are different from Europeans but that the coolie and the unemployed Berliner were oppressed by the same system. This was also the gist of his complaint against the productions which he subsequently saw in Moscow: the theatres there were actor-orientated and did not get down to the wider problems (*Inga* for instance dealt with a woman running a factory, but not with the role of factories under the Five-Year Plan), which made them basically no different from Max Reinhardt's. As for what Meyerhold in turn thought of Piscator, an interview in Barbusse's Paris paper[128] quoted him as saying that he was

> on a wrong track. I have seen photos of his sets and the plan of his theatre. I know what his plays are about. He has not grasped the problem. Piscator thought he could create a revolutionary theatre in Berlin in six months. To that end he built a modern stage and concentrated entirely on developing the *material* aspects of theatre technique. It is too one-sided. The problem confronting the director has all sorts of facets. The stage and the theatre are a framework, to which the actor's voice and gestures have to be accommodated: this is what Piscator has never attempted . . . Anyhow, from what I know of it, his repertoire doesn't strike me as likely to convince the popular masses: the story of Rasputin, for instance.

Admittedly when Meyerhold gave this interview he had not actually seen a Piscator production, but when he saw § 218 at the Wallner-Theater he did not much like it.[129] Tretiakoff, who called on Piscator around then, found his attitude like that of a child whose building bricks keep falling down: 'resignation combined with incredible tiredness'.[130]

The real sense or otherwise of a political theatre is not something to be discussed at this turning-point in Piscator's career. But certainly his relation to communist policies and the Communist Party was important and in this area nothing can be taken at its face value. Thus his statements, like the one in the Wallner-Theater programme already quoted, may not have been written by himself, while the various party organisations and authorities mentioned were far from being as unanimous (or 'monolithic') as might be supposed. For instance, *Die Linkskurve*, which under Lukács's aegis pursued a line sometimes divergent from that of its parent Association, came to criticise all use of documentary, reportage and montage, and specifically to attack the novels of Ottwalt and the *Lehrstücke* of Brecht; it also quarrelled with Maxim Vallentin, leader of the party's main agit-prop group. It had no use for Meyerhold, whom it dismissed as 'bourgeois', while Tretiakoff's influence in Germany was judged positively pernicious, since he represented the ideas of Mayakovsky and the Formalist critics, besides the assimilation of non-European techniques. On the other hand the German artists to interest Tretiakoff were not the representatives of the 'great tradition' favoured by Lukács but the innovators like Brecht, Eisler, Heartfield and Piscator, together with the interesting personalities like Plivier and Friedrich Wolf. Admittedly *Die Linkskurve* was in line with the RAPP in Moscow, which was then fighting the same avant-garde influences (and is often thought to have contributed to Mayakovsky's suicide in 1930); however, the RAPP was nearing the end of its tether. The question therefore of Piscator's political status has to be seen at this juncture in three ways: as it appeared to the party cultural authorities in the KPD, as it might appear from Moscow, and as it was likely to appear once the Moscow line changed. The overriding fact remained that he was a communist and subject to party orders. Cultural divergences within the party were not yet automatically taken as signs of political opposition.

6. The Soviet experience (1931–1936)

Into the cinema

Within two years of its foundation in 1921 Muenzenberg's IAH had begun to go into the film business in a very big way. Reference has already been made to its subsidiary the Prometheus firm in Germany, which not only handled the distribution of *Potemkin* and other key Soviet films in that country but also produced such German communist movies as *Mutter Krausens Fahrt ins Glück* and the Brecht–Ottwalt–Eisler–Dudow *Kuhle Wampe*. In Moscow however, under its Russian portmanteau name of Mezhrabpom (i.e. 'Intworkaid'), IAH ran for twelve crucial years one of the principal film studios, notable for the work of such directors as Yakov Protazanov (e.g. *Aelita*, 1924), Boris Barnet and above all Vsevolod Pudovkin, all of whose best films it produced. It had already done at least one co-production with Prometheus when Fyodor Otsep's *The Living Corpse* was made in Moscow and Berlin. Now Pudovkin's new film, *Deserter*, was to be largely shot in Hamburg, with whose social struggles its story dealt.

This was the organisation which Piscator and Katz arrived in Moscow to join in the spring of 1931. Rather more was involved here than just rescuing them from their respective troubles (and generally giving Piscator a much-needed change of work and surroundings), for this was also the time of a whole exodus of Western, and particularly German artists to work in the USSR. So far as the Russian end was concerned it looks as though the progress of the First Five-Year Plan (1928–32), the building of the new cities (like Magnitogorsk, planned by the Frankfurt city architect Ernst May) and the international successes of the Soviet cinema had created a climate of openness, almost of relaxation, in which such exchanges were temporarily welcome. For the Germans on the other hand it was not only a natural development of the aesthetic and political links of the 1920s but also a result of the worsening situation in their own country. When Hannes Meyer, for instance, was sacked from the director-ship of the Bauhaus (for permitting IAH activities there) in the summer of 1930 he was promptly put in charge of higher educational building in the USSR. Several persons and organisations were involved in giving such invitations: Tretiakoff, who had leading functions in the Society for Cultural Relations and the new Writers' Union; later Michael Koltzov of *Pravda* and his German wife Maria Gresshöhner (or Osten: a former publishing assistant of Herzfelde's); also the International Association of Revolutionary Writers or MORP, the body which embraced both the RAPP and the German Association and communicated with the latter mainly through Johannes R. Becher. None however seem to have had so ambitious a programme as Mezhrabpomfilm, which now engaged or commissioned a whole group of German writers, directors and actors, including Friedrich Wolf and Hans Richter. 'Kolonne Links', the IAH agit-prop group from Berlin, came to the Soviet Union and stayed, while among the films to be set up were Joris Ivens's *Song about Heroes*, shot in Magnitogorsk and with music by Eisler; Béla Balázs's *Tisza Burns* (never released); one written by Langston Hughes and Piel Jutzi for an imported black American cast (never made); and later von Wangenheim's *Fighters*, which was actually completed.

Rather than either of the two projects discussed the previous year, Piscator's task now was to make a film of Anna Seghers' novella *The Revolt of the Fishermen*. Originally the idea was that it should be produced in two versions, German and Russian, and to this end a German cast was engaged, including Lotte Lenya, Paul Wegener and Leo Reuss, and brought to Odessa on the Black Sea where shooting was supposed to start around the beginning of November. Not much seems to have got done during the three months of their stay there; according to Asja Lacis,[131] who acted as Piscator's interpreter throughout the making of the film, there were weeks of delays as they waited for a lens hood; then Piscator replanned the fishing town which the art director had built him (for which he roped in John Heartfield, who had come to show his work in Moscow); they had to wait again finally for the whole thing to be rebuilt after a storm had blown it down. As a result the German version had to be scrapped; since Wegener for one was due to play Mephisto in Darmstadt in January; none of the footage remains. The Russian version however went forward, though the seeming intention that Wegener should play the part of Kedennek in both versions had to be abandoned. Part was shot on trawlers in Murmansk on the Arctic, most of the rest once more in Odessa; little was done in the studio. Piscator felt that he was keeping close to the form of the book, which describes a lone agitator's arrival in a semi-mythical fishing village and his desperate, almost fatalistic, leadership of a broken strike. But much of its almost classical compactness was lost, and there was a general enlargement and intensification, not only in the severe expressiveness of the photography, but also in the intro-duction of such episodes as a storm at sea, the burning of the trawler company's offices and Kedennek's funeral procession with its hundreds

57. *The move to Moscow. Piscator* (second on right) *shooting* The Revolt of the Fishermen *for Mezhrabpomfilm in 1932, shortly before Hitler came to power.*

of mourning fishermen whose top hats (specially despatched from Mos-cow) were symbolically blown off by the storm. 1200 fishermen were involved in the strike episodes, which became near-revolutionary crowd series.

Why Piscator took two more years to finish the film is not clear, but certainly one of the things visiting Germans had to adjust to was the extremely slow pace of Soviet life. Unfortunately by the time of its completion in the spring of 1934 not only was the German market closed to it but the Russian audience too was tiring of revolutionary films with

58–59. The Revolt of the Fishermen, *1934. Two stills from Piscator's only film, based on the short novel by Anna Seghers.*

their 'emphasis on the fate of the masses, not on that of the individual',[132] instead preferring human stories in a more contemporary social setting. Released that October, *The Revolt of the Fishermen* had only a limited critical success; thus Reich found Alexei Diky's performance over-dramatic and the direction and editing time-wastingly self-indulgent for all their visual beauties, while Balázs saw it as full of errors but none the less the work of 'a great film director'.[133] Piscator himself was far from discouraged, and already had a number of new film plans pending. One was for a *Schweik* on which he wanted Brecht to collaborate;[134] another of the same time (August 1933) was for a film about education on a collective farm in the Volga German Republic, initially with Ottwalt as script writer. According to Reich[135] Piscator got Mezhrabpom to take Ottwalt under contract, but found him superficial and uncongenial to work with. Later, around Christmas 1935, the Hungarian playwright Julius Hay took over, visited the area with Piscator and wrote a story which Mezhrabpom, so he says,[136] then made him combine with one by Adam Scharrer. Provisionally entitled *Film der Wahrheit*, this film too was never finished, nor was *Des Kaisers Kulis*, which Piscator again took up when Plivier came to Russia, nor did anything come of a proposed collaboration with Brecht on *War and Peace*.[137]

By then, he seems to have been more concerned with the urgent need for short anti-Nazi propaganda films, which he proposed should start with the real story of a senior civil servant murdered by the Nazis, whose ashes were returned to his widow with a bill for cremation and other costs. This idea, approved by Mezhrabpom, evidently led to a more ambitious scheme for the production and dubbing of such shorts by several different units, which would also produce and tour plays. Reich[138] describes Piscator lobbying energetically to get this organised, paying inconclusive visits to Barbusse and Bukharin and finally spending two hours with Stalin's brother-in-law Lazar Kaganovitch, First Secretary of the Central Committee of the Soviet Communist Party, who insisted that such films must have optimistic endings. Piscator disagreed, and there the matter remained. But for the rest of the 1930s he was a frustrated film-maker.

A functionary in the theatre

Even if he had wished to work in the Soviet theatre Piscator would have found himself handicapped. For his apparent claim to have fathered the political theatre would hardly have recommended him to his Russian colleagues, who would have seen this as infringing their own hard-won position. Nor did a more direct acquaintance with the Soviet theatre lead him to appreciate it all that much better than on his first visit; thus in a report back on 'What we can learn from the Soviet theatre'[139] he stressed the vastness of the movement for workers' participation in the arts (as actors, reporters, photographers, film-makers) but above all the persistence of a tradition dating back to more bourgeois times, as seen in the work of Stanislavsky. He had nothing positive to say about the more advanced theatres, only that such use of film as he had seen there (by Meyerhold, Tairoff, Okhlopkhov and the youth theatre TRAM) was not in accordance with the principles followed in his own Berlin productions.[140] However, TRAM itself was even then being brought under control of the Stanislavskyans, while Meyerhold was marking time until his theatre had been rebuilt. An incomplete draft for a discussion between Piscator and Brecht in 1935[141] confirms both men's interest in the work of Okhlopkhov, whose productions at the Realistic Theatre in those years broke some of the last barriers between play and audience, but it also shows their concern at the generally uncritical approach to the classics seen even in so admired a production as the State Jewish Theatre's *King Lear* with Michoels. Unlike Ihering, who frankly dismissed the Bolshoi's ballet *The Red Poppy* as 'kitsch'[142] (and then returned to spend the Nazi years in Germany), Piscator put his views as tactfully as he could, emphasising that the social foundation of the Soviet theatre remained superior to anything in the West. None the less there is no evidence that he was ever asked to direct a play till after he had left, the nearest approach being in February 1934, when he helped Asja Lacis stage Wolf's *Bauer Baetz* in the Moscow Latvian theatre.

He had however a role to perform in the International Association of Workers' Theatres, where his contribution to the agit-prop movement was recognised and the principal German representative, Arthur Pieck, remained a good friend. A few weeks after Piscator's arrival in Moscow in 1931 there had been a meeting of this body's Presidium at which he read a paper 'On the international workers' theatre' (now apparently lost, like all his files from the Soviet years), then in 1932 its second congress elected him both to the presidium (along with Wolf, Wangenheim, Léon Moussinac and others) and to the secretariat to work alongside Pieck. At this meeting the association changed its name from 'Workers'' to 'Revolutionary', in line with the general shift in Soviet cultural policy then taking place, becoming MORT to match its sister association for writers, the MORP in which Becher, Aragon and the

Hungarian Béla Illés were now prominent. A year later, after the Nazis had come to power, effectively destroying the whole German movement – in other words the one workers' theatre movement comparable with the Russian – MORT staged an 'Olympiade' or festival in Moscow with nine foreign groups including Kolonne Links, which had decided to remain in the USSR. This too was attended by Piscator, who also made the odd contribution to the review, *The International Theatre*, which the association had begun to put out. It all made him the obvious man to head the association when there was once again a change of line following the establishment of a popular front, that coalition of all, from anarchists to liberal conservatives and catholics, who saw the Nazis as an overriding threat to civilisation. In the new climate MORT was reorganised to embrace the professional theatre, and Piscator became its president.

This seems to have been decided in 1934, just about when he had finished *The Revolt of the Fishermen*. That spring he went to Prague to see E. F. Burian, whose revolutionary theatre 'D 34' had just begun to make its name, and later to Paris. *Das politische Theater* now appeared in a Russian translation;[143] he issued a statement on the occasion of the First Soviet Writers' Congress,[144] a crucial meeting which brought a number of his exiled friends to Moscow, including the Pliviers; while on 5 October his film had its official premiere. From then on he concentrated primarily on the affairs of the MORT. 'The idea in appointing Piscator president', wrote Reich, whom he made his deputy, 'was to have an attractive figurehead. Piscator however took the cause, and himself, seriously.'[145] His offices off the Petrovsky Passage contained a staff of about fifteen, headed by Reich and the Piecks, with the Czech composer Robert Spitzer to look after the association's International Music Bureau (formerly International Bureau for Revolutionary Music), which had been founded on Eisler's initiative. Henceforward MORT was to be a meeting place for visitors to Moscow, combined with an information centre which would circulate translations of suitable plays, discuss problems of Marxist aesthetics and publish a journal from Zürich to which it was hoped that all anti-Nazi theatre people would contribute. In an article which was almost a policy statement he argued that MORT had been neglecting the professional theatre and its unions and should pay more attention to the avant-garde, not excluding the Surrealists. 'There are artistic elements which are simply anti-fascist by their very essence.'[146]

At the beginning of 1935 Piscator invited Brecht to Moscow,[147] where he was trying to organise a meeting of theatre directors for April. Aside from this he brought Maxim Vallentin and some of his collaborators to

Russia; he invited Hay, who came for three weeks but remained; with Tretiakoff he sent for Ernst Busch, who came from Holland and stayed two years; then in June Eisler too arrived for a few weeks, supposedly to reorganise the International Music Bureau before returning to the United States. The meeting of theatre directors evidently reduced itself to a series of encounters between Piscator, Brecht and Gordon Craig on the one hand and Meyerhold, Tairoff and Eisenstein on the other; it was on one of these occasions that Brecht saw the performance by the Chinese actor Mei Lan-fang that led him, apparently with Tretiakoff's aid, to adopt the Russian Formalist concept of the 'alienation effect'.[148] Harold Clurman and Cheryl Crawford of the Group Theatre also came around this time, when the former wrote MORT a paper on the US theatre. Piscator himself at this period remained full of ideas, obstinate in pressing them and endlessly patient with the intricacies of the Soviet bureaucracy. Unfortunately, says Reich, 'he used all his energy and imagination to set the organisation up and get it running, with the result that as an artist he stagnated . . .'.[149]

Weimar on the Volga

Although Piscator and Brecht had gone slightly separate ways after 1928, they remained allies throughout his Russian years. In 1932, when the playwright first came to Moscow for the première of his film *Kuhle Wampe*, they made an agreement not to allow their principal unperformed works – that is *St Joan of the Stockyards* and Piscator's adaptation of *An American Tragedy* – to be staged without consulting one another[150] and from then on kept one another informed about plans. Thus Piscator watched over Tretiakoff's edition of the three Brecht plays which appeared under the title *Epicheskie Dramy* in 1934, while Brecht at the end of that year wrote the 'United Front Song' for him with Eisler at the Music Bureau's request.[151] Brecht's main concerns at the time of his 1935 visit seem to have been the possibility of a production of his new play *Die Rundköpfe und die Spitzköpfe* and the chance of establishing an adequate German-language theatre in the USSR. Piscator managed to interest Michoels at the Jewish Theatre in the former, and even had hopes of being able to direct it himself.[152] So far as the latter was concerned however a first step was taken that May with the creation of a travelling theatre for German-language communities in the Ukraine under Vallentin with Curt Trepte of Wangenheim's troupe and members of Kolonne

60. *A travelling theatre for German communities in the Ukraine, set up by Piscator in 1935. The Deutsches Gebietstheater Dnjepropetrovsk prepares to perform* Wo ist Emilie? *by Hans Grach, one of its actors, directed by Maxim Vallentin.*

61. *Stuck somewhere in the Ukraine: the Deutsches Gebietstheater Dnjepropetrovsk*

Links: the 'Deutsches Gebietstheater Dnejpropetrowsk'. By the end of the year a much more ambitious plan was on foot for the creation of a first-rate German theatre at Engels in the German Volga Republic, in which not only Brecht and Helene Weigel but many other of the leading exiles from outside the USSR were hopefully asked to become involved.

The Volga Autonomous Soviet Socialist Republic no longer exists, since its population was deported during the Second World War, but in 1935 it was a none too prosperous farming district of about 650,000 inhabitants, two-thirds of them descended from eighteenth-century German settlers, five hundred miles south-east of Moscow. Like Friedrich Wolf, who regularly paid visits there, Piscator had become interested in this strange survival, but it is a moot point how far he had had any personal experience of the area when he first conceived his great design. Hay in his memoirs (which are not exactly pro-communist)[153] describes their journey in January 1936 with József Lengyel of the Mezhrabpom script department, among peasants who spoke an unintelligible German, used camels as farm animals and were nervous that their visitors might be some kind of party inquisition; Piscator, he says, 'made surprisingly little effort to adjust to his surroundings'.[154] That summer however there had been formal meetings with a special commissariat for German affairs (headed by Ernst Reuter, later mayor of West Berlin), and with other members of the local government and party in Engels, whom Piscator found willing and even eager to finance the scheme which he now unfolded. This was for a permanent company to be drawn from the finest anti-Nazi talents and grafted on to the local State Academic Theatre, whose previous actors were already due, apparently on Wolf's initiative, to be put through a special training in Moscow. From the names recalled by Reich,[155] who once again agreed to be Piscator's deputy in this project, it sounds as if the actors he had in mind to recruit were those who had worked in his own and comparable Berlin left-wing groups: for instance, Granach, Carola Neher, Maria Leiko, Busch, Lotte Loebinger and Helene Weigel.

A programme was roughed out for the opening season; Lessing's *Nathan der Weise* perhaps to start with, Gorki's *Vassa Shelesnova*, a modern Soviet play by Pogodin or Korneichuk and then, by authors closer to the company, Wolf's *Professor Mamlock* and Brecht's *Die Rundköpfe und die Spitzköpfe*. Piscator seems to have wanted Brecht to be the theatre's dramaturg; Brecht however proposed Dudow, writing that he himself 'would gladly have done it, but there are so few chances to earn a bit of money. I hope you understand that'. All the same, he and Helene Weigel spoke of visiting Engels with a view to possibly settling there, and in general he warmly welcomed 'the idea of creating a great experimental theatre in which we can resume our theatrical researches and carry them further'.[156]

In spring 1936 the twenty resident actors were packed off for two months' hard work on *Twelfth Night* under K. Subov of the Maly Theatre, after which Piscator and Reich were to decide whom to keep; in the event they found the results (and the local dialect) so uniformly depressing that they cravenly left all twenty in suspense.[157] Half the Ukraine group were then ordered to Engels to reinforce them for the first part of the season, which would begin in October. Granach (who had been working for the Jewish Theatre in Kiev), Ernst Busch and Carola Neher would join for the more serious opening in the new year. Von Wangenheim and Hans Rodenberg were invited but refused. Negotiations were started with Steckel, who accepted in principle, and others of the émigrés in Zürich, such as Erwin Kalser, Wolfgang Heinz and the designer Teo Otto. Karl Paryla too, it was hoped, would come from Prague. There were detailed discussions about pay, dates and contracts. Admittedly the housing position at Engels left something to be desired – according to Reich[158] there were two buildings with drains in a city of about 70,000 inhabitants – but six flats had been reserved in a new government block and there was a promise to build dachas. Malaria was a problem; Reich went down with it in August after moving there to supervise the first arrivals and get rehearsals going. By then Friedrich Richter and his wife Amy Frank had arrived from the Ukraine group, to be followed by Trepte and Maxim Vallentin; some training in orthodox German pronunciation was started. The Pliviers too, quite independently, had been sent from Leningrad to live in one of the villages and help 'with the construction of a self-supporting culture in the Volga German Republic'.[159] Piscator himself left Moscow in July for a trip to Western Europe, but was expected in Engels in mid-September. On 3 October he wrote from his Paris hotel to a prospective actor who seemed hesitant: 'If I had a son I would refuse to bring him up anywhere but in the USSR, because his future would be secure there.'[160]

Politics and purges

That same day Reich was wiring Piscator that he must not return.[161] All his castles were collapsing around him. First, Mezhrabpomfilm had been dissolved in June and turned into Soyuzdetfilm, a new children's film studio; so the film about the Volga Republic slid into limbo. Next MORT too was threatened with reorganisation (apparently before he left), then dissolved too; by the end of September Reich reported that it was 'really dead and shut up'.[162] Finally the whole Engels project crumbled as the émigrés outside Russia decided to let it alone. As for those within that country, Granach was arrested in Kiev, then released on Lion Feucht-wanger's intervention and allowed to leave; Carola Neher was arrested,

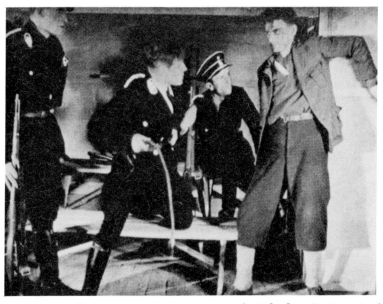

62. *Friedrich Wolf's anti-Nazi play* Das trojanische Pferd *at the State Academ-ic Theatre, Engels 1937, directed by Bernhard Reich. All that materialised of Piscator's great plans for the theatre of the Volga Republic.*

to die eventually in a camp; Maria Leiko disappeared; Busch left the fol-lowing year and went to the Spanish War; Trepte and Hermann Greid went to Sweden; the Richters to Czechoslovakia then England. Reich, who felt some responsibility to the actors already at Engels, went back there to direct them in Friedrich Wolf's new play *Das Trojanische Pferd*, which he already knew from working with Wolf on the film script. This production took place in January 1937, and appears to have been all that ever came of the whole grand scheme. After that the company was broken up, its remaining non-Soviet members returning to Moscow where they were found work in the radio's German service. There are said to have been some local arrests. At some point Reich and Asja Lacis too were deported, not to surface again until the mid-1950s. Vallentin had to battle for 'rehabilitation' in Moscow for much of 1937.[163] The Pliviers alone remained, forbidden to leave their village for the best part of two years: 'the last remaining native Germans in the Volga Republic'.[164]

It was the time of the monster purges throughout the USSR. Kirov's assassination, which sparked these off, had taken place in December 1934; the first of the big show trials, of Zinoviev, Kamenev and other 'rightists' supposed to be in contact with Stalin's exiled rival Trotsky, was held in August 1936 while Piscator was in the West. In the climate of intensified, but hopelessly confused and crudely inefficient 'vigilance' which the GPU now created the whole Russian attitude to foreign visitors and influences changed. Mezhrabpomfilm seemed one obvious danger point; MORT another; and they were dealt with in the obvious way: by suppression. The IAH was one of the first organisations to go. For the Germans in particular were suspect, and none the less so when they were party members. At the time of Piscator's first arrival they may have represented the one foreign movement capable of talking on more or less equal terms to the Russians; if they had a failed revolution behind them they also had the venerated figures of Marx and Engels. Suddenly they became the party who, with a far stronger apparatus than the Bolsheviks in 1917, had allowed Hitler to take power without even a strike to hamper him. At the same time of course they were desperate refugees, who had to be fraternally taken care of; but as Hitler ensconced himself more firmly and the threat which he represented to the USSR grew more evident they also came to be seen as potential spies. It did not help that they appeared so standoffish, setting up their own writers' organisation within the official Union, their own reviews and daily paper. As Reich points out,[165] not many made the same effort as did Friedrich Wolf to strike roots in Soviet life, and Piscator was no exception. He remained outside the Russian theatre, without ever learning Russian, though living domestically enough in his Moscow hotel with a Russian actress – Vera Vanukova, formerly of the Proletkult Theatre, who had played in his film. Reich says that he never warned her of his decision to stay in the West.

Coincidentally or not, the developing political inquisition had become tangled with the changes in aesthetic policy which had started in 1932, the year after Piscator arrived. That spring the party Central Committee abolished all the existing artistic and literary bodies, of which the RAPP had been the most powerful and authoritarian, in favour of the setting up of comprehensive Unions. Henceforward nothing was to be exclusively 'Proletarian' or 'Workers'' – which was why the international associations were now renamed – and in the course of the preparatory discussions which set up the Union of Soviet Writers that autumn (with Stalin himself and Gorki taking a hand) the doctrine of Socialist Realism was announced. The exact significance of this rather vague expression only emerged over the years: first when the Soviet Writers' Congress made it clear to the world that it meant abandoning every kind of 'Formalism', then when the theoretical writings of Georg Lukács proposed a return to the traditions of the bourgeois realist novel of the nineteenth century, parallelling the official support of Stanislavsky's methods in the theatre. Already by 1935 Piscator was open to accusations of formalism and 'vulgar sociology' in his work; and now Becher, who had come to Moscow to start the German edition of *International Literature*, accepted Lukács and his friend Andor Gábor as the exponents of the new line, which thenceforward became mandatory for the KPD. Just who first came to identify the use of avant-garde forms with Trotzkyism, i.e. a political heresy tantamount to treachery, is not certain, though Lukács for one already tended to apply such standards, for instance in his pre-1933 judgements of Tretiakoff and Ottwalt. At the beginning of 1936, however, the big guns began to go off with *Pravda* launching its attacks on 'left decadence' and 'petty bourgeois formalism' as instanced in Shostakovitch's splendid music. At the end of May a commission including Molotov and Mikoyan previewed Eisenstein's new film *Bezhin Meadow* and ordered its physical destruction on grounds that included formalism, naturalism, mysticism and slandering of the Soviet peasant.

Such was the political-aesthetic climate when Piscator left in July. Perhaps the first arrest to touch him personally was that of Erich Mühsam's widow, who was in gaol from May to October and subsequently led a semi-underground life of extreme poverty.[166] Thereafter a whole series of events followed which would have made his own future highly insecure. Ottwalt was allegedly condemned to death as a spy (but may have died in a camp). Tretiakoff was accused of spying and shot. Béla Kun, formerly leader of the Hungarian revolution and a member of the Comintern, was arrested and tortured, later shot; Piscator had got Brecht to write a message for his birthday in autumn 1935;[167] he was a friend of both men. Muenzenberg left Moscow, thanks to Togliatti's help, during a Comintern inquiry into his actions; he was expelled from the

KPD and later murdered in France by an unknown assassin. It is frequently said that Katz, who had joined him from Moscow in 1933, leaving Hans Rodenberg in charge of the German section of Mezhrabpomfilm, was now reporting back on him from Paris. Among the arrests at Mezhrabpom-film was that of Lengyel, who remained a prisoner for eighteen years. Koltzov too, who set up the review *Das Wort* in July 1936 as a counter-balance to *Internationale Literatur* (Brecht being a nominal, Erpenbeck the

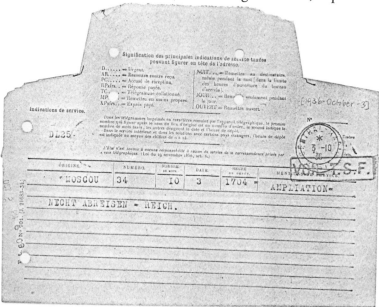

63. '*Don't leave.*' *Reich's telegram of 3 October 1936 to Piscator in Paris warning him not to come back to Moscow.* ('*Ampliation*' means confimatory copy.)

de facto editor), was arrested and executed on his return from the Spanish War; Meyerhold later still. Add the Engels victims, and it makes a long, sad list, all the sadder when set against the comparable casualties in Nazi Germany: Mühsam and the communist actor and union organiser Hans Otto, both killed in camps. Though Piscator's hostility to the Nazis remained total, on a purely actuarial basis there is not much doubt which country now held the greater risks.

7. The Paris interlude (1936–1938)

Options

At first, in his exchange of letters with Reich – and from now on, thanks largely to his widow, practically all his papers have been preserved – Piscator made considerable play with references to unspecified Authorities. It was they who were advising him to stay on in Paris; it was they who told him not to go to Spain; it was they to whom he threatened to report Reich if he did not stick uncomplainingly to his task at Engels. Difficult as it is to read the oblique language, it is clear that Piscator had left the USSR on an official mission connected less with the needs of Engels than with the changed international picture. In February 1936 a Popular Front government had come to power in Spain; in May France followed suit; on 18 July the Spanish Right under General Franco began its armed rebellion, which Hitler and Mussolini quickly supported. Muenzenberg, then still in charge of Western propaganda for the Comintern, was ordered to create a more broadly-based anti-Fascist movement, and accordingly helped organise a Rassemblement Universel de la Paix (with Lord Robert Cecil as president) which held its first congress in Brussels at the beginning of September. Piscator was sent to attend this together with Arthur Pieck, then went on to Paris to contact similar front bodies there: notably the Union des Théâtres Indépendants which were linked with the Maison de la Pensée Français under Aragon, the Association Universelle du Spectacle whose secretary he now became, and the Rassemblement's own arts committee under Francis Jourdain. On his way he had stopped off at Salzburg to see Max Reinhardt, whom he hoped to interest in the idea of a Peace Festival at Versailles which would include a stage version of *War and Peace*. There were also to be similar festivals on the First World War battlefields, including Ypres.

All these were activities deriving naturally from his presidency of MORT. However he also arranged to attend a slightly less official-sounding meeting in Prague around the end of August which Eisler too was exceptionally keen to go to;[168] and this coincided with the news of the first big Moscow trial. In mid-September he wrote to Julia Annenkova of the Moscow German-language daily to ask how she judged the prospects for his Engels undertaking:

> What do our old friends feel about it, are they bothering or haven't they any time just now, and does that mean *just* now and that things will improve later? All these are questions that particularly interest me, not least because there is a very good movement on foot here too [e.g. the Brussels congress].[169]

About this time Gustav Regler and his wife, who had joined him on a recent trip to Engels, asked to see Piscator in Paris; they brought messages from his Moscow office, and already knew that Radek too was to be tried. Then on the 29th he got a telegram from Michoels,[170] who wanted him to come and direct a play (not by Brecht), to which he replied that his movements depended 'on certain circumstances'. The same day he wrote a sad letter to Brecht saying that 'a lot of people are telling me I should under any circumstances work here and in America . . . But I'd be very sorry to abandon Engels' and finishing up 'Write me, old fellow [these two words in English], what you think. There aren't that many friends'.[171] Finally on 1 October he wrote a long but by no means equally frank letter to Reich, who had been pressing him to return and take charge, in which he reprimanded him for shirking his responsibilities in Engels and asked him 'forthwith to ring up Grete's father' (i.e. Wilhelm Pieck, the senior KPD official in Moscow) and get his advice. If there was no prospect of forming an adequate ensemble there, then he himself was 'not going to work'.[172]

Pieck gave his opinion in a typewritten letter dated 8 October.[173] The Engels project, he told Piscator, could not for the present be put into effect, and so after consulting 'the responsible authorities' he was informing him that there was no need for him to return. As for the mission which he and Arthur Pieck had undertaken, the comrades felt it would do if Arthur alone returned to report. If Piscator was needed they could always send for him. His personal advice was that it would be a waste of Piscator's time and talents to have anything more to do with MORT, which was virtually dead in its present form. 'I think you ought once again to devote yourself exclusively to your artistic activities, which I am sure are much more satisfying to you.' Cautiously, and showing the seriousness of such a warning, he signed himself 'W', inked out his son's name in the three places where it occurred, and omitted his own address.

This was the beginning of three frustrating years during which Piscator published, nothing, directed nothing and got nothing organised. In a letter to Paul Zech that summer Steckel put his finger on the root of the trouble, saying that

> I feel that Piscator has wasted some of his best years by not having had the modesty and the guts to start again from scratch, but wanting to work on a lavish scale right away.[174]

Though this was *à propos* of the Engels project, it became even more true of Piscator's activities henceforward in Paris, where he had taken up quarters in the 8th Arrondissement, at the Hotel Royal-Madeleine. His previous plan to go on to Denmark and stay with the Brechts on the way back to Russia was now postponed indefinitely while he investigated various possible schemes. Germany was ruled out; there might be theatre people close to him who had contrived to remain there – Ihering, Engel and Caspar Neher for instance, as well as such actors as Wegener, George and Venohr – but he had been horrified eighteen months earlier when Gordon Craig had suggested his going, telling him that he would be well received by Goebbels. The Spanish Civil War however offered possibilities; many of his friends were going there, including Regler, Busch and Wolf; there were two large empty theatres in Barcelona, where a programme in his honour was planned for December. After consultation with Leo Lania, with whom he was again in close touch, he wrote too to the Mexican Ambassador[175] outlining a whole scheme for the reorganisation of the cinema, theatre and propaganda services which he would be prepared to come to Mexico to put into effect. Through other contacts he hoped to get directing jobs in Stockholm and Copenhagen. And he kept his options open as regards Russia, answering an invitation (via Vera Janukova early in 1937) to direct another film there by saying that he would be at the producer's disposal later, but meanwhile 'would like to know what my situation might be with regard to work'.[176]

For a time it looked as if the most attractive field might be the United States. Already in Moscow he had been '100% set on making the crossing', according to Mrs Wolf, and had started to learn English; 'it's his best chance', she wrote.[177] This was when he had sent his adaptation of *An American Tragedy* to Wolf's agent Andrew Kertesz, together with

64–65. Piscator makes Broadway, March 1936. The Group Theatre production of his Dreiser adaptation The Case of Clyde Griffiths, *directed by Lee Strasberg. A caricature from the* New York Herald-Tribune's *review; and Wilson Barrett's design for the set.*

Schweik. In the spring of 1935 there was a successful production of the former at the small Hedgerow Theatre at Moylan, Pennsylvania, following which the Shuberts bought it for production by the Group Theatre under the title *The Case of Clyde Griffiths*. Directed by Lee Strasberg, who had met Piscator in Moscow, this took place in March 1936 and was strongly commended by Dreiser, but only ran for nineteen performances. 'A play of instruction to demonstrate a thesis', wrote Harold Clurman, who felt that the critics resented both the class emphasis and the use of an expository narrator.[178] Despite this Kertesz now felt he might arrange for Piscator to come over and direct Wolf's *Cyankali* or some other play. Both through Wolf (who attended the first American Writers' Congress in 1935) and through his work at MORT he was well aware of the progress of the American Left theatre: for instance the Theatre Union's productions of *Die Matrosen von Cattaro* and Brecht's *Die Mutter*, the Group Theatre's early Odets plays and *Johnny Johnson*, the *Schweik*-inspired musical which was Kurt Weill's first American work. When in October another agent offered him 'good possibilities'[179] if he left Kertesz, Piscator replied that any serious proposal would find him available.

Propositions

For the next eighteen months however Paris held him. One reason was the presence of the Austrian dancer Maria Ley, whom he had met in Salzburg that August when visiting Max Reinhardt. A niece of the banker Otto Kahn, she had been working at the Sorbonne, where she wrote a study of the eighteenth-century French comedy and a doctoral thesis on Victor Hugo.[180] Not long before she had lost her husband Frank Deutsch, son of one of the heads of the AEG, the great Berlin electrical engineering firm. Now she and Piscator got married, with Brecht as one of their witnesses. From early in 1937, when Piscator moved out to her Neuilly house, she was a devoted partner in all his enterprises until after his return to Germany in 1951. First and foremost among these was the plan to make a film of *Schweik*, which he had already hoped to do in the USSR. A *War and Peace* film was also still on the agenda. There were discussions about setting up a Théâtre Populaire Juif – a scheme supported by Chagall and Jean-Richard Bloch – and a plan for Piscator to take a ten-year lease of the Théâtre Pigalle.[181] With Henri Lesieur, then running a Théâtre du Peuple for the CGT (i.e. the Communist-led unions), he made a provisional arrangement to direct his 'own' *Schweik* adaptation;[182] at the same time he was proposing to put on *Rasputin* himself. He continued to be involved with the bodies whom MORT had wanted to work with, hoping for instance to direct a French adaptation of *Nathan der Weise* with Harry Baur for the 'Comité Mondial contre la Guerre et le Fascisme', and evolving a grand scheme for peace festivals to be held at Ypres and other First World War battlefield areas, on which he was required to report to the Rassemblement Universel de la Paix. The Versailles scheme was not yet dead, though Reinhardt turned it down. Moreover there were a number of plans in connection with the Paris Exposition Universelle of that summer, the chief of which was for the formation of a brilliant company of German exiles – in which Busch and some of the Zurich actors would team up with Kortner, Homolka, Albert Bassermann, Elisabeth Bergner and even perhaps Marlene Dietrich – to present a season at the Théâtre des Champs-Elysées. This project, which came to nothing, was an intermediate stage between the Engels project and the new company which he tried to set up the following year.

Either Piscator was unlucky in his efforts to break into film production or else he chose his business partners very badly. Once Alexander Korda in London had turned down the *War and Peace* idea, Piscator seems to have considered setting up a firm with Emmerich Pressburger, presumably to make *Schweik*, whose French film rights he was now trying to buy. In the event however he went into partnership with a Joseph Jacobi of Amsterdam,[183] who failed to subscribe his share of the capital (37,500 francs each by 1 July) and was later threatened with a lawsuit for fraud. In April we find Piscator investing 20,000 francs to make a French version of a Polish film called *Idl mitn Fidl*, in partnership with MM. Bystritzky, Hoffmann and Rubinstein;[184] within a month this too had fallen through. Then that summer Rudolf Leonhard, to whom he had sent his *War and Peace* treatment, put him in touch with a Swiss producer called Adolphe Forter and his firm Helgal; Forter however was primarily anxious to film *Lady Chatterley's Lover* (whose rights lay with a M. Toledo of the Banque Amar),[185] and this Piscator seems to have accepted as part of the price for *War and Peace*, for which he himself was to put up 300,000 francs. In the autumn of 1937 he considered merging their plans in a larger scheme for an international anti-war film company to be set up in Paris, for which up to 350,000 francs was to be found by M. Silberberg of Visionart Films and more by an English group headed by Oliver Baldwin MP. There was a M. Wishnewski still hoping to find backing for *Schweik* and a M. Karganski with whom Piscator was negotiating about *Rasputin*. Of all these variegated business friends the only one to become of major importance in films was the young Sam Spiegel, whom Piscator helped to get out of Switzerland that winter and sent to Mexico to look after a distributing company called France-Méxique which the Piscators had set up to show outstanding French films such as *Carnet de Bal* and Renoir's *La Marseillaise*. He also seems to have been the only one they seriously doubted and decided to break with.

In October 1936, when he wrote to tell Brecht of his intention to stay in the West he claimed that Brecht was involved in all his plans for the future.[186] After the première of *Die Rundköpfe und die Spitzköpfe* (which eventually took place in Copenhagen) Brecht replied saying that he did indeed hope they could work together.[187] However, the only scheme which he got drawn into was *Schweik*, and even here it was Lania who seems to have been Piscator's main collaborator. Quite apart from the rights problem, which was by no means simple, *Schweik* was a tricky subject to film, since not only were there political implications which could hardly be ignored but the whole setting and sense of the story needed to be determined. There were so many people to be consulted, from the Austrian and Czech embassies to the French Communist Party to Wieland Herzfelde in Prague, who told Piscator that the whole idea was out of tune with the political realities and that he should be going off instead to fight in Spain, at which Piscator was deeply affronted. Henri Jeanson, who had been brought in as a French scriptwriter, thought that the setting should be an unidentified country; Arthur Koestler, author of an unfinished neo-Schweik novel for Muenzenberg, thought Schweik should be fighting for Franco.[188] As for Brecht: when asked his opinion of the Piscator–Lania treatment he said that the beginning of a war should not be ridiculed but made more frightening, suggesting that the film should end with thousands of Schweiks making a military muddle as the nations rearm.[189] The French actor Noel-Noel was booked to play Schweik; later there was some question of using Fernandel. Brecht's work was only to begin once the backers and exhibitors had approved the initial treatment. It does not look as though they ever did.

At the end of June 1937 the Popular Front government fell. In September Piscator, writing to Jean Cassou at the Ministry of Education to ask him to make the *Nathan der Weise* adaptation, said that 'so far everything I have attempted has failed'.[190] All the same two months later he was talking (again to Cassou) about the possibility of taking French nationality,[191] and it was not until the turn of the year that he seems once more to have thought seriously of working in America. Meantime the angle of attack had somewhat changed. Though the distributors there had rejected the idea of *Schweik*, Dr Saul Colin, formerly of RKO's French office, told him that he might be welcome in the theatre:

> The impression I have had from the producers in New York is that they have a deep interest in you providing you remain in the theatrical field without any political tendencies.[192]

Before Spiegel left Switzerland he and Piscator began planning an autumn tour with a German company similar to that proposed for the Exposition Universelle: Kalser, Busch, Steckel, Langhoff, Granach, also Ernst Deutsch and Albert Bassermann, who would stay at least six months with a repertoire consisting of *Nathan der Weise* (again), *Schweik* (again) and *Faust*. At the same time the Mexicans wished him to take charge of a company to tour the US and Europe, and invited him to Mexico. Through Spiegel he made contact with Gilbert Miller, the New York and London impresario, and was able to set up two projects. First, Miller would underwrite fifty per cent of the costs of the proposed German company. Secondly, Piscator began making a stage adaptation of *War and Peace* with Alfred Neumann, then living near Florence, whose *The Patriot* Miller had previously produced.

The agreement about *War and Peace* was that the adaptation would be finished by the end of August and subsequently directed by Piscator at the St James's Theatre in London and in New York. For this each collaborator was paid an advance of $2500.[193] As with *The Patriot*, Ashley Dukes was to make the translation; first Teo Otto, then Wolfgang Roth was chosen to design the two productions; Helen Hayes and Paul Muni were to be the stars; and spring, summer and autumn of 1938 were mainly devoted to this large and difficult task. Unfortunately it was a particularly disastrous period in international relations, since it began with the Nazi occupation of Austria, saw the turn of the tide in the Spanish Civil War and ended with the Munich agreement which allowed Hitler to take the Czech border areas. Dukes, who by then was just sending the last instalment of the translation off to Miller, warned Piscator that no American producer in his senses would stage a play by two ex-Germans at such a moment.[194] On top of that, its late completion stopped its being financed out of Miller's profits for the year, which would now go in tax. But in any case when Miller (who had no German) came to read the play he thought it bad, particularly the last two acts, which included an episode with a baby that Dukes termed 'an absurdity in itself and quite unplayable for any actor'; indeed everybody whom he consulted then seems to have been against it. In September Otto Preminger estimated that the New York production would cost at least \$100,000, an immense sum for those days;[195] next Paramount, who had been interested in the film rights, turned it down; then in November Laurence Olivier, whom Miller had wanted to play Prince Andrew, read it and felt that 'a play has been used as a basis or excuse simply for the glorification of the "mise-en-scène" '.[196]

TERRIBLY DISAPPOINTED FOURTH FIFTH ACTS ESPECIALLY ANDREI ANATOLE SCENE STOP PIERRES SOLILOQUES INTERMINABLE ENGLISH AND AMERICAN AUDIENCES WOULD ONLY TOLERATE SUCH LENGTH FROM SHAKESPEARE STOP CONSIDER FIFTH ACT IMPOSSIBLE DISAPPOINTED ANDREIS DEATH SCENE AND CONSIDER FINAL SCENE WITH BABY GROTESQUE STOP DUKES CABLES QUOTE THINK PLAY FALLS DOWN AFTER THIRD ACT STOP PIERRE THREESOME AND

ENDING UNPLAYABLE STOP WOULD HAVE DECLINED TRANSLATION HAD I SEEN ENTIRE SCRIPT IN BEGINNING STOP PEPARED HOWEVER MAKE EVERY EFFORT TO SAVE SITUATION UNQUOTE STOP ALLEN SAILED TODAY STOP AS OBVIOUSLY IMPOSSIBLE PRODUCE PLAY IN PRESENT SHAPE HAVE POSTPONED MY SAILING UNTIL NOVEMBER TWELFTH TO FINISH OTHER WORK HERE STOP SEE NO POINT COLLABORATION WITH DUKES UNTIL FOURTH FIFTH ACTS COMPLETELY REWRITTEN REGARDS MILLER
[Gilbert Miller]

66. *A blow to Piscator's New York plans: Gilbert Miller's verdict of October 1938 on the Piscator–Neumann adaptation of* War and Peace, *which Piscator was expecting to direct for him in a translation by Ashley Dukes.*

With Europe crumbling around them the Piscators had banked on the success of their Mexican and American plans and had already decided to leave. They pressed Miller through lawyers to fulfil the agreement; they blamed the translation, without result; they tried to get firm financial terms out of the Mexican Education ministry, but even the travel expenses had been somehow muddled, and a visa never arrived.

The German company seems to have gone up in smoke, Granach for one finding Hollywood more attractive and advising that a tour would not succeed;[197] a Los Angeles production of *William Tell* in which he and Deutsch subsequently played in Los Angeles under Jessner's direction did much to bear this out. None the less Maria Piscator said that they now wished to become United States citizens, though they might as an alternative try to get Mexican passports.[198] They sailed for New York at Christmas, arriving on the first day of 1939. All that the previous eighteen months had achieved was to prove Steckel's verdict right.

8. New York and the Dramatic Workshop (1939–1951)

Farewell to the political theatre?

There is a note of Piscator's written in 1937 which says 'I can only work against bourgeois society, I can never work with it or through it'.[199] Similarly that summer when he met Gasbarra in Burgundy – their last meeting for some fifteen years – he got very angry and shouted 'But we said we'd never turn bourgeois!'[200] To say the least, there was some self-deception involved here, for although it is true that, unlike Gasbarra, he never became an anti-communist or even openly critical of the Russians, old friends like Wolf and Brecht had commented on the grand style of his life in Paris, and working with and through bourgeois society was precisely what he henceforth did.

Later in his American years there was good reason for him not to expose himself politically, when the House Un-American Activities Committee investigated Brecht and Eisler, to be followed by the Senate investigations under McCarthy. But there was no sudden shift in Piscator's attitude as a result of these events: he was a tactful guest from first to last, even if he never achieved the American citizenship for which he applied. Thus in the spring of 1939, when he began trying to write a second book, he recalled the heading 'Art to Politics' of the first chapter of *Das politische Theater* and decided to reverse this

> in order to say 'From Politics to Art' . . . That, finally, finally, is what you want, I said to myself.[201]

Likewise in 1942 when he wrote an article on 'The Theatre of the Future' he said no word of politics, nor even of the content of the play, but treated the theatre rather as 'an incomparable instrument for the expression of all human experience and thought'.[202] Certainly his Berlin achievements were known, as was his role in MORT, and to the American left-wing theatre of the 1930s they had been important, particularly when the Federal Theatre Project's Living Newspaper adopted projections and the documentary technique. But even before the end of the decade that theatre was in decline and its organ *New Theatre* (to which Piscator in Moscow had been a contributing editor) had ceased publication. The Living Newspaper closed in October 1938, the Federal Theatre soon after Piscator's arrival. Joseph Losey, one of the former's leading directors, could say later that he knew *Das politische Theater* well, used it and even wished to translate it; but 'the more I got to know Piscator, the less interested I became . . . In Moscow he was already half lost, in New York completely so'.[203]

All that Piscator did in his twelve years in America seems small beer compared with what he had been able to accomplish in Berlin. Yet he appears quite early on to have adjusted himself to this prospect, in a way that he had not done in Moscow or Paris. At first he still hoped that Miller might relent, and while Neumann and he revised *War and Peace* he gave readings of the script in his room at the Hotel Pierre and tried to find an American writer who would help adapt it to local requirements. However, both Sidney Howard (author of the Group Theatre's *Men in White*) and Clifford Odets turned it down. Clurman, on behalf of the Group Theatre, was not interested in the play, nor was any other Broadway producer; by March 1939 Miller had evidently rejected it once again.

67. *Transatlantic echoes of the 'Political Theatre'. The Living Newspaper show* Triple A–Plowed Under, *1936, directed by Joseph Losey for the Federal Theatre Project.*

Meantime Piscator was prepared to put up $5000 for the production of *Spell Your Name*, a refugee play on which Dorothy Thompson and Fritz Kortner were collaborating, which Kortner would eventually himself direct under the title *Another Sun*.[204] By then however he had learned that if he wanted to be admitted under the quota system he would not be able to settle in the United States as a director but only as a teacher of theatre. Accordingly he began writing off to Paris for evidence that he had been teaching at the émigré Deutsche Volkshochschule (or German People's High School) there, which once asked him to give some lectures. He asked Anna Seghers's husband, as its director, now to certify that he had held a two-year appointment there,[205] while Moussinac too seems to have written saying that he was a professor in Paris, though there is no other evidence that he was.

Thus armed, and with the experience of his own Berlin Studio behind him, Piscator in May 1939 saw Alvin Johnson, the head of the New School, to whom his wife had introductions from Sinclair Lewis, Einstein and Reinhardt. This New York adult education college did more than any other such body, either in the US or in England, to absorb eminent refugees, creating first the University in Exile and then, after the fall of France, the Ecole Libre in which they might teach and work. Now, in order to support Piscator, it made another new departure and decided to set up a drama school which he should direct. This was the Dramatic Workshop of the New School, which opened its doors at the beginning of 1940. To mark the occasion Piscator wrote an article for *The New York Times* which was his first publication since well before leaving Russia. In it he said how impressed he was with the freedom and vitality of the United States theatre, and the enviable quality of its plays. 'I am quite proud', he said, 'of the American drama.' True enough, 'the box office has its drawbacks, but one must admit that it contributes a great deal to the efficient operation of the theatre'. He thought it a pity that O'Neill's plays were so little performed, and tentatively he put forward the epic theatre, with its view of a wider world, as an alternative to the theatre of private feelings and sensitivities. Praising Gilbert Miller for his 'beautifully finished productions', he considered that achievements like those of the Theatre Guild, the Group Theater and the Playwrights' Company were 'unique in the Western world of the theatre'. The only one of his Berlin productions to which he referred at all was *The Lower Depths*.[206]

The Dramatic Workshop

The Dramatic Workshop began in January 1940 with twenty students attending evening classes and reached its numerical peak in 1947 and 1948 when it had just under 1000, of whom about a third were full-time. Among the teachers and others associated with its productions were a number of old friends from Europe. Toller had killed himself in New York the previous spring (Piscator had seem him only the day before, and found him depressed by his isolation and ill-success), while Grosz found that he and Piscator could no longer get on.[207] Zuckmayer however had just thrown up Hollywood and come East, and for the first two terms he took a slightly farcical-sounding weekly playwrights' class. Eisler ran the music theatre courses for two years (before he in turn left for Hollywood in the spring of 1942), while Ferdinand Bruckner became a house playwright and Rehfisch too joined the staff after war service with the OSS. The New School invited Brecht to come from Europe, and Piscator tried to find contributors to a fund for him,[208] but Brecht's visa application of 1940 took a year to come through and in the event he settled in California instead.[209] Initially the emphasis of the courses was very much on playwriting, which attracted forty students in the first semester as against twenty for acting and twenty-five for directing; it was run by the Theatre Guild's adviser John Gassner and in 1940/41 numbered such students as Barry Stavis, Oscar Saul and Tennessee Williams. For the first three or four years the acting was under Stella Adler, already a leading advocate of the Stanislavsky Method; Maria Piscator ran the dancing, Mordecai Gorelik the design and Piscator himself the directing. Just at first there was also a strong opera department with Georg Szell, Erich Leinsdorf and Herbert Graf, but this soon dropped off. By 1945 the actors, now numerically much stronger, were being looked after by Raiken Ben-Ari (formerly of the Habima), Maria Piscator and Margrit Wyler; design had been taken over by Leo Kerz; and in 1947 Lee Strasberg came to teach in the acting and directing courses. The aim from the outset was to make 'a school that is a theatre and a theatre that is a school', to train students for the various branches of the profession and if possible, by building up a working ensemble, 'to stimulate the development of the repertory theatre as a non-commercial institution of artistic expression with the same position in our society that the symphony or the art museum enjoys'.[210] The concept of the political theatre may have been put aside; the ideals of the Volksbühne movement were not.

The method chosen was to involve the student in every aspect of the theatre, over and above his own field of study. It was particularly important, Piscator argued, that writers should attend the design and acting classes, that designers should learn directing and acting, and that the would-be directors should have some knowledge of every field; accordingly he worked them hardest of all. Later he was to say that this collaborative approach was due to his feeling that his English was not good enough to teach actors; a practical workshop was the only solution.[211] But of course this had also been his method when he set up the Studio of the Piscatorbühne some twelve years earlier, and the link is perhaps symbolised by the incorporation of a Studio Theatre as part of the school. This was founded in September 1940 as 'A Theatre of Professional Players' (to quote its letterhead) offering subscribers 'plays which cannot be done on Broadway, because of their uncertain appeal, or sophisticated intelligence level, or overlarge cast'.[212] Piscator's intention here was that the audience too should be in some measure drawn into the work of the school, attending lectures in connection with the play given, listening to its first reading and going to one or more rehearsals. The performances would be professional ones using first-rate outside actors as well as some of those involved with the school. The theatre was to be the main hall of the old New School building on 12th Street, which Joseph Urban had designed with a great semi-circular arch above the stage and never intended or equipped for theatrical use. Here, as the rest of the New School went about its daily business around him, Piscator rehearsed his first production, to be given in mid-December. It was sponsored by a number of eminent supporters, including Muni, Robert Sherwood, George Kaufman and Sinclair Lewis. 'For the first time', wrote his wife, 'the little Playhouse on Twelfth Street had become his home.'[213]

Despite the presence of Sam Jaffé in the title part, *King Lear* was a flop, even Gassner finding its adoption of the epic approach 'singularly unsuccessful'.[214] Only one of the plays presented there over the next two years was transferred to a New York theatre, and that was *Nathan der Weise*, which Bruckner had adapted into English verse. Early in 1942 this was staged for Studio Theatre subscribers, with Herbert Berghof as Nathan directed by James Light; it was taken by the Shuberts for the Belasco Theater and ran there for about a month. Of the other principal productions Klabund's *Kreidekreis* (translated as *The Chalk Circle*), again directed by Light, with Dolly Haas as Hai-tang, was praised by the *New York Post* for its 'quaintness and delicacy' and thereafter kept in the school's repertoire; but photographs and play alike were tame compared with Wolf's 'counter-play' which Piscator had staged in 1931. Bruckner's *Verbrecher*, translated by its author as *Criminals*, was more interesting in concept, since Sanford Meisner staged it in something resembling the *Rasputin* hemisphere; the text had been considerably toned down for American consumption, but at least it was a 'Zeitstück' of the kind associated with the Piscatorbühne in the 1920s. Piscator's own plans for

68. Piscator's Dramatic Workshop in its second production at The New School, New York in March 1941: Klabund's The Chalk Circle *directed by James Light. (Compare the 'counter-play' to this work in ills. 24, 44, 45.)*

direction seem to have lain elsewhere at this time; thus he talked to the Theatre Guild about a possible production of Brecht's *Der gute Mensch von Setzuan*,[215] and persuaded H. R. Hays to make a translation of *Arturo Ui* which he hoped the CIO unions would help him to put on.[216] Late in 1941 however he started making a third version of *War and Peace* with two new collaborators, Maurice Kurtz and Harold L. Anderson, and this he finally decided to stage at the Studio Theatre, whatever its technical shortcomings, in May 1942. Though this ran for four weeks there were no offers to put it on elsewhere. Gilbert Miller was spotted among the audience, but expressed no opinions, and did not make himself known.[217]

The following year was not a good one for Piscator. To begin with he wished to stage Brecht's *Private Life of the Master Race* (a wartime version of *Furcht und Elend des dritten Reiches*) with the Studio Theatre in spring 1943, but found Brecht impossible to communicate with, complaining of him in a letter to Gorelik as a bad comrade, almost a Hitlerite. 'The necessity for all of us – in this time –', he wrote, 'is to hold together.'[218] Again the translation was to be made by Hays;[219] Leo Kerz started working on the design for the set; Brecht himself arrived for a stay of nearly four months in New York, and relations were patched up enough for a programme of Brecht's songs and poems to be put on at the school. The two men also went together to see Fritz Lang's *Hangmen also Die*, the film on which Brecht had been working and in which Alexander Granach had a part. But Hays declined to go on with the work on hearing that Brecht had authorised another translation, and after that there was a much more serious clash. For Piscator was now discussing a production of the old *Schweik* adaptation with the Theatre Guild. Brecht meantime was accepting E. J. Aufricht's commission to make a new version of the Schweik story as a musical with Kurt Weill: the scheme that finished as his play *Schweyk im zweiten Weltkrieg*. Both parties approached the same translator, Alfred Kreymborg, the poet whose *America America* had been one of the notable left-wing dramas of the early 1930s, and it was only because of this that Piscator learnt of the rival project. What made matters worse was that Aufricht (the original producer of *Die Drei-groschenoper*, who had once or twice crossed Piscator's path before), had cleared the American rights with the Hašek lawyer, as he himself had not. He thereupon drafted a furious letter to Brecht, accusing him of 'swinishness' and threatening to knock him 'off his amoral Olympus'; then thought better of it and wrote formally to all the rival group, saying that he would protect his legal rights. How this impressed Aufricht we do not know, but Weill was perhaps enough of a friend for it to weigh in his decision not to go on with the plan.

In October Piscator walked out of the only production he was ever asked to direct for the Theatre Guild, an adaptation by Paul Osborn of *A High Wind in Jamaica* called *The Innocent Voyage*. Finally the Studio Theatre was forced to close. This had been a possibility ever since its production of a new play called *Winter Soldiers* by Daniel Lewis James, whose relative success in November 1942 led the theatre unions to ask the wages appropriate to a professional theatre (such as the Studio indeed claimed to be) rather than a school. Piscator thereupon asked the New School for an additional $20,000,[220] and when this was not forthcoming decided to suspend all the theatre's activities. The unions relented enough to allow a revival of *Nathan der Weise* at the beginning of 1944, but by then Alvin Johnson had warned Piscator that the theatre would have to stop because it contravened the New School's fire regulations,[221] and after that it came formally to an end. The position of the whole Dramatic Workshop was by then threatened, for it had lost money from the outset ($8726 in 1941–42, $10,290 in 1942–43, dropping to $4945 in 1943–44), and the New School board began considering whether or not to close it down. Since no decision could be reached that year the problem was put off till February 1945.

The report which the Assistant Financial Secretary then presented summarised the arguments against the Dramatic Workshop, which at that date had around 40–60 full-time students and about 250 part-time.[222] First, this kind of professional training was inconsistent with the role of the New School, which was primarily that of adult education. The theatre students moreover were a good deal younger than all the rest. There was the fire hazard; there were also the needs of the library and the psychology laboratory, which could not at present be met. Finally there was the question of student decorum; the Workshop held too many 'egocentric anti-social individuals'. Johnson's solution was to shift it out to separate premises from the following October. It then went to the little President Theatre at 247 West 48th Street, which served not only for classes but also as a purely student theatre performing a 'March of Drama' sequence of plays as a live course in theatre history to link with Gassner's lectures. This repertory absorbed almost anything Piscator chose to put into it, and soon became converted in his mind into a form of People's Theatre which would attract subscribers over and above the ordinary students. A second and larger theatre was taken in the shape of the 800-seat Rooftop Theatre at 111 East Houston Street, where six plays could be seen for only $4, as against six from the same repertoire for $10 at the President. 'A hopeful-looking school theatre', the old Berlin critic Julius Bab called it,[223] and indeed it was mainly on block bookings by the New York high schools that it came to depend.

In 1947/48 the Workshop's catalogue referred to these performances as 'open rehearsals', and they were designed to be accompanied by lectures and discussions. Unlike those at the Studio Theatre therefore they were generally ignored by the New York critics, even though they were liable to include students who later became important, for instance Elaine Stritch and Walter Matthau in *The Little Foxes* that year. Among the exceptions were Piscator's own staging of Sartre's *The Flies*, which used the revolve, threw projections on a gauze, made the actors enter and exit through the auditorium, and began with a film prologue showing the German occupation of France; Piscator bought the rights for a year, and tried unsuccessfully to set up a Broadway production. Others were

69. Erwin and Maria Piscator (right) *with members of the cast of Sartre's* The Flies *at the President Theatre in 1947: Dramatic Workshop students directed by Paul Ransom.*

Robert Penn Warren's *All the King's Men*, which Piscator adapted and directed from the novel, shorn of its irony and turned into a straight conflict between dictatorship and proletariat, and Wolfgang Borchert's *Outside the Door*, which was opposed by Gassner as 'decadent' and 'inept',[224] but none the less was important as the first post-war German play to be seen in New York. Unfortunately however the cost of running both these theatres was such as to offset all the financial gains of the immediate post-war years. While student numbers shot up after the ending of the European war in May 1945 (so that between 1944 and 1947 income is said to have quintupled)[225] thereafter the deficit was such as to make the New School trustees seriously alarmed. Johnson by now had retired as president, but even he criticised the administration of the Workshop, and in March 1948 it was decided that the New School would have to shed it.[226] An independent board of trustees was set up, with Piscator as

70. *Piscator's adaptation of Robert Penn Warren's novel* All the King's Men *at the President Theatre in March 1948, shortly before the Dramatic Workshop's severance from the New School.*

chairman and a membership that included Gassner, Johnson, Penn Warren and Kurt Weill. What happened after the formal separation in 1949 is still not entirely clear, but it seems that despite a reduced scale of operations the Dramatic Workshop and Technical Institute, as it renamed itself, had gone too far into debt to recover. Even if Piscator himself had not decided to slip back to Germany in 1951 it would hardly have survived more than a year or two.

European voices

Apart from his abandoned job for the Theatre Guild Piscator did scarcely any directing outside his own school except in their seasons at Sayville and other summer stock theatres, where the plays were routine fare. His one Broadway production, Irving Kaye Davis's *Last Stop* (1944), was a failure whose première he refused to attend. In the spring of 1945, how-ever, just as the war in Europe ended, he once again agreed to direct Brecht's *The Private Life of the Master Race*, this time in a new translation by Eric Bentley, for an off-Broadway group called 'The Theatre of all Nations' before a mainly CIO audience. Extensive notes and sketches[227] show how he now proposed to set about staging this no longer topical play: it would begin informally with actors and stage hands preparing the stage; the pianist would then play 'The Star-Spangled Banner', till a giant SS man with a revolver forced him to break into the Nazi Horst-Wessel Song; then there would be a discussion about dictatorship and democracy, leading into an exposition of the ideas of the epic theatre and so to the play proper. Piscator did the casting, which included the Bassermanns (whose English was none too intelligible), and conducted the first rehearsals. Then Brecht arrived from California, disliked what he saw and tried to have the performance cancelled. On 29 May, a fortnight before the opening at City College, Piscator walked out, telling Brecht that he couldn't afford 'the luxury of an artistic failure'.[228] Brecht called in Berthold Viertel, who had directed a German reading of the play in New York some years earlier, and together they took the direction over, scrapping all the planned introduction.[229] Piscator and the critics alike found the result amateurish, though it seems questionable whose fault this was. 'Our ideas on epic theatre are so different', he wrote of Brecht to his colleague Leon Askin, 'that I preferred to leave him alone.'[230]

All the same this time they remained friends and allies, and early in 1947, when Brecht was clear that he wanted to go back to Berlin, he wrote to Piscator saying that 'whenever I have mentioned the possibility of a visit I have raised the question of your making one too, because with-out you I find it difficult to envisage a successful attack on provincialism, hollow emotionalism etc. in favour of great, mature political theatre'.[231] There was a further exchange of letters – almost of testimonials – that March, Brecht formally saying

Just to get things straight, let me tell you that of all the people who

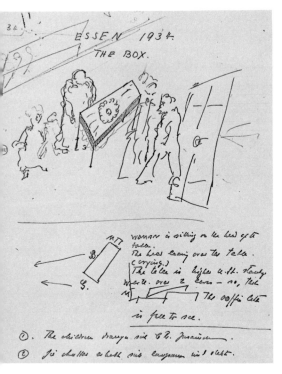

71–72. *The clash over Brecht's Private Life of the Master Race, 1945. Sketches by Piscator for his rejected New York production at City College showing,* above, *the arrangement of the coffin scene;* below, *the general disposition of the chorus etc. Piscator's notes are in a mixture of English and German.*

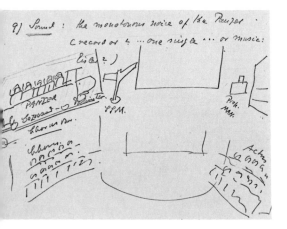

have been active in the theatre over the past twenty years no one has been so close to me as you.[232]

– to which Piscator replied 'I too believe that I've still to come across any author who comes nearer than you to the sort of theatre I have in mind'.[233] Whereas Brecht's idea however was that they should run two separate theatres in Berlin, Piscator wanted both to cooperate in one. By that time Piscator was once more in touch with Friedrich Wolf, whose son Lukas was working in the Dramatic Workshop, and who, after being rescued from French internment by the Russians (who declared him a Soviet citizen) had come back to the Soviet sector of Berlin. Wolf suggested first that Piscator should come on a visit and perhaps direct a film for DEFA, then that he should come as a guest director to the revived Volksbühne, in which Karlheinz Martin, Lotte Löbinger and other old friends were now involved.[234]

Brecht left the United States in the autumn of 1947, and a year later went to Berlin to stage that historic production of *Mutter Courage* which led to the formation of the Berliner Ensemble. The position at that time was that both the Deutsches Theater and the Theater am Schiffbauerdamm were in the Soviet sector, as was the Volksbühne's bombed-out theatre on the former Bülowplatz. Wangenheim had reopened the Deutsches Theater in 1945 with a production of (yet again) *Nathan der Weise* in which his father and Wegener appeared; but he was too ill for that job and had been replaced as Intendant by Langhoff, with Ihering as chief dramaturg. Ernst Busch, interned by the French at the same time as Wolf, was less lucky and was handed over to the Gestapo; an intervention by Gustav Gründgens, Intendant of the Staatstheater under the Nazis, saved him from execution, but before the Russians arrived he had been badly injured in the bombing; none the less he now helped to get the Volksbühne movement back on its feet by directing and acting in a revival of *Die Matrosen von Cattaro*, with two other old Piscator actors, Venohr and Friedrich Gnass, at the Theater am Schiffbauerdamm. This theatre had been allotted to the Volksbühne, with the previously little-known Fritz Wisten as Intendant (which was why Brecht could not at first use it as he had hoped). From the Soviet Union Maxim Vallentin had returned to head a new theatre school at Weimar, where he became the chief German advocate of Stanislavsky's method; Erpenbeck became editor of the magazine *Theater der Zeit* and was responsible for supervising the East German repertoire; Rodenberg in 1948 was made theatre adviser at the House of Soviet Culture. The Arthur Piecks also came back, but no longer had anything to do with the theatre. Pieck senior was of course to be President of the German Democratic Republic when it was constituted in October 1949.

To Wolf's first approaches Piscator replied that he felt too old to start again from the beginning and mistrusted Wolf's eternal optimism.[235] In 1948 however Wolf told him that they would want him for the Volks-bühne once its theatre had been rebuilt, saying 'I know of no objection to you on the part of the Party'; the only doubt was whether Piscator would accept the job.[236] Then after the production of *Mutter Courage* in January 1949, i.e. during the Berlin Airlift and just when the Dramatic Workshop was having to prepare for its separation from the New School, Brecht and Wolf got together to try to lure him over. Brecht asked if he would come that autumn to direct a play for the Berliner Ensemble, perhaps Nordahl Grieg's Paris Commune play *The Defeat*;[237] in March he added that he himself was adapting the Grieg play (as *Die Tage der Commune*) and that he would get Piscator a production at the Zurich Schauspielhaus on the way. 'It is a good moment', he said, 'it mustn't be left much longer, everything is in a state of flux at the moment and its direction will be determined by the capacities available.'[238] Wolf for his part wrote that

> the crucial point for us, so far as a major invitation goes, has always been whether we could take it on ourselves, in our present tran-sitional state of things, to fish you out of your two theatres and bring you to a ruined Berlin where you would find many things lacking but at the same time an infinite number of new and genuine tasks. Could you give me your honest reactions to this: could/would you wholeheartedly abandon the security of your position over there in favour of our somewhat loose situation here?[239]

Piscator drafted replies to both men, telling Wolf 'Yes, of course. There is hardly anything to decide . . .',[240] but saying to Brecht that while he would like to come 'if my affairs here let me'[241] there were a lot of unknown factors involved. There was thus still an element of hesitation. However, there is no evidence that either letter was sent, and it seems that the expected formal invitation from the Volksbühne never arrived.

One of the difficulties in judging Piscator's American achievements is that so much of what has been written about the Dramatic Workshop has been like an exercise in public relations. Thus a careless reader might conclude that its numbers reached 7700, its income $500,000, the number of subscribers to the 'March of Drama' repertory 30,000 and the repertory itself a hundred plays, performed to professional standards: it was, in Piscator's words to an ITI conference later, not only the best repertoire he had known but 'the best theatre I've ever had'.[242] In this light it becomes difficult not to look at the record with a certain scepticism and wonder just how much of it is due, like Piscator's alleged three years as 'lecturer in dramatic art at the German University in Paris', to the over-selling common to so many ventures in the US. And yet even today Lee Strasberg considers that as a school the Workshop had 'great value', while Stella Adler concurs. Of the alumni claimed for it,[243] Harry Belafonte spent a semester there. Walter Matthau was asked to leave. Marlon Brando attended for a year as one of Miss Adler's most memorable pupils before an agent spotted him at Sayville in the summer of 1944, just when Piscator had asked him too to leave on disciplinary grounds.[244] Tony Curtis likewise in the early 1940s was a student under his own name of Bernard Schwartz. Rod Steiger completed the course slightly later. Aside from Brando, the person who most impressed Piscator was Tennessee Williams, who was still nominally a student at the time of the Theatre Guild's production of his first play *Battle of Angels* and subsequently asked to become Piscator's secretary.[245] He was turned down because Piscator thought it more important for him to do his own work, but he none the less helped on the staging of *War and Peace*, and his use of a narrator and projections in *The Glass Menagerie* clearly reflects Piscator's methods. Perhaps the most impressive testimonial from any of these people came from Judith Malina, who told Piscator in 1947 that

> I have learned to believe what you believe in, to strive for that for which you strive. You are my *teacher*: the one in whom I have most faith, in whom I trust, from whom I learned and still seek to learn.[246]

The Living Theatre, which she and Julian Beck went on to found, is further evidence that his teaching could stimulate students in directions quite different from his own.

The Dramatic Workshop filled a gap between the decline of the American Left theatre and the rise and recognition of 'Off-Broadway', whose way it helped to pave. It is primarily this that determined its historic role rather than any particular methods or principles that can be related to Piscator's work in pre-Hitler Germany. True, he and his European collaborators did much to introduce students to the general traditions of the modern European theatre, not excluding a measure of expressionism; but the Workshop never had the technical resources to stage plays on the old scale, nor was the New York theatre (and its unions) used to working so intensively as had been the case in Berlin. Vestiges of the old documentary approach remained in their use of narrators, inscriptions and projections, but its impact was blunted by the abandonment of any extreme political stance and there was some tendency to the kind of symbolism visible in Piscator's film. Where acting was concerned he called for 'objectivity' rather than Stanislavsky-style naturalism; the actor must tell a story instructively, and tell it to an audience of whose presence he must remain aware, concentrating on them rather than on the middle of the stage. But he did not go so far as Brecht, whose notion of 'alienation' he never accepted, and he was so little inclined to impose these views on his acting teachers that a recent biography of Brando positively identifies Piscator with Strasberg and Stella Adler as 'leading exponents of the Method style of acting in America'.[247] Thus when the Actors' Studio was set up in 1947 it no doubt seemed perfectly logical for one of his leading performers, Herbert Berghof, together with such ex-students as Steiger and Eli Wallach, to go on to work there in the Stanislavsky tradition; indeed Strasberg himself feels that Piscator's opposition to the latter was based on its production style rather than on its acting techniques.[248]

What did remain of the old Piscator, however much he might play down the political theatre and his communist past, was the concept of theatre as a moral force. Thus in February 1944 when he revived *Nathan der Weise* in face of the growing evidence of anti-semitism in the US he told the New York *Daily Worker* that

> it is the business of the theatre to deliver a social message and this is as important as that it should be 'entertaining' . . . Mere entertainment, 'art for art's sake', is not a reason for a theatre production.[249]

None the less he emphasised that it would be 'dramatically a magnificent evening in the theatre' as well as socially right. Once he would have assumed that these were the same thing.

9. The long road home
(1951–1966)

————◆————

'The cold shoulder'

When Piscator flew back to West Germany at the beginning of October 1951 he was nearly fifty-eight and had been away for over twenty years. 'I don't know if I've ever in my life felt smaller', he noted. 'Nobody had asked me to come, neither the lot in the West nor those in the East. . . .'[250] His whole position at this juncture was indeed extremely insecure; thus he summarised his civic status:

1. Germany: deprived of citizenship
2. France: identity card
3. America: denied citizenship
4. A German once more
5. Israel: no answer
6. Likewise from the East: no answer
7. They recommend: Chile or . . .

Among his few remaining links in the Federal Republic were first and foremost his old family home above a shop at Dillenburg in Hesse-Nassau, which now became the firm base where he planned his productions, and secondly the Hamburg Schauspielhaus, where Weisenborn and Rehfisch were dramaturgs. In his luggage he had brought *All the King's Men* and *War and Peace*, which he wanted to revise with Alfred Neumann in the hope that either Hamburg or the newly founded West Berlin Schiller-Theater would put it on. Meantime he attended the Hamburg dramaturgical discussion group run by Weisenborn – a writer who had remained close to the Communists and been imprisoned by the Gestapo for his resistance activities – and did two productions there, of which the first, Fritz Hochwälder's *Virginia*, was in Ludwig Hoffmann's words 'a

73. *Piscator's return (1). Schiller's* Die Räuber *as staged by him in West Germany to inaugurate the Mannheim National-Theater, thirty-one years after his controversial production of 1926.*

resounding failure which became a great liability'.[251] Whether or not there was also a political intrigue against him, as he himself suspected,[252] he lost his foothold in Hamburg almost immediately and for years was unable to establish himself in the major West German theatres.

Working as a freelance director, he was dependent for the rest of the 1950s on the lesser and middle-grade provincial theatres – first of all in his own area (Marburg and Giessen), then at Tübingen and later at Essen – where he had little or no choice of play and might find himself doing two or three productions of the same work. He also did a few productions outside Germany, including one at last in Zurich where he was unfortunately out of sympathy with the play. But he was offered strikingly few chances in the major theatres and when the first arrived he noted in his diary that he felt like saying that he no longer had the confidence to go through with it: only he needed the money.[253] This was an adaptation of Sartre's *L'Engrenage* which Harry Buckwitz had asked him to direct in the smaller of the Frankfurt municipal theatres in September 1953, and in the event it was a moderate success, remarkable for the introduction of a new technical device in the shape of a stage lit from beneath: the 'Lichtbühne' which was also to feature in the Berlin *War and Peace*. This was Piscator's only production at Frankfurt for some eight years, though he was given a number of productions at the Mannheim National-Theater, of which the most interesting were Arthur Miller's *The Crucible* (a play he also staged in several other theatres) and the 175th anniversary production of *Die Räuber* with which he inaugurated their new smaller theatre in January 1957. This time he saw Schiller's play not as a topical political drama but as a more meditative reflection on the problem of freedom, using a central stage (again partly lit from beneath) and concentrating on the great monologues which he had telescoped in 1926.

The first effective step towards Piscator's comeback however was the belated acceptance of *War and Peace* in January 1955 by Boleslav Barlog at the Schiller-Theater, for it was this that not only brought him back to Berlin but put him once again before an international public. By now the script was in its third form, having been reviewed yet again with the Hamburg dramaturg Guntram Prüfer after Neumann's death in 1952; there had also been some inconclusive negotiations with Jean Vilar and the Paris TNP for a translation by Adamov in which Gérard Philipe would play Prince Andrew. When he got Barlog's message Piscator was rehearsing *The Crucible* in Sweden; and this only left him six weeks to prepare the production of which he had been thinking for the best part of twenty years. With H. W. Lenneweit as designer he devised a rather clumsily symbolic division of the stage into a 'destiny-stage', lit from beneath, a circular 'action-stage' in front of it and, almost in the auditorium, three quasi-pulpits or 'reflection-stages' for Pierre, Natasha and Prince Andrew. Originally the idea had been to make Pierre function as a narrator, but now a separate narrator was installed at a desk between the 'destiny' and 'action' stages to function almost as a master of ceremonies. There was no film: where once Piscator would have used projectors to show the battle of Borodino, now he had Pierre and the narrator demonstrate it with model soldiers on the 'destiny-stage'. The West Berlin critics found this whole approach dreadfully oversimplified, but it was a success with the public, and the following year the whole production went to the Paris international theatre festival. There too the audience were enthusiastic, giving Piscator himself a very warm reception; but the critics were hostile, sometimes in unpleasantly nationalistic terms, Gabriel Marcel being a notable exception.

74. The new symbolic division of the stage: the 'destiny', 'action' and 'reflection' stages in War and Peace.

Though Barlog followed this up by engaging Piscator for three further productions the results were none too happy for him. That autumn for Faulkner's *Requiem for a Nun* he used the 'Lichtbühne' again, and insisted that his leading actress Joana Maria Gorvin should adopt a critically detached attitude (almost à la Brecht) to her part.[254] Again the production was invited to Paris, but this time Piscator, feeling that the adaptation had been weakened by the absence of a narrator, told the French press that he thought it a wrong choice: a statement which naturally offended the theatre. Also during the 1955–56 season he directed Büchner's *Dantons Tod*, this time with Caspar Neher as his designer, but the notices were bad, he felt that the theatre had not given him the co-operation he needed, and he found Barlog's objections to the length of his rehearsals insulting.[255] There had been some question of his doing *Faust* part II (which would have been not only an immense challenge but also his first Goethe production); instead however Barlog now offered him a triple bill of Russian one-acters – 'flies offered to a gaffed fish'[256] in the words of his diary – and the fact that the critics liked this much better than his major productions made it all the more galling. Thereafter he directed nothing more in Berlin until the 1960s, when he at last appeared as a serious candidate for a permanent job there.

In the meantime Piscator had been applying for a number of provincial *Intendant*-ships: at Duisburg, at Bremen, at Saarbrücken and even at Heidelberg.[257] In each case he was turned down on grounds that never seem to have been specified, though he himself felt that his loss of citizenship in the 1930s might be a factor. Also he would have liked to set up some kind of teaching academy which would have been an improved continuation of the Dramatic Workshop, possibly in collaboration with his wife, who had remained based on New York. He discussed the idea first at Frankfurt, with Buckwitz and with Max Horkheimer, the university Rector; then in 1955 he published the 'Proposal for a Theatre Academy' which can be found in the second volume of his collected *Schriften*.[258] Three years later he was hoping that it might be founded at Essen under the wing of the Folkwang-Schule there, and asking Ferdinand Bruckner to teach a playwrights' class.[259] However, this ambition too never materialised, and as a result it was altogether ten years before he achieved any position of influence in the post-war German theatre. One reason for the delay was perhaps that he was so largely out of sympathy with its ruling preoccupations: the drama of Anouilh, Giraudoux, Fry and Eliot, like that of Beckett and Ionesco which followed, was utterly uncongenial to him and he had no way of dealing with it. 'I must get clear in my own mind', says a sad note after the failure of *Danton* in May 1956,

1. Whether my talent as such has declined . . .
2. Whether it is the audience that has changed, rather than myself!
3. Where to find an audience still: here in the West, or there in the East?
4. And plays and authors for it: which ones?[260]

Linked with this sense of uncertainty was his dislike of much that he saw in the society around him. Thus one of his last letters to Alfred Neumann in Switzerland about seven months after his return, when he was preparing the Marburg production of *Nathan der Weise*:

> Unfortunately it is too mild to express the feelings I myself have here on seeing, hearing – and smelling: it stinks, like the American says.[261]

This last phrase was written in English.

Taking stock

In 1948 he had told Schulz-Norden, the original publisher of *Das politische Theater*, that he was doubtful about the value of reissuing that work.[262] Now however, while continuing to steer clear of the old catchphrase, he began to reformulate his ideas in terms of *Bekenntnistheater*, a confessional theatre, or theatre that makes a statement of faith. Dismissing most American drama as 'technically on the level of the naturalistic theatre of the 1890s', he accused the prevalent European playwrights of the early 1950s of 'breathing the air of an unhealthy and reactionary period'.[263] In face of an attitude of 'art for art's sake' whose consequences he thought must be disastrous, he looked for evidence that the Germans were trying to see what had gone wrong in the Nazi era, and felt its absence to be 'the great disappointment of my return home'.[264] A fortnight after his sixtieth birthday, therefore, it came like a solemn resolution when he noted in his diary of 1 January 1954 that the basic attitude of the theatre should be grounded in morality and *Bekenntnis*. At first he seems to have envisaged this new confessional theatre as an independent organisation under that name, with theatres in some of the major West German cities where plays about the main problems of the time would be staged: 'the theatre of the positive people – against existentialists, degenerates and those who have given up hope. I have now been in Germany for 3 years', he noted. 'There is no conscience.'[265] The necessary process, so he told *Crucible* audiences at Mannheim that autumn, would be *Kenntnis – Erkenntnis – Bekenntnis*;[266] knowledge, recognition, and confession or nailing one's flag to the mast (unfortunately there is no comprehensive term in English). For the present it was not easy for him to realise this aim, though he tried only to direct plays which would not conflict with it. However, the very concept owed something to Tolstoy, and in publicly answering critics of his *War and Peace* production the following spring he accused them of being unable to come to terms with a performance that was in effect a period of meditation, without the fashionable ambiguities and symbols which they felt qualified to interpret. This talk, given before an SPD forum in West Berlin, was called 'Confessional Theatre and the Discomfort of the Critics'.[267]

The new formulation cannot be disentangled from the mixed state of his political ideas around that time. Shocked though he had been by the repression of the East Berlin demonstrations of 16–17 June 1953, he could not but feel that 'the Berlin workers have struck their mother. An unpleasant, severe mother, and possibly a bad one, but a mother none the less'.[268] Six months later he was dreaming of a new Communist party which would be 'a party of human beings'.[269] Even now he could see himself as an opponent of the bourgeoisie and the SPD as its 'stirrup-holder – or rather, its pimp!'[270] He regretted not having been given the overall direction of the Volksbühne in East Berlin, which in his view had been denied him by the hostility of Wangenheim, Rodenberg and Vallentin.[271] He realised however that he had been harmed by Otto Katz's ludicrously fabricated evidence at the Slansky trial in Prague in 1951, when Katz not only denounced Claude Cockburn and the late Konni Zilliacus as British imperialist agents but accused Piscator of leading him into Trotzkyist ways. And so when at last he ventured into East Berlin with Ihering at the end of October 1955 he was quite surprised to get a friendly reception. Though there is no record of any further meeting between him and Brecht, he saw Eisler, Heartfield, Anna Seghers, Arnold Zweig, Wangenheim, Langhoff and others, went to the Brecht productions of *Mutter Courage* and *Der Kaukasische Kreidekreis* and even wondered whether he should not write to Wilhelm Pieck 'to see if they realised what they missed by not bringing me back'.[272] Certainly his stock in East Berlin seems to have improved, for early in 1957 he was invited to direct *Richard III* at the Deutsches Theater with Ernst Busch, while the following year Vallentin hoped to stage *The Case of Clyde Griffiths* at the Maxim Gorky Theatre.[273] He was elected to the (East) German Academy of Arts, as one of the small group of Western members along with Masereel, Feuchtwanger and Heinrich Mann. Out of the past, Ehm Welk wrote regretting that he had not taken a job in the GDR. And, more significantly for the future, he met the Deutsches Theater dramaturg Heinar Kippardt who became keen to work with him.

At the same time Piscator's attitudes were certainly affected by resentment at his treatment in the West. Throughout the 1950s his diaries are spattered with sour reflections about his lack of recognition, critical remarks about other West German theatre people and gloomy musings on old age and death. They make depressing reading, and are not free from plain ordinary jealousy, such as sometimes unbalances his remarks about Brecht. All the same it must have been wounding to read Ernst Schumacher's big East German Brecht study of 1955 and find his own brand of epic theatre dismissed as 'a petty-bourgeois radical theatre movement' whose effective principles had all been anticipated in the USSR.[274] A certain grudge remained even after John Heartfield had reassured him that Brecht himself disowned this view, exclaiming 'but Piscator was my teacher'.[275] As for the attitude of the main West German *Intendanten*, it was quite simply unwelcoming. Himself a punctilious man, if at times an irritable one, he could not forgive those who ignored his letters, kept him waiting or pretended to be too busy to see him; and this led him to write off a steadily increasing list of the leading theatre men: Gründgens, Schweikart, Buckwitz, Schalla, Stroux, Hilpert and others who had worked under the Nazis and risen to positions of power before his return. Personally, as well as artistically and politically, he disliked much of the West German theatre; happy as he was to be back in his right language and region, in other ways he felt out of place.

Such at least are the thoughts which seem to have occupied his solitary walks at Dillenburg, and they might easily have dominated the second book which he repeatedly planned to write. From about 1954 on he sketched numerous schemes for this, and some of the longer passages in the diaries were designed for incorporation in it. It was to be called *My Second Theatre Diary*[276] or *The Theatre I Have in Mind*,[277] dedicated to the deer around Dillenburg (as against *Das politische Theater*'s dedication to the proletariat of Berlin), and among the chapters envisaged were '25 years of *War and Peace*'; 'My film: not a masterpiece but the work of a master'; one on the American theatre, which would deal with his two Broadway jobs and the 'undue power of the unions'; one looking 'Towards a Theatre Academy, together with a backward glance at the Dramatic Workshop'; and one which would be a form of 'Debate with Brecht', defining their differences with respect to Epic Theatre and Alienation. 'The cold shoulder' was to have been his heading for the chapter on his work to date in West Germany, while the final chapter on 'My Critics' was subtitled in one draft 'Malice, ignorance, or outdated aesthetics?'. Fortunately, perhaps, for his reputation, the book never came to anything; such passages as he wrote were too rambling (his principal punctuation mark being the dash), so that Helmut Schlien, whom he engaged as a collaborator, complained of his inability to think logically, and threw up the job. Later, with Gerd Semmer, Piscator began tape-recording some of his recollections, and as late as 1962 was still preparing a second book, this time centring on his Russian years.[278] Meanwhile he had become reconciled with Gasbarra, who was living in Italy after running the German service for Rome radio under the Fascists, and now edited the slightly modified West German version of *Das politische Theater* for publication in 1963. Though he wrote many articles and speeches in these fifteen years, it remained Piscator's only book.

Indian summer of the political theatre

At what point Piscator began to set his sights on the West Berlin Freie Volksbühne we do not know, but evidently it followed Willy Brandt's election as SPD Mayor of that city in the autumn of 1957. Brandt not only had a different attitude to the problem of relations with the East from previous Socialist leaders, but was also unusually conscious of Berlin's artistic originality in the 1920s, naming Piscator (in his book *My Road to Berlin* 'as told to Leo Lania' who by then was a successful American journalist) along with Brecht, Toller, Gropius and Schoenberg as one of those most responsible.[279] Already that year we find Piscator in his diary roughing out a programme for taking over a theatre, with a repertoire including a *Hoppla 1957* to be written by Mehring, the same author's *Der Kaufmann von Berlin*, his own *War and Peace*, *The Case of Clyde Griffiths* and *All the King's Men* plus the Brecht plays, aided by Busch and Erich Engel.[280] Since 1949, when the division of Berlin became permanent, the Volksbühne in the Western half had occupied the Theater am Kurfürstendamm, mainly under Oskar Fritz Schuh, an excellent if unpolitical director who could call on some of the best German-speaking actors and worked closely with the designer Caspar Neher; their productions of Büchner's *Woyzeck* and *Leonce und Lena* were seen in England. In 1952 Dr Siegfried Nestriepke, one of Piscator's old enemies in the battle of March 1927, had become head of the new Free Volksbühne organisation (as distinct from the unfree one based on the old Bülowplatz theatre in the East); then in 1958 Schuh left and an evident deterioration set in. In four successive seasons the theatre had three different *Intendanten*, starting with Leonard Steckel in 1958–59. Piscator, who had at long last been invited back to Berlin to direct a new opera with Boris Blacher, was already a candidate for the post in 1960. The following year he staged his first guest production there – Miller's *Death of a Salesman*, with Steckel heading the cast – and in the spring of 1962 it was announced that he would take over. For the Volksbühne as for himself this was the beginning of a second fruitful era, only interrupted by his death.

'What I need to find', he then noted in his diary, 'is tough, weighty plays soaked in reality, of a kind that never previously existed. Back to the style of the 1920s.'[281] The secret of his success at the Volksbühne was that he managed to do precisely that, and not least because a new generation had meanwhile become interested in his old achievements. Even as he had been lamenting what he called the 'avant-gardist re-action'[282] of Beckett and Ionesco and other absurdist authors, whose vogue he identified with a general rejection of hopeful concepts like pacifism, idealism and progress, the climate had been changing under his nose. First of all, a powerful group of younger West German writers had emerged who were bitterly obsessed by the Nazi past and by the conduct of their parents: Catholics, Socialists, Marxists, resident in or out of Germany but united by a common awareness of guilt. Secondly, and quite as important, it had been established that there was an audience for such themes; here Barlog's production of *The Diary of Anne Frank* in 1956 was a vital pointer. Thirdly, since Brecht's death that same year there had been a nucleus of younger directors, operating in both halves of Germany but largely trained in his Berliner Ensemble, to whom the political theatre of the 1920s was highly congenial. Suddenly, it seemed, it was no longer true that Piscator would be forced to stage dramatised novels in view of the lack of suitable plays, as he still argued. He did eventually approach Mehring with a view to an updated version of *Hoppla, wir leben!*, but the timing of his appointment was such that the playwrights he most needed now came to him spontaneously. Thus Kipphardt wrote more than two years previously to tell him that he was working on a play about Robert Oppenheimer and planning *Der Hund des Generals*, a play whose use of projectors, narration and different acting areas is clearly based on Piscator's methods.[283] Then in February 1962 an unknown thirty-year old author called on him to discuss a play which their common publisher thought might be of interest. This was Rolf Hochhuth and the play *Der Stellvertreter* or *The Representative*. If Piscator had missed the boat in 1951 he had caught it now.

For the first time in his life he was able to stage plays that met his requirements, so that the author's text dominated the production. Not that this was the case with all his productions, by any means, let alone all those staged under his aegis by other directors. His opening production, for instance, of the four late plays by Gerhart Hauptmann known as the *Atriden-Tetralogie*, was criticised much as *War and Peace* had been for its

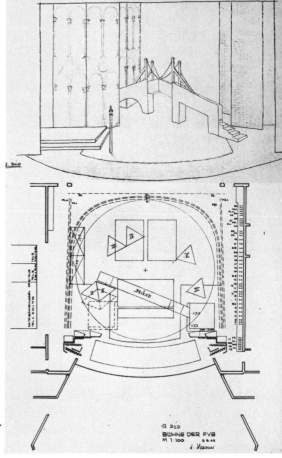

*75–76. Piscator's return (2). Pro-
ductions for the Volksbühne once
more in 1963 at its new West Berlin
theatre, with Hans-Ulrich Schmückle
as designer.* Above Rolland's
Robespierre *adapted by Piscator
and Gasbarra, showing use of projected crowd background (compare
ill. 9).* Right, *plan and perspective
drawings for* The Merchant of
Venice. *The prisms (marked with
Roman figures) rotate for changes of
set.*

telescoping of a vast cycle into a single evening and its oversimplification of the writer's veiled allusions to Nazism and the war (during which the cycle had been written) by the projection of documentary material; once again it used the 'Lichtbühne'. Rolland's *Robespierre*, with which the Volksbühne's new West Berlin theatre opened the following spring, was more successful, not least because it began his period of collaboration with the designer Hans-Ulrich Schmückle, but it was even less modern a play, while his *Merchant of Venice* seems to have been too heavy and the

77. *The new documentary drama of Piscator's last period. His production of* In the Case of J. Robert Oppenheimer *by Heinar Kipphardt, 1964/65 (here seen at The Hague), showing projection of Senator Joseph McCarthy.*

new comedy *Mohrenwäsche*, which tried to combine a serious anti-racialist theme with a farcical treatment, something of a disaster.

The three major new plays however were of the first importance, their effects felt far outside Germany. Thus Hochhuth's well-founded and sensitive study of the Vatican's policy towards the Nazi extermination camps is a great work, if only because whatever its structural faults its language and handling are worthy of its immense theme; 'thanks to this play', said Piscator even before the rehearsals began, 'there is some point in working in the theatre'.[284] Kipphardt's *In der Sache J. Robert*

Oppenheimer, which followed early in his third season, was less a work of art, being a television-derived documentary of Dr Oppenheimer's hearings before the US Atomic Energy Commission; but again it took an all-absorbing subject and treated it with dignity and skill. Finally Peter Weiss's *Die Ermittlung* was a sober, beautifully written presentation, in the form of an almost Dantesque 'scenic cantata', of characteristic facts and self-justifications, unadorned and shocking, drawn from the chief German war crimes trial, that of former members of the SS at Frankfurt in 1963–65. More than anything which Piscator had previously directed, these three works corresponded to the *Bekenntnistheater* which he had envisaged, and their power is such that they have been performed all round the globe.

Not long before he took over at the Freie Volksbühne Piscator was again in correspondence with Bernhard Reich, who was re-emerging as an elderly Soviet critic after his 'rehabilitation' in 1955. Answering Reich's inquiries as to his present style of production he replied that conditions in the West German theatre made it impossible to evolve a distinctive 'method'; he could only describe his approach as 'analytical criticism making use of epic elements'.[285] He was also very conscious that the standard of his actors was not as high as it might be, and for this he blamed the attraction of television contracts in the Federal Republic, which drained much of the talent from Berlin.[286] Certainly the three plays which established the 'documentary theatre' of the 1960s made their way almost irrespective of direction and performance: something that could not have been said of any of the new plays directed by him before 1933. None the less these were the three which he felt to be material for 'an epic, "political" theatre such as I have been fighting for for thirty years and more', and in the controversies which they provoked he fought valiantly for them, shielding Weiss, for instance, from right-wing critics who objected to his mentioning the links between the extermination camps and heavy industry, the regrettable past and the blooming present. Meantime the revised edition of *Das politische Theater* had come out, as well as its French and Italian translations, prompting him only a few months before his death once more to define his notions of 'Political Theatre Today'. The old political theatre, he then told readers of the Hamburg *Die Zeit*, 'had followed a Marxist ideology, without however strictly adhering to the party line, from which indeed it frequently departed'. The political theatre that had become internationally known in connection with authors like Hochhuth, Kipphardt and Weiss was somewhat different:

The paradox of today's political theatre lies in the fact that its topicality is primarily focused on the immediate past.

This brought him back to the original political conception of the Volksbühne, which seventy-five years earlier had set out to concentrate on topical problems, leading him to insist that his repertoire there still needed to be visibly different from that of other theatres: it must express a *Bekenntnis zum Politischen*, a statement of faith in politics. And to do so it demanded a style of production which would turn it into 'a modern think-theatre'.[287]

By then Piscator was seventy-two, and a certain change in his energies and concentration by comparison with the 1920s was only to be expected.[288] None the less it is striking how far he returned to his old interests. Already there had been something symbolic in his inaugural

78. Climax of the 'confessional theatre'. Rehearsing The Investigation *at the Volksbühne, 1965, with, left to right, Luigi Nono (composer), Peter Weiss (author) and, behind the seventy-one year old Piscator, Hans-Ulrich Schmückle (designer). The material of the play was drawn from the principal German war crimes trial of former members of the SS.*

speech in the new theatre,[289] where he addressed himself to Nestriepke and Tilla Durieux, who were in the audience and personified the two aspects of his original break with the Volksbühne; and indeed in the 1960s he was able to turn that body into something like the political force its founders had wished it to be. Though the new version of *Hoppla* never materialised he asked Schmückle to devise a hemisphere set *à la Rasputin* for his adaptation of the novel *Der Aufstand der Offiziere*, the last of his productions and the first time he had so deliberately echoed the old techniques. What is more, at the end of 1965 he was planning a new production of *Schweik* to follow, and was negotiating with Max Brod in Tel Aviv to settle the question of the rights; once again there would have been treadmills, though this time with photomontages by Heartfield instead of the drawings by Grosz.[290] Meanwhile he decided that he was not satisfied with the revisions to *Das politische Theater* (which were partly the result of typographic simplification but also played down the 'proletarian' emphasis and omitted the reference to his membership of the KPD). Accordingly during his last rehearsals he arranged with the East German Academy to republish the original work as it stood, together with a second volume of 'Writings' (*Schriften*) drawn from his occasional lectures, programme notes and articles.[291] That March, shortly before going into a Bavarian nursing home for a gall-bladder operation, he wrote a new postscript to the book, explaining his dissatisfaction and incidentally saying that

> I don't think I am devaluing those authors who worked with me in the 1920s if I say that the type of play I ideally had in mind at that time is only now being written by people like Hochhuth, Kipphardt and Weiss . . .[292]

Kipphardt's *Der Hund des Generals* was to be staged in the autumn, and already he planned to do another play with Weiss, whom he wanted to write a work with Jesus as the central figure. Quite unexpectedly he died before this could be properly discussed.

10. Legacy of a political theatre

Piscator's impact

Since 1966 many things have combined to give Piscator an influence which the experiences of his fifties and sixties would hardly have led him to expect. Not only has the documentary drama continued, stimulated in part by the realism of television (and indirectly of the documentary film movement by which the latter was nourished), but the 1950s dramatists to whom he took such exception have largely disappeared from the repertoire. Among leading German directors there are now few survivals from the Nazi theatre; instead many of the key positions in both East and West have fallen to such products of the Berliner Ensemble as Angelika Hurwicz, Monk, Palitzsch, Wekwerth and Besson, with Kipphardt too for a time as a controversial *Intendant*. So in the GDR we find Manfred Wekwerth, today again principal director at the Theater am Schiffbauerdamm, testifying to the impression made on him, even before its re-publication, by an old copy of Piscator's book, which he ranked with Brecht's 'Kleines Organum' as a seminal work;[293] nor is it a coincidence that he should now like working with Schmückle, who left the Volksbühne after Piscator's death. Likewise on the occasion of the East German Academy's Piscator exhibition in 1970 the theatre historian Werner Mittenzwei wrote how, on discovering Piscator's work, 'I found him just as exciting a personality as did those who had known him in the 1920s'.[294] Even more does this seem to be so in the West, where the most exciting new theatre is outspokenly political, Peter Stein's Schaubühne am Halleschen Ufer in West Berlin. Particularly given the radicalisation of student politics since the upheavals of 1968, the example of Piscator's early productions there is a powerful one. In the Federal Republic, as elsewhere in the Western world, he fits the demand for a kind of Marxism, and a Marxist approach to the arts, which shall not be identified with strict party control or the Stalin-imposed Socialist Realist aesthetic.

And yet Piscator, unlike Brecht, never seems to have produced disciples. Paradoxically it has been said that where Brecht, the writer, left his mark primarily on directors, actors and designers – i.e. on the staging of the play – Piscator, the director, left his on the drama itself; and there is something in this. One reason perhaps is that he was not a theorist and did little to set out his principles of direction for others to follow. Even *Das politische Theater*, written when he was at the height of his powers, is a disorderly collage functioning not by logical argument but by infection and illustration: it catches your imagination, or it doesn't. And indeed he could never have found it all that easy to theorise about what he did. Thus where acting was concerned he may or may not have been a good director to work under – most of the first-hand evidence seems to be that he was – but he certainly imposed no distinctive or uniform approach on his actors, nor was he ever able to build up a coherent ensemble, though it has been argued (both by Reich and by the Volksbühne dramaturg Hermann Kleinselbeck) that this is something that he would have been well fitted to do. He could perhaps have codified his demands on the author, if they had not been overshadowed by his insistence on reshaping the play (or adapting the novel) through collective discussion. So far as the more technical side of his method went, however, he did indeed set out his ideas about the use of film, but much of his staging depended on an empirical appreciation of new mechanical devices and he was anyway too anxious about the one-sided reputation which this earned him to want to write at length about it. His influence was exerted primarily by force of example, and that example was most stimulating when set against the conditions under which he had to work.

Piscator, in other words, was not a Thinker in the Theatre but a man who combined exceptional theatrical talents with a strong political drive. Foremost among those talents was his grasp of stage technology, which far excelled that of any other director of his time. Less remarkable in certain directions – such as the handling of individual actors and crowds, where Reinhardt had been pre-eminent – he was outstanding in several qualities which could have served him well in almost any field: his thoroughness, his optimism, his power to convince others, and his imagination. It was these that enabled him to bring off highly complicated operations against almost hopeless odds, and to sweep a variety of more or less temperamental collaborators into working for him. Thus Reich, who might well have resented being left to face the music in 1936, recalled thirty-odd years later that

> Working with Piscator was unusually rewarding. One's first sight of him was not deceptive: a young-looking man with strongly phosphorescent blue-green eyes and, for a city-dweller, a very fresh complexion. Piscator was normally in a good mood and at the top of his form. He was like one of those toy figures you can't knock over: accepting defeats and setbacks with defiance, and ready for a return match at any moment.[295]

Absurd as it may look in retrospect, the Engels project remains a testimony not only to his high hopes but also to his infectious advocacy of them: nobody else could have taken so improbable a scheme so far towards realisation. As Reich goes on to say,

> I had opportunities to work with Brecht and Wolf, I rehearsed with Bassermann, Moissi and Werner Krauss and spent hours in Paul Wegener's company, but none of them had so riotous and free-flowing an imagination as Piscator. He played with his ideas like a cat with a mouse, and was unable to stop once he had started.[295]

Of course such qualities needed keeping within realistic bounds if the result was not to be a disappointment which sooner or later might lead to depression. But once harnessed to a theatrical task and directed to a clear objective their impact could be stunning. Thus Friedrich Wolf to his wife at the time of *Tai Yang erwacht*:

> I have never enjoyed rehearsals more, never been so freshly confronted with the theatre; they alone have taught me an awful lot. Truly, quite new things are involved, not sensational effects but real objective necessities, new points of view to correspond to our new awareness and approach to work and life. And even if it remains at the experimental stage an experiment like this is a hundred times richer and more important than those refined trifles put on by Reinhardt and Klein with Käthe Dorsch or Werner Krauss. I'm extremely glad to have worked with Piscator . . .[296]

Whose epic theatre?

Brecht's verdict, though not precluding occasional jibes at the first Piscatorbühne's technical mishaps and capitalist finances, was on the whole even more impressive, for more than once he ranked Piscator among 'the greatest theatre men of all time'.[297] Why Piscator should have felt that Brecht failed to acknowledge his debt to him is not clear, though the fact that so much of Brecht's theoretical writing remained un-published till the 1960s may have had something to do with it. In fact if one adds up the references to Piscator in the collected Brecht edition they are only noticeably exceeded by those to Shakespeare, while in the unfinished *Messingkauf Dialogues* he made the debt explicit, calling the adaptation of the theatre to politics 'Piscator's achievement, without which [Brecht's] theatre would hardly be conceivable'.[298] As early as 1926 Brecht was seeing Piscator as a contributor to that 'great epic and documentary theatre'[299] which was on the way, and thereafter he wel-comed his 'electrification'[300] of the theatre (a significantly Leninist phrase for the technological revolution) as a means of encompassing new areas of subject-matter and making a new drama at least technically possible. In various notes he found that *Sturmflut* turned the 'background' into an active participant by means of film; that *Konjunktur* tackled a major economic theme such as he himself had tried and failed to master in *Joe P. Fleischhacker*, the play which made him a Marxist; that *Schweik* used a moving stage to keep the episodic narrative flowing; while the third company's productions showed that once the mechanical devices had been subdued 'a lovely simplicity'[301] could infect the acting. To him, as to Reich, Piscator was a kind of de facto dramatist, 'inspiring scenes and projects by other writers, supplying them with documents and scenic performances, and making a montage of them'.[302] But because he said so little about the 'epic theatre', confining his references mainly to Paquet's *Fahnen* as interpreted by Lania and Alfred Döblin,[303] Brecht was right enough to recognise him as its 'master builder' while making clear that 'the actual theory of the non-Aristotelian theatre' was to be attributed rather to himself.[304]

However, it is often the people who talk most about an idea who become most commonly associated with it, and so it is not surprising that Brecht should in many eyes have appeared to be the epic theatre's sole originator. This does not seem particularly to have disturbed Piscator so long as he was the more famous director of the two, and even later he normally respected their alliance in public. In 1936 they tentatively planned some joint theoretical statements to set against the spread of the Stanislavsky method:[305] possibly an illustrated brochure, as suggested by Brecht (later to be treated by Piscator as an unfulfilled project for a collaborative book). After the Second World War however there are numerous notes or diary entries which show Piscator's growing resentment of the younger man's reputation for originality, starting with the shrewd (but undated) comment that

> Whenever I read Brecht's notes to his plays, I notice that the examples chosen by him correspond much more to the plays directed by me than to those authored by him.[306]

Brecht's half-curtain then is copied from Piscator's projection screens, and his use of the revolve an imitation of the treadmill stage. In 1955 his second production of *Mutter Courage* is 'Schweik's anabasis, dragged out interminably',[307] while its success in Paris prompts the reflection that Brecht 'has taken over my legacy – by not entirely fair means'.[308]

More constructively, Piscator at various times addressed himself to the problem of how his own and Brecht's conceptions of epic theatre differed, something that had been brought home to him by their disagreement of 1945 over *The Private Life of the Master Race*. This sequence of realistic sketches he then termed 'un-epic, disconnected, disunified – a series of coincidental scenes written one after another and laid side by side',[309] even though such a structure was exactly what 'epic' meant to Brecht. Similarly a note of 1955:

> B.'s starting point is episodic succession.
> P.'s is political fatality.
> B. demonstrates it in miniature.
> P. on the big scale. I wanted to comprehend fate as a *whole*, showing how it is made by men and then spreads beyond them. (Hence the machinery, film etc.)[310]

He rejected Brecht's later doctrine of alienation, which he regarded mainly as an excuse for his failure to deal directly with actual political issues; thus again

> B. wants a parable.
> P. wants the essence.

Like many people, he seems not entirely to have grasped what Brecht meant by the new term, but as to its application to acting he compromised, arguing that the actor needs both emotion (à la Stanislavsky) and reason (à la Brecht) 'without making the usual sharp distinction between the two'[311] – a position in fact much like Brecht's own in the 1950s.

Jealousies apart (and it should perhaps be noted how one-sided they were) the two men were theoretically much closer to one another than to anybody else; thus the excerpt on p. 107 from Piscator's 'Rechenschaft' statement of 1929 seems to match Brecht's contemporary table showing the differences between epic and dramatic theatre, while his diary note of 1955 'I believe in *Reason*'[312] reiterates their common creed. That being so it may seem strange that despite all their recurrent plans for collaboration Piscator never directed a single Brecht play until after Brecht's death (when he staged *Mutter Courage* at Kassel). If this was partly because the writer was none too confident of Piscator's ability to realise his works as he wanted (actually barring their use by the Dramatic Workshop in 1948, according to Eric Bentley),[313] it was also due to the fact that Piscator, while acknowledging their merits in principle, found them at bottom to be uncongenial. In the 1930s, according to Reich, he dismissed them 'as purely intellectual constructions . . . he got no fun out of them';[314] then at the end of Brecht's life he seemed to veer round and attack him (as also Eisenstein) for being ultimately an aesthete who fell short in *Bekenntnis*.[315] 'Brecht is my brother', he told a French interviewer at the time of the Paris *War and Peace*,

> but our views of totality differ: Brecht unveils significant details of human life while I attempt to give a conspectus of political matters as a whole. In a sense you can say that his Mother Courage is a timeless figure. I'd have tried to portray her more historically by showing the Thirty Years' War.[316]

Likewise *Der Kaukasische Kreidekreis* in Brecht's production struck him as confusing, artificial and unrealistic; in his diary he rejected the over-operatic music, the eclectic influences and the use of masks, refusing to accept Brecht's assumption that the rich are automatically bad and the poor good.[317] Behind this incompatibility lay perhaps their very real difference in temperament: the one man choosing the plebeian stance, the other the patrician; the one unkempt, the other elegant; the one a sardonic debunker, the other an optimist with an under-developed sense of the ridiculous. And so when Brecht died in August 1956 and the East German government invited Piscator to the memorial ceremony, he hesitated in terms which summarise their ambiguous relationship before coming down on the right and generous side:

shall I
brother in spirit
gave help none the less

he stood by the cause
a great poet
simple, beautiful, best culture of
   language
discovered 'epic theatre'

but he was able to develop the
   theory and write plays
then he was the greater one after
   all
he was the only man who, through
   his art, managed to represent
   Germany during its division.
   he has become influential across
   all borders. his plays are also
   performed in the West – one
   can only appreciate him.[318]

shall I not
not always a good one
when I was unsuccessful
when I had success he was far away
but never became a party member
sceptical and romantic

the word – after he saw its funda-
   mental application in my
   theatre

too formal

Sense and nonsense of the political theatre

If Brecht's ideas of epic theatre were essentially political (being grounded
in a wish to look critically and instructively at the world's complex
mechanisms), in Piscator's case all such notions were subordinate to the
political theatre. Here there is no doubt about his proprietorial rights in
the expression, which is one that even now has the power to stimulate
new generations of directors, actors, writers and those more generally
interested in the relationship between society and the arts. Over the
years its significance for Piscator may have changed, first the Communist
Party and then the Marxist ideology losing the dominant roles originally
allotted them, till the term itself fell in abeyance (much as did 'epic
theatre' with Brecht, if for quite different reasons), to be revived in
modified form some twenty years later. But what it effectively meant was
that the theatre must deal with the great political themes most relevant
to its time – i.e. with social and economic revolution in the 1920s, with

overcoming the Nazi past in the 1950s and 60s, and with combating militarism always – and do so in such a way as to expound the issues in depth, and set the audience debating. Using every technical resource to increase that depth and to clarify the historico-economic connections, it must confront such topical problems directly, as Brecht for one generally did not; art must be subordinate to the main aim, and would itself learn in the process.

What then was the aim to be? Originally Piscator's motive force was revolutionary, arising from his war experiences and nourished by the Russian and (to some extent) Hungarian examples; 'when I became a Marxist', as he paradoxically put it, 'I had no notion of Marx'.[319] From this derived an emotional drive which lasted right through the 1920s, to be revived (perhaps a little too deliberately) in his Soviet film. Gradually however a more objective, intellectualised form of Marxist analysis took over, starting with *Trotz Alledem!* in 1924 and gaining ground as he acquired better informed advisers (often from outside the theatre) and new technical aids. It tended indeed to be too objective for the party, who cared more about short-term propaganda and the fluctuating interests of the Soviet Union, but once he had broken away from the Volksbühne Piscator accepted this and felt that it was legitimate to slant the evidence in the communist cause. If he had not he could never have worked in the USSR in the 1930s; however after that experience the drive slackened in favour of rather more abstract ideals: tolerance, for instance, as seen in *Nathan der Weise*, or what he termed 'the right to build a country free together'.[320] Though it remained true that 'the main thing is always the play's message',[321] there is something almost apologetic in his note of 1955 to the effect that:

> Once I believed commitment was truth: the others were wrong and my side was right. Today one should at least be able to demand the right to say 'truth is neutral'.[322]

If his concern with the post-war German conscience gave him a fresh impetus in his last years it lacked the old force; it was not he who took the lead this time but the writers; such drive as he brought to the new German theatre was largely that of his earlier productions.

In Piscator's conception of the political theatre the theatre in question was always tacitly assumed to be something like the Volksbühne, with its roots in the popular culture movement of the 1880s and 90s. And this at once distinguished him from the more practical Marxists of the Weimar Republic, for whom the only theatre of political significance to the proletariat was to be found among the small agit-prop groups. For of course what should by rights lead the workers to organise and take action is not what any play says but the conditions of their daily life, even if a few militant songs and sketches can be as effective as oratory in crystallising their conclusions. As for the large traditional theatres, unless one has nothing to escape from, they are there primarily for escapism, which to the bored or exhausted is a simple human necessity even if it can be of a more or a less improving kind. It was on his failure to accept such humdrum functions that Piscator's political theatre first foundered, for it was essentially a bourgeois theatre dependent on attracting an experiment-conscious bourgeois audience, even though the bourgeoisie was what it was out to overthrow. Grosz, who was more cynical and saw such anomalies much more clearly, expressed it in a short exchange in his autobiography, where Piscator is depicted talking to one of his rich backers:

> 'Hah, Erwin, insult me, will you? Say something really foul.'
> 'You unscrupulous capitalist.'
> 'Hah, again. Hah, isn't that charming? Erwin, here's a blank cheque. Any amount, any amount. . . .'
> 'Mud in your eye, Mr Grosz, and here's to the Decline of the West. . . .'

As Piscator even then realised, 'a revolutionary theatre without its liveliest element, a revolutionary audience, is a nonsense on which no one ought to embark'.[323] Revolutionary sentiment among the actors and stagehands, moreover, can be a two-edged weapon, to say the least. Piscator was not happy when a virtual *putsch* by his actors deposed him from the third Piscatorbühne, while neither in Germany nor in America was he enthusiastic about the theatre unions, whose militancy spoilt his plans for *Singing Jailbirds* just as their rigidity destroyed the Studio Theatre.

Brecht, that great puncturer of other people's inflations, diagnosed the problem in a short note of the late 1920s characterising the Piscatorbühne:

> Not politics trying to take over the theatre, but the theatre politics. Currently there is a tendency to see Piscator's attempt to revitalise the theatre as a revolutionary one. In fact it is revolutionary with respect neither to productivity nor to politics, respect to theatre.[324]

For the politicians are no more anxious than are the workers to have theatre depart from its traditional role, and for anyone who really wishes to influence politics there are plenty of better means. But even if the political theatre is thus politically much less significant than television or radio, it none the less represents an important extension of the theatre, by enabling it to handle fresh subjects, by driving it to devise fresh methods and techniques, and last but not least by giving its members a rewarding and productive sense that they are neither hired entertainers nor devotees of a private cult. Faced with industrial society's assumption that the theatre exists for distraction, education or national prestige (with which is incorporated the tourist business), theatre people need a spirit of inquiry, of involvement in outside affairs, and a sense of purpose. And these things Piscator could give.

They are always given at a price, however, and the value of the historical background in the present case is that it allows us to judge what the price may be. For the Weimar Republic and its aftermath were not only a fertile ground for politically-inspired art of all kinds, but also a terribly strenuous testing-ground for it and the people who practised it. Piscator himself saw clearly enough how ineffective the political theatre had been in stopping the Nazis from coming to power in 1933, but he never asked how far it, together with its incidental splitting of the Volksbühne movement, had helped in that disintegration of the Left which allowed the great German tragedy to develop unchecked. This is one factor which has to be borne in mind by anybody interested in political art today; it must not be used to divide potential allies who may one day need to join forces against another major evil. Nor can it be discussed at all constructively without some awareness of the personal and artistic cost to the people who practised it in Piscator's time. First the Nazi repression cut the soil from under their feet; then the political nature of their commitment laid them open to attack in the Soviet Union, the very country which had in many cases been their example; then if they went West they risked being victimised as Reds, and soon found themselves in the hateful position of 'enemy aliens' in a war against their own compatriots; finally they returned (if they survived all this) to a divided country neither of whose conflicting halves corresponded to the ideals by which they themselves had been guided. Admittedly there were one or two exceptional people who continued to work along their own lines despite all, and somehow kept their personalities intact. But for those who had been most deeply committed to politics – Piscator in the theatre, Grosz in art and Eisler in music – sooner or later uneasy compromises and renunciations were unavoidable, and in the wear and tear which such adjustments involved their talents, like their energies, suffered.

Piscator worked in the theatre at a crucial time and place, when the tensions of our time were at their strongest, and went on to apply his new methods in a variety of quite different political climates and systems. Brilliant as were his early achievements, we have seen that what came later might be different, inappropriate or unrealistic. The danger for the present day is to base our expectations of the political theatre only on the former, without taking their sequel into account or asking how far its flaws were already implied in his initial approach. If we are to have a politically committed art of any but the most general kind it must be tough and sophisticated enough to face the problems which he posed. Otherwise it might be better not pursued.

Notes

———◆———

1. Grosz 'Randzeichnungen zum Thema' in *Blätter der Piscatorbühne* no. 2 (the programme for *Schweik*). 'Marginal Notes on the subject' in the Arts Council's *Erwin Piscator* catalogue, p. 33.

2. Wieland Herzfelde: *John Heartfield*. Verlag der Kunst, Dresden, second edition 1971.

3. Which Piscator saw. See his interview with Gerd Semmer of 10 June 1959, transcript in the West Berlin Academy headed 'Deutsche und russische Theaterleute'.

4. Letter in the West Berlin Academy.

5. Piscator: *Schriften 2*, p. 239.

6. Piscator: *Das politische Theater*, p. 46. (All page references to *Das p.T.* are to the 1929 edition, reproduced in his *Schriften 1*, 1968.)

7. Reich: *Im Wettlauf mit der Zeit*, Henschel, East Berlin 1970, p. 201.

8. 'Über Grundlagen und Aufgaben des proletarischen Theaters' in *Der Gegner* (1920–21) no. 4, pp. 90–93, reprinted in *Schriften 2*, pp. 9–12.

9. *Das p.T.*, press handout cited on p. 35.

10. *Die Rote Fahne* of Oct. 1920, cited in Fähnders and Rector: *Literatur in Klassenkampf*, Hanser, Munich 1971, pp. 196–9.

11. 'Über die Aufgaben der Arbeiterbühne.' Message to the 10th Bundestag of the DATB, 8–9 April 1928, reprinted in *Schriften 2*, p. 44.

12. *Das p.T.*, p. 38.

13. A drawing is (poorly) reproduced on p. 41 of *Das p.T.*

14. *Das p.T.*, p. 39.

15. Report by K.G., reprinted in Ludwig Hoffmann and Daniel Hoffmann-Ostwald: *Deutsches Arbeitertheater*, Henschel, East Berlin, second edition 1971, Vol. 1, p. 160.

16. Programme in *Das p.T.*, pp. 66–7. Amplified in Hoffmann: *Deutsches Arbeitertheater*, Vol. 1, pp. 170–79.

17. Otto Steinicke in *Die Rote Fahne*, 14 July 1925, reprinted in Hoffmann:

Deutsches Arbeitertheater, Vol. 1, pp. 181–2 and Günther Rühle: *Theater für die Republik*, Fischer, Frankfurt 1967, pp. 646–9.

18. Fritz Engel in *Berliner Tageblatt*, 13 July 1925. Reprinted in G. Rühle, pp. 649–50.

19. So Max Osborn alleged in his review in *Berliner Morgenpost*, 28 May 1924, reprinted in G. Rühle, pp. 541–2.

20. Albert Venohr, in conversation, 1973.

21. *Leipziger Tageblatt*, 5 June 1924, cited in *Das p.T.*, p. 58. The whole article is reprinted in Döblin's *Griffe ins Leben*, Berliner Theaterberichte, Henschel, E. Berlin 1974, p. 250 ff. See also Ulrich Weisstein's account of play and production in Sigrid Bauschinger *et al.* (eds.): *Amerika in der deutschen Literatur*, Reclam, Stuttgart (?1975), p. 272 ff.

22. See note 18 above.

23. *Schriften* 2, p. 57.

24. Knellessen, cited by Weisstein (as in 21).

25. *Arbeiterzeitung*, Vienna, 2 June 1924, cited in *Das p.T.*, p. 57.

26. See Babette Gross: *Willi Muenzenberg*, DVA, Stuttgart, 1967, pp. 184–5. There are also accounts suggesting that Fairbanks and Pickford saw the film in Moscow.

27. 'Piscator über die Regie', 1926, reproduced in *Schriften* 2, p. 15.

28. In *Berliner Börsen-Courier*, 22–3 February 1926, reprinted in G. Rühle, p. 694.

29. According to Albert Venohr, in conversation 1973.

30. For details of Piscator's adaptation and interpretation see Hugh Rorrison: 'Piscator directs Schiller's "Die Räuber" ' in Margret Dietrich: *Regie in Dokumentation, Forschung und Lehre*, Otto Müller, Salzburg 1975, p. 168 ff.

31. Reproduced in *Das p.T.*, p. 85.

32. Cited in *Das p.T.*, p. 102.

33. Maria Ley-Piscator: *The Piscator Experiment*, James H. Heineman Inc., New York 1967, p. 74.

34. Toller 'Berlin 1919' in *Volksbühne*, Berlin, 1 March 1927. In all fifteen scenes were completed.

35. Herbert Ihering (or Jhering): *Reinhardt, Jessner, Piscator oder Klassikertod?*, Rowohlt, Berlin 1929.

36. *Das p.T.*, pp. 104–5.

37. 'Bühnen der Gegenwart und Zukunft' in *Die Rote Fahne*, 1 January 1928, reprinted in *Schriften* 2, pp. 32–7. Cited from section headed 'Das politische Theater'.

38. Bernhard Reich: *Wettlauf mit der Zeit*, Henschel, East Berlin 1970, p. 203.

39. The letter is in the West Berlin Academy.

40. In *Das p.T.*, p. 123.

41. 'Wieder Piscatorbühne!' in *Die junge Volksbühne*, Berlin, no. 1 (1929). Reprinted in *Schriften* 2, p. 47.

42. *Das p.T.*, p. 154.

43. See Hans Reimann: *Mein blaues Wunder*, List, Munich 1959, p. 409 ff.

44. Reproduced in *Das p.T.*, p. 127.

45. In Weisenborn: *Der gespaltene Horizont*, Desch, Munich 1964, p. 159.

46. Cited in G. Rühle: *Zeit und Theater 2*, Propyläen, West Berlin 1972, p. 800.

47. *Das Programm der Piscatorbühne*, no. 1, 1927.

48. e.g. *Neue Freie Presse*, Vienna, 8 June 1928.

49. From Diary 5 (Autumn 1952) in West Berlin Academy.

50. Fritz Sternberg: *Der Dichter und die Ratio*, Sachse und Pohl, Göttingen 1963, pp. 33–6.

51. Brecht: *Ges. Werke. Schriften zum Theater 2*, Suhrkamp, Frankfurt 1967, pp. 272–92.

52. In *Die Junge Volksbühne*, Berlin, no. 5, reprinted in *Das p.T.*, pp. 250–51.

53. 'Rechenschaft', speech held at the former Herrenhaus, Berlin, on 25 March 1929. Extract in *Schriften 2*, pp. 54–5.

54. See Jung's account in his *Der Weg nach Unten*, Luchterhand, Neuwied 1961, pp. 319–21.

55. Date from G. Rühle. The programme gives September 3rd.

56. According to G. Rühle's note, *Zeit und Theater 2*, pp. 805–6.

57. Letter Gasbarra–Piscator in West Berlin Academy.

58. Jung: *Der Weg nach Unten*, p. 326.

59. Reports in *Die Rote Fahne*, 9 and 18 July 1930.

60. See the account in Harry Wilde: *Theodor Plivier*, Desch, Munich 1965, pp. 236–43.

61. Jung: *Der Weg nach Unten*, p. 326.

62. Diary 17 (1957) p. 182, in the West Berlin Academy. He there calls it 'mein Tiefstand'.

63. Albert Venohr in West Berlin has the relevant ledgers.

64. Act 2, scene 1. Kiepenheuer edition of 1927, p. 58.

65. 'Hoppla, wir leben' or 'In diesem Hotel zur Erde'. Printed in G. Rühle: *Zeit und Theater 2*, pp. 787–90.

66. Monty Jacobs in the *Vossische Zeitung*, Berlin, 5 September 1927, quoted in G. Rühle: *Theater für die Republik*, p. 794.

67. Ihering, in *Berliner Börsen-Courier*, 5 September 1927, reprinted in G. Rühle: *Zeit und Theater*, p. 798.

68. Bertolt Brecht's *Arbeitsjournal*, Suhrkamp, Frankfurt 1972, entry for 26 June 1943.

69. The only known copies are in the Brecht-Archive in East Berlin. It is not clear how far this script, which is printed in Herbert Knust's 'Materialien' volume to the Brecht *Schweyk*, is as actually performed.

70. For the use of film see Knust's notes to the catalogue *Theatrical Drawings and Watercolors by George Grosz*, Busch–Reisinger Museum, Harvard 1973. This reproduces many of the drawings (which differ from the better-

known lithographed versions) and cites Grosz's pencilled animation instructions.

71. 'Muschel von Margate'. Text in the programme (*Blätter der Piscatorbühne* no. 3, 1928).

72. S. Fischer, Berlin, 1929, reprinted in G. Rühle's *Zeit und Theater 2*, whose notes, pp. 803–9, describe the circumstances of its production.

73. Moholy's scene-by-scene designs are in the Cologne University Theatre Museum at Porz-Wahn.

74. Reich mentions the four screens in his *Wettlauf mit der Zeit*, p. 210.

75. Cited in G. Rühle: *Theater für die Republik*.

76. See the published text of the play (Dietz, Berlin 1930), which includes the 'Alterations for the Piscator-Bühne' in smaller type.

77. In *8-Uhr Abendblatt*, Berlin, 4 April 1930, cited in C. D. Innes: *Erwin Piscator's Political Theatre*, CUP 1972, p. 137.

78. See Harry Wilde: *Theodor Plivier*, pp. 234–42.

79. According to Herbert Ihering's review, reprinted in his *Von Reinhardt bis Brecht*, Rowohlt 1967, p. 318.

80. In the programme of *Mond nach Links* (*Blätter der Piscatorbühne*).

81. According to Innes, p. 117.

82. *Berliner Börsen-Courier*, 16 January 1931, cited in G. Rühle: *Theater für die Republik*, pp. 1067–8.

83. *Berliner Tageblatt*, 17 January 1931, cited in G. Rühle, p. 1063.

84. 'Rechenschaft', from a speech of 25 March 1929, in *Schriften 2*, p. 50.

85. 'Das Theater von Morgen' in *Berliner Börsen-Courier*, 31 March 1929. *Schriften 2*, p. 48.

86. 'Bühne der Gegenwart und Zukunft' in *Die Rote Fahne*, 1 January 1928. *Schriften 2*, p. 34.

87. Arts Council catalogue: *Erwin Piscator*, p. 44.

88. Given in *Das p.T.*, pp. 106–7.

89. p. 149. This is modified in the revised edition of 1963, p. 149.

90. Kiepenheuer, Berlin 1930, pp. 293–4.

91. *Brecht on Theatre*, Methuen, London 1964, p. 30.

92. See letter Brecht–Piscator of 1927, Brecht-Archive no. 219/12.

93. Brecht-Archive no. 219/11.

94. 'Das ABC des Theaters', radio discussion with Ihering on 22 April 1929. *Schriften 2*, p. 62.

95. Das Programm der Piscatorbühne no. 1.

96. Fr. Kranich: *Bühnentechnik der Gegenwart*, Vol. 2, Oldenbourg, Munich 1932, pp. 294–5.

97. Kranich, Vol. 1, 1929, p. 268.

98. 'Paquets Sturmflut in der Berliner Volksbühne' in *Der neue Weg*, Berlin, I, 3 (1926), pp. 1–2. *Schriften 2*, p. 18.

99. Kranich, Vol. 2, p. 132.

100. *Das p.T.*, p. 171.
101. *Das p.T.*, p. 193.
102. Cited in *Das p.T.*, pp. 136–9.
103. Walter Gropius: *Theaterbau* (IV Convegno 'Volta', Rome 3–14 October 1934), Reale Accademia d'Italia, Rome 1934, p. 7.
104. Reproduced in Gropius: *Theaterbau*.
105. Brecht, interviewed in *Exstrabladet*, Copenhagen, 20 March 1934. Reprinted in *Brecht on Theatre*, p. 69.
106. 'Das politische Theater' in *Der neue Bücherschau*, Berlin, 7 Jahr, 5 Folge no. 4, pp. 168–71. *Schriften 2*, p. 29. Translation in Arts Council catalogue, pp. 44–7.
107. Cited in 'Meyerhold à Paris' by Stefan Priacel in *Monde*, Paris, 7 July 1928. (Note that this was Barbusse's review, not *Le Monde* the daily paper.)
108. Sternberg: *Der Dichter und die Ratio*, Sachse & Pohl, Göttingen, p. 33. He dates this episode 1932, but it probably occurred in 1929.
109. Letter for Piscator's sixtieth birthday (17 December 1953) in West Berlin Academy.
110. 'Protokoll der Gründungsversammlung des Studios am 16 Oktober 1927' in *Das p.T.*, p. 145.
111. Jung: *Der Weg nach Unten*, p. 317.
112. *Blätter der Piscatorbühne Kollektiv*, no. 8, Berlin, April 1930, p. 12.
113. See note 102 above.
114. *Das p.T.*, p. 211.
115. Postscript to the Soviet edition of *Das p.T.* (Moscow 1934) dated May 1933. In *Schriften 2*, p. 106.
116. See note 102. Arts Council catalogue, p. 47.
117. *Das p.T.*, p. 245.
118. Reich: *Im Wettlauf mit der Zeit*, p. 204.
119. Brecht: *Ges. Werke Gedichte*, Suhrkamp, Frankfurt 1967, p. 154. Trans. in *Poems 1913–1956*, Eyre Methuen, London 1976, p. 112. The poem is dated by the Brecht-Archive 'c. 1925'.
120. Reich, p. 217.
121. 'Der Durchbruch das politischen Theaters' in *Die Linkskurve*, Berlin, 2, 12 (1930), pp. 10–11. *Schriften 2*, p. 77.
122. 'Die Piscator-Bühne' in the September 1929 issue (p. 4 f.) attacked him for the content of the plays performed by his company; 'Zwei Theaterabende' the next month (p. 17) condemned *Der Kaufmann von Berlin* and contrasted Piscator unfavourably with the Gruppe junger Schauspieler; then in the January 1930 issue (p. 19 f.) Berta Lask in a review dismissed his book as 'appallingly subjective and individualistic'.
123. See Ludwig Hoffmann's note in *Schriften 2*, p. 368.
124. Jung: *Der Weg nach Unten*, p. 315.
125. Diary 1 (1951–2) in West Berlin Academy.

126. See *Das p.T.*, illustration opposite p. 145. Arts Council catalogue, opposite p. 40.
127. Interview with Lotte Schwarz in *Moskauer Rundschau*, 5 October 1930. *Schriften 2*, pp. 75–6.
128. Priacel: 'Meyerhold à Paris'. See note 107 above.
129. According to Albert Venohr, in conversation, 1973.
130. Arts Council catalogue, p. 37.
131. Asja Lacis: *Revolutionär in Beruf*, Rogner und Bernhard, Munich 1971, pp. 74–6.
132. See Erwin Sinko: *Roman eines Romans*, Wissenschaft und Politik, Cologne, p. 271.
133. Balázs: 'Piscator's First Film' in *New Theatre*, New York, December 1934, p. 14. Piscator himself was on the board of this journal.
134. Letter to Brecht of 1 August 1933. Brecht-Archive no. 477/115.
135. *Im Wettlauf mit der Zeit*, p. 337.
136. Julius Hay: *Geboren 1900*, Wegner, Reinbek 1971, pp. 195–202 and 207–9.
137. Undated letter from Brecht, c. July 1936. Brecht-Archive no. 2155/08.
138. *Im Wettlauf mit der Zeit*, pp. 337–9, 346–8. Piscator's recollection in his diary for 1956 is different (Diary 15, p. 155 in the West Berlin Academy). He thinks the visit to Kaganovitch had to do with the completion of *Aufstand der Fischer*, though he recalls Reich acting as his interpreter.
139. *In Die Welt am Abend*, Berlin (a Muenzenberg paper), 17 December 1932. Reprinted in *Schriften 2*, pp. 89–92.
140. 'Theater und Kino' in *Das internationale Theater*, Moscow 1 (1933) no. 3. *Schriften 2*, p. 95.
141. In the Brecht-Archive (no. 331/05–09).
142. Ihering article of 23 June 1931, reprinted in *Von Reinhardt bis Brecht*, p. 340. See also p. 335.
143. *Politicheskii Teatr*, Moscow 1934.
144. 'Euer Vorsprung muss sich vergrössern' in *Deutsche Zentral-Zeitung*, Moscow, 17 August 1934. Reprinted in *Schriften 2*, pp. 116–17.
145. *Im Wettlauf mit der Zeit*, p. 345.
146. 'Über die Lehren der Vergangenheit und die Aufgaben der Zukunft' in *Das internationale Theater*, Moscow, 2 (1934), nos. 5–6, pp. 3–7. *Schriften 2* p. 119.
147. Letters to Brecht of 8 and 27 January 1935. Brecht-Archive numbers 477/83 and 477/114.
148. Brecht: 'Alienation Effects in Chinese Acting'. In *Brecht on Theatre*, p. 91 ff.
149. *Im Wettlauf mit der Zeit*, p. 345.
150. Agreement of 17 April 1932. Copy in the Brecht-Archive.
151. See Piscator's letters to Brecht of 27 August 1933 and 21 December 1934. Brecht-Archive numbers 477/101 and 477/118–19.

152. Letter Piscator–Brecht of 9 September 1935 (Brecht-Archive no. 477/100) and letter Brecht–Piscator of 25 September (ditto no. 477/99).
153. *Geboren 1900*, pp. 195–202.
154. Ibid., p. 198.
155. *Im Wettlauf mit der Zeit*, pp. 349–51.
156. See Piscator's letters of 3 July 1936 to Brecht and Helene Weigel (Brecht-Archive number 477/111–12). Brecht's undated response (ditto 2155/09–09), and the letter from him tentatively dated ?July 1936 in the Morris Library at Carbondale.
157. According to Curt Trepte, in conversation in East Berlin, 1973.
158. *Im Wettlauf mit der Zeit*, p. 350.
159. Harry Wilde: *Theodor Plivier*, p. 355.
160. Letter to Otto Wallburg, in Morris Library, Carbondale.
161. Telegram in the Morris Library, reproduced on p. 141.
162. Undated letter from Reich in Morris Library, provisionally dated 27 September.
163. See Hermann Haarmann *et al.*: *Das 'Engels' Projekt*, Georg Heinz, Worms 1975, p. 96.
164. Wilde: *Theodor Plivier*, p. 367.
165. *Im Wettlauf mit der Zeit*, p. 315.
166. See Harry Wilde's account in *Theodor Plivier*, p. 359 ff.
167. Letter to Brecht 9 September 1935, Brecht's reply 25 September. Brecht-Archive numbers 477/100 and 99 respectively.
168. Letter: Eisler–Piscator 2 August 1936 in Morris Library, Carbondale.
169. Piscator to Julia Annenkova, 14 September 1936, letter in the Morris Library.
170. Also in the Morris Library.
171. Brecht-Archive number 477/104–5.
172. Letter in the Morris Library.
173. Ditto.
174. Dated 22 July 1936: in West Berlin Academy.
175. Letter of 1 December 1936, in the Morris Library.
176. Letter to Comrade Babitzky, of 13 January 1937, in Morris Library.
177. Letter to Friedrich Wolf, in the latter's *Briefwechsel*, Aufbau, East Berlin 1968.
178. Clurman: *The Fervent Years*, Dobson, London 1946, pp. 174–6.
179. Telegram of 13 October 1936 from Helen Airoff, in Morris Library.
180. *Le Théâtre au dix-huitième siècle* and *Les Gueux chez Victor Hugo*, both published by Droz, Paris, 1934.
181. Draft lease agreement dated 1 March 1937 in Morris Library.
182. Part-agreement of 27 January 1937 in Morris Library.
183. Contract Piscator–Jacobi dated 26 February 1937 in Morris Library.
184. Agreement of 4 April 1937 in Morris Library.

185. For the *Chatterley* project see files 31/97 and 31/98 in the Morris Library.

186. Letter to Brecht 26 October 1936 (original in Brecht-Archive).

187. Pencil note by Brecht on a letter of 18 January 1937 from Helene Weigel (Morris Library).

188. See undated memorandum 'Welche Fragen sind prinzipiell über den Schweik-Film zu klaeren?' (Morris Library).

189. Undated letter from Brecht (about 10 June 1937) in Morris Library.

190. Letter to Cassou of 9 September 1937 (Morris Library).

191. Ditto 20 November 1937 (ditto).

192. Letter from Colin, 15 December 1937 (Morris Library).

193. Contracts of 2 and 8 June 1938 in Morris Library.

194. Letter from Dukes of 28 November 1938 in Morris Library.

195. Preminger to Miller 21 September 1938 in Morris Library.

196. Letter: Olivier to Miller 11 November 1938 in Morris Library.

197. Undated letter from Granach (?10 May 1939) in the West Berlin Academy.

198. Letter: Maria Piscator to Milton Diamond, 9 December 1938, in Morris Library.

199. On the back of a letter of 18 January 1937 in Morris Library.

200. Cited in letter from Gasbarra dated September 1946 in West Berlin Academy.

201. 'Der Schrei nach der Kunst' unpublished typescript of May 1939, in West Berlin Academy.

202. In *Tomorrow*, Vol. 1 (1942) no. 14, pp. 1–6.

203. *Théâtre Populaire*, Paris, no. 53 (1964), p. 6.

204. Draft contract dated 29 January 1939, in Morris Library.

205. Letter to Johann Schmidt of 9 February 1939 in Morris Library.

206. 'The American Theatre. A Note or two on Playwrights. The Box Office and the Ideal.' *New York Times*, 21 January 1940.

207. Letter: Piscator–Brecht 3 March 1939 (Brecht-Archive no. 911/71–86): 'Grosz chucked me out of his house the first night because I still believe in progress and he doesn't.'

208. Letters to Elmer Rice and Klaus Mann, 17 April 1940 in Morris Library. Neither contributed.

209. See letters: Brecht–Piscator of 8 March 1939 (above), 17 May 1940 and undated (c. 5 August 1941) in the Morris Library.

210. Dramatic Workshop catalogue, cited in Maria Ley–Piscator: *The Piscator Experiment*, p. 104.

211. 'Zur Berufsausbildung des Schauspielers'. Lecture to the Third Congress of the ITI at Essen, published in *Die deutsche Bühne*, Darmstadt, no. 10, 1965.

212. Cited in *The Piscator Experiment*, p. 150.

213. *The Piscator Experiment*, p. 162.

214. John Gassner: *The Theatre in Our Times*, Crown Publishers, New York 1954, p. 95n.

215. See letters: Brecht–Piscator undated, *c.* 14 September 1941 (Morris Library) and Piscator–Brecht 15 April 1943 (Brecht-Archive no. 1185/11).
216. See letter: Hays–Piscator 23 September 1941 in Morris Library.
217. *The Piscator Experiment*, p. 193.
218. Letter to Mordecai Gorelik 21 January 1943 in Morris Library. See also Diary 15, p. 99 (in West Berlin Academy), which suggests that Brecht disliked Piscator's conception of the staging.
219. Contracts with Ann Elmo, Hays's agent, and with Brecht 23 April 1943, in Morris Library. The question of Brecht's relationship with Piscator, as revealed by the Carbondale papers, is discussed at greater length in my article 'Brecht and Piscator' in *IcarbS*, Carbondale, Vol. I, no. 2.
220. Piscator to Alvin Johnson, 1 December 1942 (Morris Library).
221. Letter from Johnson, 7 February 1944 in Morris Library.
222. Report on Survey of the Dramatic Workshop, January 1945, by Mr Rubinow, in Morris Library.
223. In *New Yorker Staatszeitung*, 25 November 1945.
224. *The Theatre in Our Times*, p. 15.
225. Letter: Paul Ransom–H. S. Hunnewell 8 May 1949 (in Morris Library) gives summary of student figures, repertory subscriptions and income for period 1944/45 to 1948/49. This was a letter designed to impress.
226. See letters from B. J. Hovde, 14 July and 26 October 1948 and from Alvin Johnson, 3 and 17 December, all in Morris Library.
227. Box 31/114 at Morris Library.
228. Letter to Brecht, 29 May 1945 in Morris Library.
229. *Bertolt Brecht Arbeitsjournal*, entry for June–mid-July 1945. For Viertel's previous production concept see Viertel: *Schriften zum Theater*, Kösel-Verlag, Munich 1970, pp. 216–21.
230. Piscator to Askin, 2 July 1945 in Morris Library.
231. Brecht to Piscator, February 1947 in West Berlin Academy.
232. Ditto, March 1947, ditto.
233. Piscator to Brecht, 29 March 1947, ditto.
234. Letters: Wolf–Piscator of 4 June 1946 and 17 March 1947 in West Berlin Academy. Latter printed in Wolf, *Briefe*, p. 223.
235. Undated letter to Wolf, not completed, in West Berlin Academy. Wolf letter of 23 May 1947 in his *Briefe*, p. 234.
236. Wolf to Piscator, 9 June 1948, in West Berlin Academy.
237. Brecht–Piscator, 9 February 1949, in West Berlin Academy.
238. Brecht–Piscator, letter of March 1949 in West Berlin Academy.
239. Wolf–Piscator, 2 February 1949, West Berlin Academy.
240. Undated draft letter to Wolf (West Berlin Academy).
241. Ditto, Brecht (ditto).
242. 'Zur Berufsausbildung des Schauspielers', *Die deutsche Bühne*, 10, p. 189.
243. Listed in *The Piscator Experiment*, pp. 99–100.

244. See Diary 14, p. 53 and diary for December 1955, in West Berlin Academy.

245. *The Piscator Experiment*, pp. 236-7.

246. Letter: Malina–Piscator, 12 June 1947, Morris Library.

247. Ron Offen: *Brando*, Henry Regnery Co., Chicago 1973, p. 26.

248. Lee Strasberg in conversation, New York, 1974.

249. *Daily Worker*, New York, 12 February 1944.

250. Note 'Abflug von Amerika' in West Berlin Academy.

251. Postscript to *Schriften 2*, p. 360.

252. See Diary 17 for 28 September 1957 in West Berlin Academy.

253. Diary 9, 5 September 1953, in West Berlin Academy.

254. See the account of this production in Klaus Schulz's thesis *Das 'politische Theater' Erwin Piscators*, Göttingen 1956, pp. 173-6.

255. Diary 16 for 3 and 5 May 1956, also letter to Barlog dated 4 May in West Berlin Academy.

256. Diary 17, entries for 15 April and 21 May 1957.

257. See Diary 15, end February 1956.

258. 'Vorschlag zu einer Theaterakademie' in *Lebendige Kunst*, Pädagogische Blätter, Beilage zu Heft 5-6, 1955. Reprinted in *Schriften 2*, pp. 179-84.

259. Letter to Bruckner, 20 June 1958, in West Berlin Academy.

260. Diary 16, entry dated 8 May 1956 (West Berlin Academy).

261. Letter to Neumann, 9 April 1953 (East German Academy).

262. Letter to Schulz-Norden, 12 February 1948 (East German Academy).

263. 'Die Dramatisierung von Romanen'. English and French versions in *World Theatre/Le Théâtre dans le monde*, Brussels, 5, 4, pp. 291-304. *Schriften 2*, p. 211.

264. Interview in programme for *The Crucible*, Nationaltheater Mannheim: *Bühnenblätter* 1954-5, 2, 10-11, 14-15. *Schriften 2*, p. 174.

265. Diary 14, 10 November 1954 et seq. (West Berlin Academy).

266. As note 264, *Schriften 2*, p. 176.

267. 'Bekenntnistheater und das Unbehagen der Kritik'. In *Schriften 2*, pp. 188-95.

268. Diary 7, p. 25, June–July 1953 (West Berlin Academy).

269. Diary 12, 29 January 1954 (ditto).

270. Diary 14, mid-November 1954 (ditto).

271. Diary 13, end April 1954 (ditto).

272. Diary 15, entries covering 24-7 October 1955 (West Berlin Academy).

273. Maxim Vallentin to Piscator, 27 March 1958, in West Berlin Academy.

274. Ernst Schumacher: *Die dramaturgischen Versuche Bertolt Brechts 1918–1933*, Rütten und Loening, Potsdam 1955, pp. 125-30.

275. Diary 15, entry for 3 November 1955 (in West Berlin Academy).

276. 'Mein zweites Theater-Tagebuch', plan in West Berlin Academy.

277. 'Das Theater, das ich meine', ditto.

278. So he said in a letter to me of 9 January 1962.

279. Brandt: *My Road to Berlin*, p. 14.

280. Diary 17 for November 1957, in West Berlin Academy.

281. Quoted by Ludwig Hoffmann in his postscript to *Schriften 2*, p. 361.

282. 'Volksbühne heute'. Speech to the 1962 Volksbühne conference at Kassel. *Schriften 2*, pp. 290–91.

283. Letter: Kipphardt–Piscator of 1 July 1959 in West Berlin Academy.

284. 'Vorwort zum "Stellvertreter".' *Schriften 2*, p. 303. Included in several editions of the play.

285. Letter of 4 May 1961 cited in Reich: *Wettlauf mit der Zeit*, p. 224.

286. Interview in *Berliner Morgenpost*, 25 October 1964, reprinted in *Schriften 2*, p. 313. See also his unpublished essay on 'Ensembletheater'.

287. *Die Zeit*, Hamburg, 26 November 1965, reprinted in *Schriften 2*, pp. 333–40.

288. Dealing with the established Volksbühne officials, Dr Walter Huder has suggested, was 'too much for his failing powers'.

289. 'Verherrlichen wir den Menschen', in *Schriften 2*, pp. 306–10.

290. Hans-Ulrich Schmückle/Sylta Busse: *Theaterarbeit*, Hanser, Munich n.d. (1975), p. 122 ff.

291. These are the two volumes of *Schriften* which appeared in 1968. See Ludwig Hoffmann's editorial postscripts to both.

292. *Schriften 2*, p. 267.

293. Manfred Wekwerth: *Schriften*, Henschel, East Berlin 1973, pp. 30–31.

294. 'Piscator and the Theatre of the Twenties' in the Arts Council *Erwin Piscator* catalogue.

295. *Im Wettlauf mit der Zeit*, p. 340.

296. Undated letter in Wolf *Briefwechsel*, Aufbau, East Berlin 1968, p. 42.

297. Section 'Piscator's Theatre' in Brecht's *The Messingkauf Dialogues*, Methuen, London 1965, pp. 64, 67. Also his article 'The German Drama, pre-Hitler' in the *New York Times*, 24 November 1935, reprinted in *Brecht on Theatre*, p. 77.

298. Section 'The Augsburger's Theatre' in *The Messingkauf Dialogues*, p. 69.

299. Brecht: *Ges. Werke Schriften zum Theater*, 1967, p. 104.

300. Ditto, p. 135.

301. 'On Experimental Theatre', a lecture of 1939. *Ges. Werke Schriften zum Theater*, p. 305; *Brecht on Theatre*, p. 134. Several pages are devoted to Piscator.

302. *The Messingkauf Dialogues*, p. 68.

303. In *Das p.T.*, pp. 53–9. In the revised version of 1963 Lania's report of the production is heavily cut, while Döblin's remark about a 'halfway house' is followed by a new conclusion which starts: 'I now had a chance to evolve a form of production which years later was proclaimed from another quarter to be "epic theatre".'

304. See *Messingkauf Dialogues*, pp. 68–9 and *Ges. Werke Schriften zum Theater*, p. 316.

305. Letter: Brecht–Piscator of about July 1936, in the Morris Library, Carbondale.

306. Cited by Herbert Knust in Mews and Knust (eds.): *Essays on Brecht*, University of North Carolina Press, 1974, p. 66.

307. Diary 15, entry for 2 November 1955, in West Berlin Academy.

308. Ditto, undated entry around January 1956.

309. Letter to Brecht cited by me and partly illustrated in *IcarbS* I, 2, pp. 91–2.

310. 'Wie unterscheidet sich das *Epische* bei Brecht-bei mir?', in Diary 15, p. 110. Marked 'Wichtig' (important) in Piscator's hand.

311. 'Zur Berufsausbildung des Schauspielers' in *Die deutsche Bühne 10*, Darmstadt 1965, p. 188.

312. Diary 14, p. 119 (West Berlin Academy).

313. Letter Bentley–Saul Colin, cited by Juergen Stein in the Morris Library's catalogue *Erwin Piscator Exhibit*, 1974.

314. *Im Wettlauf mit der Zeit*, p. 358.

315. Diary 15, p. 99 (West Berlin Academy).

316. Interview in *Théâtre Populaire*, 1956, no. 19, translated in *Schriften 2*, p. 207.

317. Diary 15, entry for 27 October 1955, cited by Knust in *Essays on Brecht*, pp. 64–5.

318. Translated and cited by Knust in *Essays on Brecht*, p. 67.

319. Diary 14, entry for 23 May 1955, in West Berlin Academy.

320. Playbill for 'Rally of Hope', New York, 6 June 1943, cited by Stein in catalogue of *Erwin Piscator Exhibit*.

321. 'Das Gesicht des heutigen deutschen Theaters' in *Fuldaer Volkszeitung*, 26 October 1955.

322. Diary 14, entry for 17 January 1955.

323. 'Rechenschaft 1', speech of 25 March 1929 in *Schriften 2*, p. 55.

324. Brecht: *Ges. Werke Schriften zum Theater*, p. 139.

Bibliography and acknowledgments

————◆——

The following is a selective list only. Further bibliographies are given in the books by C. D. Innes, Maria Ley-Piscator and Heinrich Goertz named below, while Piscator's own writings are listed as completely as possible in Juergen Stein's 'Erwin Piscator. A Checklist' in *IcarbS*, Carbondale, Vol. I, no. 2, 1974 (pp. 95–120).

1. Primary materials

Erwin Piscator: *Das politische Theater*, Adalbert Schulz Verlag, Berlin 1929.

Erwin Piscator: *Das politische Theater*, neubearbeitet von Felix Gasbarra, mit einem Vorwort von Wolfgang Drews, Rowohlt, Reinbek bei Hamburg 1963.

Erwin Piscator: *Schriften*, edited by Ludwig Hoffmann for the Deutsche Akademie der Künste, Henschelverlag, East Berlin 1968. (Volume 1 is a photo-reprint of *Das politische Theater*, 1929 edition, with notes by the editor and a 'Nachwort 1966' by Piscator. Volume 2, subtitled 'Aufsätze Reden Gespräche', contains seventy-two more occasional items, in chronological order with notes and a full list of Piscator's productions.)

Erwin Piscator: 'Objective Acting' in Toby Cole and Helen Chinoy (eds.), *Actors on Acting*, Crown Publishers, New York 1949.

Blätter der Piscatorbühne, Berlin, 1927–31. Programmes of Piscator's three companies, containing writings by himself, Gasbarra, Lania, Grosz and other close collaborators. The series begins with *Rasputin*, that for *Hoppla!* having been entitled *Das Programm der Piscatorbühne*.

The International Theatre, Moscow, 1933–5(?). Started as Bulletin no. 2 of the International Workers' Theatre Olympiad, initially with S. S. Podolsky as editor. In 1935 Piscator announced that it would become a twice-yearly almanac, but only one issue seems to have materialised.

2. Some texts of plays and adaptations

Lajos Barta: *Russlands Tag*. In Hoffmann/Hoffmann-Ostwald, Vol. 1, pp. 57–68.

Jean-Richard Bloch: *Le Dernier empereur*. Une histoire, Gallimard, Paris 1926.

Carl Credé: *§ 218. Gequälte Menschen*, J. H. W. Dietz, Berlin 1930.

Theodor Dreiser: *Amerikanische Tragödie*, adapted by Piscator, Ahn and Simrock, Wiesbaden and Berlin n.d.

Jaroslav Hašek: *The Good Soldier Svejk*, translated by Cecil Parrott. Heinemann, London 1973. Dramatisation by Max Brod and Hans Reimann, Zsolnay-Verlag, Vienna 1967. Version attributed to Brecht, Gasbarra, Piscator, Grosz, in Herbert Knust (editor) *Materialien zu Bertolt Brechts 'Schweik im zweiten Weltkrieg'*, Suhrkamp, Frankfurt 1974.

Rolf Hochhuth: *Der Stellvertreter*, Rowohlt, Reinbek bei Hamburg 1962 (includes foreword by Piscator). English translation by R. D. Macdonald: *The Representative*, Methuen, London 1963. American adaptation by Jerome Rothenberg: *The Deputy*, Samuel French, New York 1965.

Franz Jung: *Wie lange noch, du Hure bürgerliche Gerechtigkeit?* and *Die Kanaker*. Malik-Verlag, Berlin 1921 (in 'Sammlung revolutionärer Bühnenwerke').

Heinar Kipphardt: *In der Sache J. Robert Oppenheimer*. In *Stücke I*, Suhrkamp, Frankfurt and also separately by Fischer Taschenbuch Verlag, Frankfurt 1971. English translation by Ruth Spiers: *In the Matter of J. Robert Oppenheimer*, Methuen, London 1967.

Hans Helmut Kirst and Piscator: *Aufstand der Offiziere*, Desch, Munich 1966.

Peter Martin Lampel: *Revolte im Erziehungshaus*, Kiepenheuer, Berlin 1929.

Rudolf Leonhard: *Segel am Horizont*. In *Ausgewählte Werke II*, Verlag der Nation, East Berlin 1963.

Walter Mehring: *Der Kaufmann von Berlin*, with notes, in Günther Rühle: *Zeit und Theater. Von der Republik zur Diktatur 1925–33* Band II, Propyläen, West Berlin 1972. Additional songs in Mehring's *Arche Noah SOS*, Fischer, Berlin 1931.

Alfons Paquet: *Fahnen. Ein dramatischer Roman*, Dreimasken-Verlag, Munich 1923. *Sturmflut*, Berlin 1926. Republished in Reinhold Grimm and Jost Hermand (eds.): *Deutsche Revolutionsdramen*, Frankfurt n.d.

Theodor Plivier: *Des Kaisers Kulis* (novel), Malik-Verlag, Berlin 1929. The dramatised version appears to be unpublished.

Romain Rolland: *Robespierre*, adapted by Gasbarra and Piscator, Desch, Munich 1964.

Anna Seghers: *Der Aufstand der Fischer* (novel), Kiepenheuer, Potsdam 1928. Translation by Margaret Goldsmith: *The Revolt of the Fishermen*, Matthews and Marrot, London 1929.

Ernst Toller: *Hoppla, wir leben!* with notes, in Günther Rühle: *Zeit und Theater* (as for Mehring, above). Translation by Hermon Ould: *Hoppla!*, Benn, London 1928.

Leo Tolstoy, adapted by Neumann, Piscator and Prüfer: *Krieg und Frieden*, Rowohlt, Reinbek bei Hamburg 1955. English version by R. D. Macdonald, *War and Peace*, MacGibbon and Kee, London 1963.

Robert Penn Warren: *All the King's Men*, translated and adapted by Piscator and Hellmut Schlien as *Blick auf den Mond*, Lechte, Ensdetten 1957. Adaptation by Warren: Random House, New York.

Peter Weiss: *Die Ermittlung*, Suhrkamp, Frankfurt 1965. Translation by Alexander Gross: *The Investigation*, Calder and Boyars, London 1966.

Friedrich Wolf: *Tai Yang erwacht*. In *Gesammelte Werke 3: Dramen*, Aufbau-Verlag, East Berlin 1960.

Paul Zech: *Das trunkene Schiff. Eine szenische Ballade*, Schauspiel-Verlag, Leipzig n.d. (1920s).

3. On Piscator

Herbert Jhering: *Reinhardt, Jessner, Piscator, oder Klassikertod?*, Rowohlt, Berlin 1929.

Heinrich Goertz: *Erwin Piscator in Selbstzeugnissen und Bilddokumenten*, Rowohlt, Reinbek bei Hamburg 1974.

C. D. Innes: *Erwin Piscator's Political Theatre*, Cambridge University Press 1972.

Maria Ley-Piscator: *The Piscator Experiment*, James H. Heineman, Inc., New York 1967; reprinted by Southern Illinois University Press, Carbondale and Edwardsville 1970.

4. Catalogues

Akademie der Künste, West Berlin: *Erwin Piscator 1893–1966* (Compiled by Walther Huder, Hannelore Ritscher and Ilse Brauer), West Berlin 1971.

Ditto: *Theater in Exil 1933–1945* (Same compilers), West Berlin 1973.

Arts Council of Great Britain: *Erwin Piscator Political Theatre 1920–1966* (Compiled by Ludwig Hoffmann), London 1971. (Based on the *Schriften*, some of whose material is translated and included.)

Southern Illinois University: *Erwin Piscator Exhibit* (Compiled by Juergen Stein and Katharine Lockwood), University Graphics, Carbondale, for Friends of the Morris Library, 1974.

Busch-Reisinger Museum, Harvard University: *Theatrical Drawings and Water-colors by George Grosz* (Compiled by Hedy B. Landman and Herbert Knust), Harvard 1973.

5. Unpublished dissertations

Klaus Schulz: *Das 'politische Theater' Erwin Piscators*, Göttingen 1956.

Hans Joachim Fiebach: *Die Darstellung kapitalistischer Widersprüche in Erwin Piscators Inszenierungen 1920–1931*, Berlin 1965.

Jürgen Stein: *Die Archivierung theatralischer Quellen am Beispiel der Erwin Piscator Papers an der Southern Illinois University*, Vienna 1973.

Thea Kirfel-Lenk: *Erwin Piscator im Exil in den USA. Studien zu seiner antifaschistischen Theaterarbeit am Studio Theatre des Dramatic Workshop der New School für Social Research* (1939 bis 1943), East Berlin probably 1978.

6. Relevant memoirs and biographies

Harold Clurman: *The Fervent Years*, Dobson, London 1946.

Tilla Durieux: *Eine Tür steht offen*, Herbig, West Berlin 1954.

Babette Gross: *Willi Muenzenberg*, Deutsche Verlags-Anstalt, Stuttgart 1967.

George Grosz: *Ein kleines Ja und eine grosses Nein*, Rowohlt, Reinbek bei Hamburg 1955. English translation (abridged): *A Little Yes and a Big No*, Dial Press, New York 1946.

Julius Hay: *Geboren 1900, Erinnerungen*. Christian Wegener Verlag, Reinbek bei Hamburg 1971.

Franz Jung: *Der Weg nach unten*. Luchterhand, Neuwied 1961.

Beth Irwin Lewis: *George Grosz. Art and Politics in the Weimar Republic*, University of Wisconsin Press, Madison 1971.

Bernhard Reich: *Im Wettlauf mit der Zeit*, Henschelverlag, East Berlin 1970.

Harry Wilde: *Theodor Plivier*, Desch, Munich 1965.

Friedrich Wolf: *Briefwechsel. Eine Auswahl*, Aufbau-Verlag, East Berlin 1968. *Briefe. Eine Auswahl*, Aufbau-Verlag, East Berlin 1969.

There are also allusions in various other autobiographies, such as those of Ernst-Josef Aufricht, Kortner, Reimann, Toller (*Quer Durch*), Zuckmayer *et al.*

7. Other relevant works

Bertolt Brecht: *Schriften zum Theater*. In *Gesammelte Werke*, Suhrkamp-Verlag, Frankfurt 1967. English translations in *Brecht on Theatre* and *The Messingkauf Dialogues*, Methuen, London 1964 and 1965 respectively.

Walter Fähnders and Martin Rector (eds.): *Literatur im Klassenkampf. Zur Proletarisch-revolutionären Literaturtheorie 1919–1923*, Hanser, Munich 1971.

Helga Gallas: *Marxistische Literaturtheorie*, Luchterhand, Neuwied 1971.

Hermann Haarmann, Lothar Schirmer, Dagmar Walach: *Das 'Engels' Projekt.* Ein antifaschistisches Theater deutscher Emigranten in der UdSSR (1936–41). Georg Heinz, Worms 1975.

Ludwig Hoffmann and Daniel Hoffmann-Ostwald (eds.): *Deutsches Arbeitertheater 1918–1933.* Two vols., Henschelverlag, East Berlin 1961. Second edition 1972.

Herbert Jhering: *Von Reinhardt bis Brecht.* Three vols., Aufbau-Verlag, East Berlin 1961. One-volume condensation Rowohlt, Reinbek bei Hamburg 1967. (Collected theatre criticisms.)

F. W. Knellessen: *Agitation auf der Bühne.* Das politische Theater der Weimarer Republik. Emsdetten 1970.

Fr. Kranich: *Bühnentechnik der Gegenwart.* R. Oldenbourg, Munich and Berlin. Vol. 1 1929, Vol. 2 1933.

Asja Lacis: *Revolutionär im Beruf.* Berichte über proletarisches Theater, über Meyerhold, Brecht, Benjamin und Piscator. Rogner und Bernhard, Munich 1971.

Siegfried Mews and Herbert Knust (eds.): *Essays on Brecht.* Theater and Politics. University of North Carolina Press, 1974. (Contains Knust's paper on 'Piscator and Brecht. Affinity and Alienation.')

Günther Rühle (ed.): *Theater für die Republik 1917–1933.* Im Spiegel der Kritik. Fischer, Frankfurt 1967. (See also under Mehring in section 2 above for *Zeit und Theater*, which contains illuminating notes.)

Jürgen Rühle: *Das gefesselte Theater.* Kiepenheuer and Witsch, Cologne 1957. Shortened paperback version under title *Theater und Revolution*, DTV, Munich 1963.

Hans-Ulrich Schmückle and Sylta Busse: *Theaterarbeit.* Eine Dokumentation. Hanser, Munich n.d. (1975).

Ernst Schumacher: *Die dramatischen Versuche Bertolt Brechts 1918–1933.* Rütten und Loening, East Berlin 1955.

Frank Trommler: *Sozialistische Literatur im Deutschland.* Ein historischer Überblick. Kröner, Stuttgart 1976.

8. Sources and acknowledgments

Other references to articles, etc. are given in the Notes. For an account of unpublished archive material, see Jürgen Stein's checklist cited earlier. Briefly, Piscator's own papers are divided mainly between the Morris Library at Southern Illinois University, Carbondale, and the Akademie der Künste in West Berlin. There are also important scripts, cuttings and other items in the Akademie der Künste of the GDR in East Berlin. I am grateful to have had opportunities to work in all three, thanks primarily to the kindness of Professor Kenneth Duckett, Dr Walter Huder and Dr Ludwig Hoffmann. Most of these papers were made available in the first place by Dr Maria Piscator, to whom all Piscator students are permanently indebted, and I have to thank her (as well as the various archives concerned and the Brecht Estate) for permission to make quotations, as well as for seeing me in London and New York.

Through the kind offices of Dr Brigitte Lohmeyer of the Federal German Embassy in London and Dr Klaus Schulz (a former collaborator of Piscator's and author of the dissertation listed above) of the London Goethe Institute, Inter Nationes were my hosts for the bulk of my researches in Berlin and West Germany. Others who helped me in various ways, either by seeing me or in correspondence, included Miss Stella Adler, Denis Bablet, Eric Bentley, Mrs Sonia Bogs-Hessdörffer, Bernard Dort, Miss Joanna Drew (of the Arts Council of Great Britain), Henry Glade, Mel Gordon (of TDR), Professor Mordecai Gorelik, Helmut Grosse (of the Institut für Theaterwissenschaft at Cologne University), Peter M. Grosz, Mr Bro Herod (of the New School), Professor Herbert Knust, David Koch (of the Morris Library), Wolfgang Roth, Malcolm E. Scheer (of the Raymond Fogelman Library, the New School), Hans-Ulrich and Sylta Schmückle, Jürgen Stein, Lee Strasberg, Curt Trepte, Albert Venohr, Robert Penn Warren, Peter Weiss, the Bertolt Brecht-Archiv, the Institut für Theaterwissenschaft of the Freie Universität Berlin (which holds some of Traugott Müller's designs and photographs) and the Lincoln Centre Library, New York (for documents relating to Piscator's U.S. productions). Many thanks to all of them.

Index

DATE DUE

DEMCO 38-297

Germany
Showing relevant theatre sites

0   100   200 km

Oldenb

● Hamburg

Elbe

NETHERLANDS
● The Hague

● Bochum

Krefeld ● ● Essen

● Kassel

BELGIUM

● Brussels

HESSE

Dillenburg ● ● Marburg

Wetzlar ● ● Giessen

Rhine

● Frankfurt

● Darmstadt

● Mannheim
● Heidelberg

Saarbrücken ●

FRANCE

● Tübingen

BAVARIA

● Mü
● Star

Zurich ●
SWITZERLAND